POWER AND THE
GOVERNANCE OF
GLOBAL TRADE

A volume in the series

Cornell Studies in Political Economy
edited by Peter J. Katzenstein

A list of titles in this series is available at www.cornellpress.cornell.edu.

POWER AND THE GOVERNANCE OF GLOBAL TRADE

From the GATT to the WTO

SOO YEON KIM

Cornell University Press

ITHACA AND LONDON

First published 2010 by Cornell University Press

Printed in the United States of America

Library of Congress Cataloging-in-Publication Data

Kim, Soo Yeon.
    Power and the governance of global trade : from the GATT to the WTO / Soo Yeon Kim.
        p. cm. — (Cornell studies in political economy)
    Includes bibliographical references and index.
    ISBN 978-0-8014-4886-7 (cloth : alk. paper)
    1. International trade—Political aspects. 2. General Agreement on Tariffs and Trade (Organization) 3. World Trade Organization. I. Title.
II. Series: Cornell studies in political economy.
    HF1379.K568 2010
    382'.92—dc22   2010001009

For Erin and Helena

Contents

Acknowledgments

As I look back on the journey of this project and the many people who have made this book possible, I am grateful first and foremost to Joanne Gowa, who as mentor and friend has been the most influential figure in the development of this book and in my intellectual development since completing my doctorate. Our paper on the distributive consequences of the General Agreement on Tariffs and Trade (GATT), included as a chapter in this book, provided the initial inspiration for this book and spurred my interest in great power politics and the distributional consequences of international institutions. Joanne's intellectual discipline, work ethic, and dedication to her children have been and continue to be my model of scholarly excellence and of the often elusive balance between work and parenthood. With great affection and respect, I thank Joanne for her unfailing support and for the tough questions that have made this book all the better.

I enthusiastically acknowledge the support of the Niehaus Center Globalization and Governance, directed by Helen Milner, at the Woodrow Wilson School of Public and International Affairs, Princeton University. This book was completed while I was a Niehaus Fellow, and in addition to the invaluable research time I received through the fellowship, the project benefited enormously from engagement with the intellectually community of the Woodrow Wilson School. I thank my dear friend Sophie Meunier, who encouraged me to think about the GATT, the WTO, and trade from the perspective of globalization and governance more broadly. Our many conversations over the course of this project have helped to ground the book in the "real world" and to find the meaning of this project in the pressing debates on governance in the twenty-first century. As a Niehaus Fellow, I was also fortunate to meet the extraordinary Bob Keohane, who encouraged, or more accurately, challenged me to think more deeply about the role of power in institutions. I also thank the participants of the Fellows Workshop, a weekly gathering of Fellows in residence at the Woodrow Wilson School. I am especially grateful to Tim Bartley, Carmela Lutmar, Dan Gingerich, Raymond Hicks, Tobias Hofmann, Karen Long Jusko, Jonathan Monten, Bumba Mukherjee, Ato Onoma, Chris Rudolph, Injoo Sohn, Tom Wright, and Vineeta Yadav for their helpful comments on various chapters. Special thanks are also due to Raymond Hicks for methodological advice and data compilation.

This book has benefited greatly from the colleagues and friends who generously gave their time to comment on various parts of this book. I thank David Baldwin, Christina Davis, Bob Erikson, Erik Gartzke, Virginia Haufler, Scott Kastner, Kathleen Knight, Margaret Pearson, Anne Sartori, Robert Pahre, Brian Pollins, George Quester, and Alex Wendt. I am especially grateful to the ever affable and cheery David Andrew Singer, who pushed me to stand my ground, and to Stephanie Rickard for a timely reading of the manuscript.

I also received valuable feedback on various parts of this book from presentations at the Workshop on Power and Institutional Design in the 21st Century, organized by Bob Keohane and myself; the Workshop on the Effectiveness of International Institutions, organized by Helen Milner, Tobias Hofmann, and Bumba Mukherjee; the International Relations Faculty Seminar at the Woodrow Wilson School, Princeton University; the Columbia University International Politics Seminar (CUIPS); seminars at the University of Virginia and the University of Maryland; and meetings of the International Studies Association and the American Political Science Association.

My acknowledgments would not be complete without special thanks to the main figures at Cornell University Press: Roger Haydon and Peter Katzenstein. I join many others in high praise of Roger's professionalism and efficiency. Peter Katzenstein has been instrumental in fostering a greater interest and understanding of the word "identity" in power politics, and I thank Peter for overseeing revisions that have brought only good things to the book. Thanks are also due to the two reviewers of the manuscript for their constructive and detailed comments and suggestions. I am also grateful to Martin Schneider, copyeditor, and to Karen Laun, production editor, for excellent editing and management of the publication process at Cornell University Press.

Last but certainly not least, this book would not have been completed without the support and encouragement of Deborah Guber, whose good spirits I always turned to when my own were not; Dorothee Heisenberg and Amy Richmond, my "sisters"; David Cameron, and Don and Ann Green, who have cheered me on since my early days as a graduate student at Yale. I am also indebted to Thomas Chung and especially to Sungju Cho and Youngok Choi for stepping in as uncle and aunt on many weekends. This book is dedicated to my two daughters, Erin Kim Chung and Helena Kim Chung, whose love and understanding I could not have done without through this project. They are my constant reminders of what is truly important in life, and a happier person wrote this book because of them.

POWER AND THE
GOVERNANCE OF
GLOBAL TRADE

Introduction

The "Battle of Seattle," now familiar to many, marked an inauspicious beginning in the efforts of the World Trade Organization to launch its first round of trade talks. To protest against an organization which had before then garnered little public attention, nearly fifty thousand activists descended on the city of Seattle in November 1999, at the site of the WTO's Ministerial Meeting, where member countries' trade negotiators had congregated for four days in the hopes of coming to agreement on an agenda.[1] The magnitude and intensity of the protests effectively shut down the city: a state of "civil emergency" was declared and a nighttime curfew was imposed, turning this city known for its liberal lifestyle and the home of Starbucks Coffee houses into something akin to Fort Seattle. The motley group of activists included anarchists, environmentalists, union members, and religious and human rights activists gathered under a common banner, labeling the WTO as the "World Takeover Organization" or "Way Too Orwellian." The activists were united in their opposition to the WTO as an inherently unfair institution that puts profits ahead of people and the planet, harmful to the various causes in the name of which they had gathered.

Rather than opening a new era of liberal trade in the global economy, the WTO suffered a major public relations disaster, and to make matters far worse, the talks themselves ended in failure, as representatives of the

---

1. *BBC News*. WTO Protesters Win Seattle Case. Available at http://news.bbc.co.uk/2/hi/americas/6317469.stm, accessed 8 September 2007.

135 member nations left the meeting without agreement on an agenda. The United States and the European Union, the world's two leading traders, faced their usual deadlock over agriculture, having come to Seattle after months of unsuccessful talks to resolve disagreements and present a unified front. The developing countries took advantage of the deadlock between the United States and the EU and, given that the WTO relies on consensus to make decisions, used their veto power to block the expansion of the agenda and thus any decision on the agenda itself, leading to the collapse of the talks and the suspension of negotiations. Indeed, developing country delegates, though present in name, were effectively excluded from the talks in Seattle. Virtually all of the negotiations took place among the representatives of twenty-five key countries, as even U.S. Trade Representative Charlene Barshefsky admitted, with the remaining 110 countries remaining well outside the meetings.[2] There was harsh criticism from delegates such as Clement Rohee, foreign minister of Guyana: "We from developing countries were invited to this meeting, and asked to participate, but then treated like delinquents.... We didn't come here to sit outside and drink coffee while the decisions were taken by the richer countries."[3]

Though WTO members would launch the Doha Round two years later in Qatar in 2001, the Seattle demonstrations successfully put the WTO and the globalization it represents on the map of the general public's political consciousness. They resulted in a newfound interest in the activities of an organization that, though its rules and regulations governing commerce profoundly affect lives all across the world, had traditionally conducted its negotiations away from the public eye, in relative obscurity, even secrecy. Since the events of Seattle, the WTO has become a focal point for the public's emerging interest in questioning the merits of free trade and, with it, the good and especially the bad side of globalization. Yet the strident criticisms seem almost misplaced when one considers the target: the WTO, an institution expressly committed to the conduct of liberal trade. The *Agreement Establishing the World Trade Organization* devotes the beginning of its preamble to the goals of liberal trade, which involve the expansion of trade and the elevation of living standards while balancing these benefits of trade with developmental needs and environmental sustainability.

The WTO and the General Agreement on Tariffs and Trade (GATT) that preceded it have constituted the premier multilateral trade governance

2. BBC News. WTO Tarnished by Seattle Failure. Available at http://news.bbc.co.uk/2/hi/special_report/1999/11/99/battle_for_free_trade/549794.stm, accessed 9 September 2007.
3. Ibid.

regime since the end of World War II. As the WTO's predecessor, the GATT took the world through the period of reconstruction after World War II and the Cold War years, ensuring nondiscrimination in the conduct of trade and spearheading efforts to liberalize trade through the reduction of tariffs, which fell from double-digit levels to 4 percent over six rounds of multilateral trade negotiations (Gallagher 2005, 2).[4] Indeed, the early years of the GATT witnessed a sixfold increase in global trade, as the volume of world trade grew at an annual average rate of 7 percent (Finlayson and Zacher 1981, 602). Yet in spite of its laudable success in promoting economic growth and prosperity through the liberalization and the expansion of trade, the scenes of Seattle have replicated themselves in subsequent WTO meetings, from Genoa to Hong Kong, with no sign that the strident critiques of the WTO—or of globalization—have been appeased.

Power and Governance of the International Economy: A Study of the GATT

The starting point for this book is thus a key puzzle in today's ongoing debate about the merits and perils of globalization. That is, given that this global trade governance body is expressly devoted to the promotion and expansion of liberal trade and the benefits it accrues for those who participate, why is there so much opposition to it, as evidenced so prominently in the Battle of Seattle and the other protests that followed? In this sense, this book is something of an "anti-globalization" project, intended to assess in a systematic way the major criticisms of the GATT/WTO regime and globalization writ large. That is, is the global trading system really geared toward the rich and the powerful? If so, how did it happen, and what have been the consequences? These are the questions that form the heart of this book. The motivation for this project comes in large part from the enduring questions about why Seattle was important and what the important issues vis-à-vis globalization and governance are, as seen from the vantage point of the critics of the global trade regime. The book investigates the institutional

---

4. Eight rounds of multilateral trade negotiations took place under the GATT. These, and the number of Contracting Parties participating in each, included the Geneva Round (1947, 23 Contracting Parties); Annecy Round (1949, 13); Torquay Round (1951, 38); Geneva Round (1956, 26); Dillon Round (1960–1961, 26); Kennedy Round (1964–1967, 62); Tokyo Round (1973–1979, 102); and the Uruguay Round (1986–1994, 123). From http://www.wto.org/english/thewto_e/whatis_e/tif_e/fact4_e.htm, accessed 16 December 2009. The Uruguay Round, the last under the GATT, established the World Trade Organization (WTO) with the signing of the Final Act on 15 April 1994, in Marrakesh. The WTO Agreement went into effect on 1 January 1995.

and empirical bases of their claims, attending to the multilateral institutions that have governed trade since the end of World War II and how their rules have shaped the evolution of the global trading system.

In analyzing the impact of the global trade regime on international trade, this book offers a twenty-first-century reading of the origins and development of global trade governance under the GATT and the WTO. It seeks to bring to the contemporary political arena the very questions that informed the construction of our global trade regime. The book's theoretical focus is on the distributive consequences of regimes, or how the construction of governance mechanisms, in spite of the resolution of collective action problems, leads to inequalities in the benefits they confer. The prevailing view of regimes favors their voluntaristic components, emphasizing the ability of regimes to produce cooperation among participants and generating positive-sum, Pareto-optimal outcomes that benefit all with absolute gains. Less attended to in this debate, however, has been the consideration of the non-positive-sum dimension of international institutions, brought to the fore in Gruber (2000) in an emergent "power politics" theory of international institutions that privileges the role of powerful actors in institutional formation and institutional durability. The arguments developed in the book, then, link the criticisms that have found such favor among opponents of the global trade regime with non-positive-sum, distributional issues of institutional design and development, providing key insights into the following two questions: Why does global trade governance under the GATT and the WTO look the way it does? And what have been its consequences? On the way, this book develops the central finding that the trade-creating benefits of the GATT and the WTO have indeed been skewed disproportionately in favor of major powers and industrialized countries.

This trading system is now more than sixty years old, as the GATT of 1947 went into effect on 1 January 1948. The voluminous body of literature on the GATT and its origins and economic fundamentals now includes the diplomatic documents compiled by Irwin, Mavroidis, and Sykes (2008) detailing the intent of the regime's creators and the subsequent legal provisions that were written into the text of the GATT. This book focuses on the distributional aspects of these provisions, that is, the rules that produced inequalities between the powerful trading nations and the less powerful developing countries and, as a consequence, how these rules impacted the course of commercial relations for members of the regime. It is an investigation of the GATT primarily as a political institution established to govern economic relations among its participants, encompassing its "level of institutionalization" (Boin 2008, 91): its origins, evolution, and effects as a political institution. The political questions confronted by the GATT's and now the WTO's members are those of any society that must find its own resolution to its fundamental political problem—"who gets what, when, and how" (Lasswell 1936).

The analytical focus of the book is on the nexus of three key factors—power, institutions, and international trade. The confluence of these factors demonstrates the distributive consequences of the GATT/WTO regime in several respects. First, it brings power "back into the analysis" of international institutions, chiefly by emphasizing the importance of who designs—who the principal architects are at the time of regime formation—and, as a consequence, how the power relations that determine institutional choice become embedded in institutional development. In this connection, this project is first and foremost a study of power and governance of the international economy in which the trade regime of the post–World War II period—the GATT and to a lesser extent the WTO—occupies the primary focus of empirical inquiry. It seeks to bring up to the present day the governance questions that confronted the GATT's creators so as to gain insight into the particular exigencies that characterize our particular era of the international economy and the governance issues that arise from them. It applies, in particular, the theoretical framework offered in Barnett and Duvall (2001, 2005a) to examine the role of "compulsory power" wielded by the leading actors in fashioning the institution and the "institutional power" they derive from the institutional rules themselves, which in combination produce and reproduce the power relations that characterize the non-positive-sum dimension of international institutions.

Moreover, the book offers an empirical assessment, using quantitative analyses, of the distributive consequences of the regime in terms of how it actually affected international commerce since its inception. From the perspective of the GATT's principal architect, the United States, the objective of constructing a multilateral trade regime was to expand trade among its participants. As noted eloquently by Herbert Feis, who served on the U.S. delegation to the Geneva negotiations of 1947, "If each country could be attracted by the chance of securing new opportunity from *all* the rest, it might be bolder and more assured in granting opportunity to others. The impelling thought was, could not the course of trade expansion be hastened and extended through one universal accord?" (Feis 1948, 41; emphasis in original). The analyses offered in the second half of the book are directed at this question: to what extent has the GATT/WTO regime fulfilled its original task of trade expansion? In providing an empirical assessment of this question, the analysis fits in squarely with the emerging and often controversial debate on the effects (and effectiveness) of international institutions such as the GATT and the WTO. This book offers a full-length assessment of the effects of the GATT and the WTO on international trade, combining a quantitative analysis of its effects on international trade with a qualitative analysis of the historical context within which it occurred.

Examining the distributive consequences of regimes from the perspective of power relations raises important issues more broadly for global governance, in particular the question of how, in the twenty-first century, the world must deal with the institutional and great power legacies of the Cold War period. The existing "triad" of international institutions of global governance—the UN, the IMF/World Bank, and the GATT/WTO—was established for the post–World War II world, one in which the United States was pitted against the Soviet Union. With that world now gone, superseded by 9/11 and global pandemics, the question arises as to the viability of these institutions, so embedded and entrenched in the Cold War politics that gave rise to them in the first place. A response to these questions demands a closer look at how institutions are constructions of power and what this means in the twenty-first century. It also requires an assessment of the extent to which "old" power relations have given way to new ones, this time perhaps along developmental lines, and how institutional reform may proceed accordingly, if possible without completely abandoning the institution itself. As the first post–Cold War construct in international cooperation, the WTO's success, or lack thereof, in expanding global trade carries important implications for how powerful countries can design institutions and the tradeoffs they face among preserving power, promoting economic efficiency, and leveling the playing field for all.

The Accidental Institution

Governance of the existing global trading system originates with the General Agreement on Tariffs and Trade, signed in 1947. Since its inception, the GATT has been a rule-setting mechanism for the governance of international trade, focusing its efforts on the reduction of trade barriers such as tariffs in "reciprocal and mutually advantageous" (Hoekman and Kostecki 1995, 11) arrangements through multilateral negotiations. The GATT has been a means as well to expand international trade, making the "promotion of interactions" (Finlayson and Zacher 1981, 601) in the form of trade exchanges the very raison d'être of its existence. The GATT and its eight rounds of negotiations since 1947 have defined the nature and rules of the international trading order after World War II. It continues to shape the course of international trade in the form of the WTO, created by the Final Act of the Uruguay Round in 1994.

The creation of the GATT was something of a historical accident. It started as a humble trade protocol attached to the Havana Charter for the creation of the International Trade Organization (ITO).[5] As is well known, the ITO, along with the International Monetary Fund and the International Bank for Reconstruction and Development (IBRD/World Bank), made up the set of institutions designed to govern international trade and finance after World War II to aid in reconstruction and recovery and to ensure stability in the global economic order. When the Truman administration withdrew the ITO Charter for consideration and ratification by the U.S. Congress, the GATT was adopted instead.[6] The first round of trade negotiations that would become the GATT of 1947 was held while the Preparatory Committee was still drafting the ITO Charter. The refusal of the United States to ratify the ITO Charter doomed the body, and the GATT emerged as the trade-governing body because the first round of tariff bargaining had been concluded; the Protocol of Provisional Application of the General Agreement on Tariffs and Trade went into force in 1948. Until the creation of the WTO, the GATT became the de facto standard-bearer with respect to the rules of international trade.

The GATT was never intended to become the international postwar trade regime. Had the ITO Charter been ratified in the United States, reconstruction and liberalization in the global trading system would have taken place under a proper formal international organization, one that provided a global trade policy forum and a legal framework. Because it was merely the trade protocol of its parent organization, the "entirely accidental international institution" (Finlayson and Zacher 1981, 562) was virtually devoid of formal institutional features. Given its temporary and supplementary status, its legal standing was unclear, and it contained no provisions for a budget or a fully fledged secretariat. According to Gardner, for nearly a decade the GATT headquarters greeted visitors with the sign "Interim Commission for the International Trade Commission" (Gardner 1956[1980], xxv). It also did not help matters that in the United States, the GATT never received formal congressional approval. Indeed, the U.S. contributions to the GATT administrative budget were regularly camouflaged as "international conferences and contingencies" in the State Department's budget (Gardner 1956[1980], xxv). It was not until 1968 that Congress received a formal request for permanent authorization for contributions to the GATT Secretariat.

Yet in spite of its lack of formal structure, the GATT emerged as the de facto governing organization as its Contracting Parties authorized several administrative bodies, including a small but permanent secretariat, a

5. For a first-hand account of the negotiations over the ITO Charter, see Wilcox (1949).
6. On the reasons for the failure of the ITO Charter's ratification in the United States, see Diebold (1952) and also Zeiler (1999).

permanent council to maintain operations between meetings, and a network of specialized committees. In the course of its almost five decades of existence, it developed into the authoritative body governing trade, whose role Gardner describes as having four parts: "as a forum for trade negotiations, as a body of principles for governing trade policy, as a center for the settlement of trade disputes, and as a vehicle for the development of trade policy" (Gardner 1956[1980], xxvi).

The goals of the GATT, as noted by its Contracting Parties in the preamble to the original General Agreement of 1947, included "raising the standards of living, ensuring full employment and a large and steadily growing volume of real income and expanding the production and exchange of goods" (GATT 1947). Due in part to its original role as the supplementary trade protocol to be attached to its parent organization, the ITO, the GATT was not intended to be a vehicle for *free* trade as such. This also reflected the general goals of the postwar planners. Indeed, as Hoekman and Kostecki note, "Nowhere is any mention made of free trade as an ultimate goal" (1995, 11). Rather, the GATT was devoted to promoting *liberal* trade in the postwar period, emphasizing liberalization in two main areas of international trade. First, it sought the reduction of trade barriers, that is, "state policies or practices that impede the access countries enjoy to each other's markets for their exports" (Finlayson and Zacher 1981, 562), mainly in the form of tariff reductions. Members—Contracting Parties, as they were called—negotiated reductions in tariffs on the basis of reciprocity in an effort to form "mutually advantageous" arrangements.

Second, the GATT sought to eliminate discriminatory treatment in international trade, focusing the efforts of members on removing quantitative restrictions and preferential tariff systems such as that between Great Britain and its dominions. The GATT's rule-making function thus relied on its two main pillars of reciprocity and nondiscrimination (Bhagwati 1990); as such, the GATT was devoted less to the promotion of free trade than to the removal of trade barriers and the establishment of equality in market access for its members. In doing so, however, the GATT also left out a substantial number of trade issues that would have been covered had the ITO Charter been ratified. Issues such as trade in commodities and private business practices, covered in the ITO Charter, were thus excluded from regulation and supervision, as they were left unaddressed in the GATT, which would largely remain the case until the advent of the WTO.

Power and Time

The central focus of this study is well captured in terms of the independent and dependent variables of interest: the effect of the global trade regime—the GATT and the WTO—on international trade, measured primarily as the extent to which, consistent with its initial goals, the regime has been successful in expanding trade among its members. How member countries have fared in their trade relations provides the clearest and most concrete indication of whether the GATT and the WTO have been effective governance mechanisms for promoting liberal trade. Moreover, patterns in trade among members of the GATT and the WTO illustrate the distributive consequences that that regime has had on the trade of its members. This book thus assesses the distributive consequences of the regime through an examination of actual trade flows, with particular attention to the divide between the developed and the developing worlds. The claims of critics of the trade regime that the rules of international trade are "slanted" in favor of rich industrial countries highlight an important but neglected by-product of regimes. That is, while regimes bring about cooperation among otherwise noncooperative actors and resolve collective action problems, they have larger distributive consequences to the actors that choose to participate in them, creating "winners" out of some while marginalizing others. For its proponents, the GATT was, and continues to be in the form of the WTO, the champion of liberal trade, promoting the benefits of prosperity and peace that attend a stable international economic environment. For its opponents, of which there are more than a few, the regime is still little more than an "exclusive country club," a means to protect the economic interests of the richest countries, which results in the marginalization of the developing world.

In assessing the distributional dimensions of the GATT and the WTO, this book advances arguments about institutional design, institutional development, and institutional effects, privileging the theoretical importance of two key variables: power and time. These variables provide invaluable insight into questions such as why the rules of bargaining over trade in the GATT and the WTO look the way they do, how they have remained so entrenched since the inception of the regime, and what effects they have had in the evolution of the global trade order. In framing the rich and voluminous literature that exists on the General Agreement in terms of these key variables—power and time—this book makes several important contributions to the existing literature and to ongoing debates on institutions, globalization, and governance.

Power and Principal Architects

First, this book emphasizes the role of institutions as constructions of power in which who designs greatly affects the kinds of rules that are installed and the kind of governance mechanism that is brought to bear in a particular issue area. That is to say, the identity and characteristics of the principal architects that bring an institution into existence are given their due. In emphasizing the distributional dimensions of institutions, this book thus plays down the voluntaristic and cooperative components of institutions while directing attention to the more contested and conflict-laden dimension of institutional formation, one that is greatly affected by the politics of power. As much as institutions reflect the resolution of collective action problems, they also figure importantly as arenas of political contestation among powerful actors, who must, as principal architects, resolve their cooperation problems and bring the institution into existence. This book argues that the identity of the principal architects determines how their influence is exercised, whether at the moment of institutional choice or in the course of an institution's development. The characteristics of the principal architects determine the kinds of cooperation problems that arise, how they are resolved, and ultimately, the kind of institution that emerges to govern.

The emphasis on power, in particular, places this book squarely in the "power-politics" paradigm of international institutions propounded in Gruber (2000) and others. This book offers a study of power in the GATT's creation, thus providing a key case study for this theoretical approach. At the same time, it delves deeper into the identity and attributes of the principal architect itself—the United States—to demonstrate how identity, as much as objective considerations of power, fashion institutional outcomes. Applied to the institution in question, this book argues that it was, and is, as much "*American* hegemony" as it was "American *hegemony*" (Ruggie 1992) that determined the normative and functional contours of the existing multilateral trade regime. Indeed, as Robert Pollard, writing more than three decades after the establishment of the GATT, notes:

> The ideas and institutions that govern the world economy today are a direct legacy of the Truman administration. Postwar American leaders—Harry S. Truman, Dean Acheson, William L. Clayton—deliberately fostered the economic interdependence of the major powers in order to ensure U.S. security and prosperity. Even with the momentous changes in the international economy since 1945, the system still functions largely as the postwar generation of policymakers anticipated it would. (1980, 2)

The early outcomes in the GATT spanned the Roosevelt and Truman administrations. They had in common a commitment to a multilateral international economic order as a key to U.S. security. In planning for the postwar order to follow the end of the Second World War, policymakers were chiefly concerned with the reconstruction of Europe, which they believed was critical. As it faced the beginnings of the Cold War, the Truman administration in its grand strategy subsumed foreign economic policy to its main security goals—"the preservation of democracy in Europe, the support of friendly governments in the Far East, and the containment of the Soviet Union" (Pollard 1980, 4).

The imprint of U.S. leadership on the GATT was very much a function of the degree of "compulsory power" (Barnett and Duvall 2005a) the United States wielded at the time of institutional formation. Barnett and Duvall define power generally as "the production, in and through social relations, of effects that shape the capacities of actors to determine their circumstances and fate" (8). In offering a taxonomy of power, "compulsory power" is distinguishable from other forms of power in that it is direct and expressed in the interactions among actors, encompassing "the range of relations between actors that allow one to shape directly the circumstances and/or actions of another" (13). It is the form of power most closely associated with Dahl's (1957) classic definition of A's ability and intent to get B to do something B would otherwise not do. Compulsory power relies as well on commonly used measures of power that are derivable from market size and military capabilities. Barnett and Duvall's classification of different forms of power is valuable for the analysis in this book because it separates "compulsory power" from "institutional power," the diffuse or indirect form of power that operates in social interactions, specifically in the formal and informal institutions that mediate interactions between actors. The powerful actor, through the "rules and procedures" that define the institution, "guides, steers and constrains" (15) other actors, whether in their behavior or in their very existence, with or without intent. Though there is little question as to the endogeneity of compulsory and institutional power, the analytical distinction is useful for, in the first instance, distinguishing what is attributable to the principal architects—the most powerful actors—and what is attributable to the institution itself—the rules that privilege the powerful. The governance question underlying institutional formation thus becomes one of the principal architects utilizing their compulsory power at the moment of institutional choice and transforming it into institutional power, in which prevailing power relations and disparities become embedded in the institutional arrangements.

Time and Longitudinal Effects

In addition to power, this book also privileges the role of time, as it highlights the longitudinal effects of the GATT and the WTO, in analyzing both institutional development and institutional effects. While the role of power demonstrates how principal architects, at the moment of institutional choice, embed prevailing power relations in institutional arrangements,

time is equally important in understanding and explaining how these institutional arrangements constructed through power become reproduced,
generating a feedback process that reinforces those power relations and
contributes to institutional continuity and resilience. This book offers an
analysis of the trade regime's institutional development that emphasizes its
historical context and how the regime was "shaped by its times" (Pomfret
1988). It uses a historical approach to illustrate the resilience in the rules of
bargaining over trade and trade barriers in the GATT and the WTO. The
analyses are devoted, in particular, to identifying the sources of continuity
in the regime, in an effort to identify the causal mechanisms most significant in explaining institutional resilience over time in the trade regime.

The analytical distinction between "compulsory power" and "institutional
power" noted in the previous section is of great value in understanding
the role of temporality in the process of institutional development, as the
analytical distinction allows as well for a temporal separation of these two
different conceptualizations of power. As noted earlier, the endogenous nature of these two forms of power renders a causal feedback loop in which
one form of power not only explains the other but is also partly explained
by it. It is the compulsory power wielded by the principal architects that
installs the institutional power of these actors, giving them privileged positions with respect to the rules, norms, and procedures that define the institution. At the same time, it is also the institutional power they enjoy that
enhances their compulsory power, their positions of power and influence.

Modeling a causal process in this manner runs the risk of circular reason-
ing, as Büthe warns, proposing instead modeling such endogenous causal
processes as a sequence (2002, 485–486), which necessarily brings time
into the picture. The temporal separation of compulsory and institutional
power involves linking the two in a sequence, in which one form of power
is taken as a starting point from which to delineate the feedback process.
Sequencing in this manner illustrates the respective roles of compulsory
and institutional power in the institutional evolution of the GATT/WTO
regime. It allows one to clarify the causal connections between the power
relations that create institutions and the institutional power wielded by the
powerful without having to abandon the assumption that these are mutually
causative. This is not to say that such is the causal sequence that definitively
encapsulates the relationship between compulsory and institutional power.
Indeed, Barnett and Duvall soundly "reject the idea of sequencing," as it
cannot be assumed that "one form of power necessarily and always precedes
the other" and argue instead that these forms of power are jointly present
in many social contexts (2005b, 67). Nevertheless, in this book about the
GATT and the WTO, sequencing is an appropriate approach for analyzing

the role of power in institutional design and institutional development, as the former does precede the latter.

In analyzing the institutional development of the GATT/WTO regime, this book begins with the end of World War II, a critical juncture in which the institutional slate had been wiped clean and a "postwar winning state" (Ikenberry 2001) holding a preponderance of power—the United States—constructed a new international political and economic order. It is thus the compulsory power wielded by the United States at this time that provides the starting point for this temporal sequence. U.S. leadership in the institutional design of the GATT demonstrates how compulsory power is transformed into institutional power. The importance of time, however, is best illustrated in the resilience of the latter—institutional power. Institutional power is strongly resilient and resistant to change in the "rules of the game" (Barnett and Duvall 2005a, 23). It reflects the autonomous aspects of institutions, whose ability to govern continues "after hegemony" (Keohane 1984) in the face of shifts in the power relations that produced them in the first place. Institutional resilience, or the persistence of institutional power over time, explains continuity in the GATT/WTO regime, even with significant and substantial changes in the constituency of its members. For example, to take the puzzle presented by the regime's critics, if the GATT/WTO regime is the premier institution for liberalizing trade and promoting prosperity and peace, it explains why and how developing countries were marginalized. It explains as well, despite the large influx of developing country members, why the global trading system never corrected its deficiencies vis-à-vis the developing countries. The answer lies in the institutional features of the GATT itself, especially the critical role played by early outcomes in the Geneva, Annecy, and Torquay Rounds that made the GATT into an instrument for cementing the Western subsystem against communism. Because the GATT's institutional mechanisms continued to persist throughout the Cold War and even today, in the WTO era, the divide between industrial and developing countries has continued to be a defining institutional feature.

Another important way in which this book privileges the role of time is in its empirical analysis, which emphasizes the longitudinal effects of the GATT and the WTO on actual trade flows. On the effects of the WTO on international trade in particular, the book investigates the impact of *when* countries accede to the regime, which is hypothesized to be directly linked to the scale of the regime's trade-creation effects. More central in terms of the overall methodological approach of the study is the modeling of the effect of the regime as a "treatment effect," in which a country's trade is observed before and after the "treatment," in this case accession to the GATT and/or the WTO. Comparing the levels of trade for countries before and after their accession to the regime is an effective means of gauging the success of the regime in expanding trade. Modeling the effect of the regime in this manner has the advantage of controlling for unit heterogeneity, or those idiosyncratic factors that are attributable to the particular unit under analysis, so it avoids the statistical bias that results from not controlling for these unobservable and intrinsic factors (Green, Kim, and Yoon 2001). In doing so, the analysis essentially compares countries with themselves, before and after they enter the regime, thus enabling the analysis to hold constant those factors that are attributable solely to the countries themselves. In emphasizing the longitudinal dimension of the effects of the GATT and the WTO, the analysis directs greater attention to within-group variation, or how trade is affected in countries that become members of the regime. This stands in contrast to the cross-sectional dimension, which is less emphasized in the analysis, as it compares countries in the regime with those that remain outside it.

The Plan of the Book

The arguments and analyses offered about the GATT and the WTO in this book are framed broadly in terms of "Rules" and "Consequences," thus bridging the gap in existing studies that focus on one or the other—but rarely both. The book is divided into two main parts, each focusing on a different aspect of the story about the GATT/WTO regime. The first part, consisting of two chapters on the "Rules," is a largely qualitative analysis of the regime's inception and evolution. Chapter 1 examines closely the role of power in institutional design, as seen in the institutional preferences of the principal architect, the United States, and how they influenced the most important features of the GATT—namely the bargaining protocol for tariff reductions. The focus of chapter 2 is the role of time, specifically how the institutional arrangements put in place by the powerful nations became entrenched and resistant to change over the years. The core of the analysis examines the persistence of a power-based bargaining protocol through the various negotiating rounds as an important source of institutional resilience. Part 2, on the "Consequences," looks in turn at the GATT and the WTO to assess, through quantitative analyses, their distributive consequences, that is, the actual effect of the regime on international trade. The chapters address the question of how countries have fared as they became members of the GATT and later the WTO, namely whether they experienced a boost in trade following their entry into the regime. The central findings of these chapters are that the largest economies and major powers experienced the greatest gains in trade. Even with the advent of the WTO, little has changed to ameliorate the inequality in trade between industrial and developing countries.

Rules: The Power-Based Bargaining Protocol

In the first part of this book, on "Rules," the analysis examines how power, in the forms of U.S. leadership and great power politics, constructed the rules of the GATT and contributed to their continuation over time. Of particular interest are the origins and persistence of the bargaining protocol: bilateral negotiations on a product-by-product basis among principal suppliers. This is essentially a power-based bargaining protocol (Steinberg 2002), in which market size provides the basis for power in trade negotiations.

The principal supplier rule involves one country offering concessions to the chief source of imports for a particular good and receiving in return concessions on its main exports to that country. It is based on the assumption that each party to a trade negotiation may both offer and receive tariff concessions; however, the ability to offer and receive concessions was limited to countries that were the principal suppliers of the products under negotiation and thus excluded those that were not. As such, small economies, especially developing economies that had little in the way of offering large import markets and thus were not principal suppliers of most of the goods subject to negotiations, wielded little influence and were effectively excluded from the bargaining process. Though never formalized as a "rule" in the trade regime, the principal supplier rule, accompanied by bilateral negotiations and item-by-item negotiations, has been the chief bargaining protocol over the lifetime of the regime. It has also been a major target of criticism from the regime's opponents, who argue that it is the main cause of blame for the resulting "globalization gap" (Isaak 2005, 173–174). The first part of the book is devoted to examining the origins and the resilience of this power-based bargaining protocol.

Chapter 1 is an analysis of the first General Agreement on Tariffs and Trade, signed in 1947, relating it to the broader question of why global trade governance looks the way it does today. Its theoretical focus is on the relationship between power and institutional design, in particular how the process of institutional formation is driven by the leading country and its cooperation problems with other great powers. The analysis focuses on the key institutional arrangements that were installed in the first round of negotiations in Geneva. The institutional preferences of the United States capture the main effect of power in the design of the General Agreement. U.S. preferences also clashed with those of other leading actors, especially Great Britain, and intensified cooperation problems. The institutional

arrangements reflecting U.S. preferences and the resolution of cooperation problems among the great powers determined the normative and
functional contours of the General Agreement. Over time, they generated
strong points of institutional resilience and stability in the regime's development. The chapter also includes a brief discussion of institutional alternatives proposed by developing countries during the negotiations over the
International Trade Organization.

Chapter 2 addresses the question of why the GATT's power-based bargaining changed so little over the course of some five decades and in the
face of changes in U.S. trade politics and integration efforts in Europe. The
analysis thus focuses on the sources of institutional resilience in the GATT
over time, across the rounds of multilateral trade negotiations ending with
the Uruguay Round and the formation of the WTO. The theoretical argument of the chapter emphasizes the regime's path-dependent development
in which opportunities for institutional reform—critical moments—result
in the persistence of the rules established in the original agreement. The
analysis traces the staying power of two power-related institutional arrangements: centralization and flexibility. Centralization is the concentration of
the main task of the GATT—tariff reductions—among the major economies, demonstrating the continuation of power-based bargaining practices
in the GATT. Flexibility refers to the set of exceptions installed in the GATT,
chiefly at the behest of the United States, of which the exceptions for agriculture and the sanctioning of free trade areas and customs unions have
had the most significant effects on the evolution of global trade.

Consequences: The Distributive Divide

The second part of the book, on "Consequences," examines the impact
of the rules of trade. The rules of trade established through the GATT were
directed toward its primary goal of expanding trade in the post–World
War II global economy. The GATT performed three important functions
in this regard. It facilitated the conclusion of trade agreements by providing a multilateral forum for negotiations. The rules of trade installed in the
GATT served to constrain its members, thus reducing the uncertainty inherent in trade relations by encouraging compliance with trade agreements.
The GATT also provided smaller economies with opportunities to participate in and to influence, to a modest degree, the management of trade
barriers. Underlying these key functions of the GATT was the firm belief
among its members that the expansion of international trade would benefit
all states (Finlayson and Zacher 1985, 602). There is little question as to
the success the GATT achieved in reducing tariff levels. At the first round
of negotiations in Geneva in 1947, the United States took the lead, cutting

tariffs on its imports by an average of 35 percent (Irwin 1995, 326). Though subsequent rounds would see progress in tariff cuts only in fits and starts, overall in the five decades since the GATT's inception, tariff rates had fallen substantially, from 40 percent at the end of World War II to 5 percent by the mid-1990s (Irwin 1995, 326).

Yet there is equally little question that the GATT has led to a distributive divide in the global trading system, one in which most of the trade takes place among developed countries and within the industrialized world, while the developing world remains largely marginalized. Gardner (1956) noticed the decided lack of benefits for the developing world in the postwar economic order early in the GATT period:

> For the world economy as a whole, the third of a century since Bretton Woods has been a period of unprecedented prosperity and growth. In very round figures, world production has soared from $300 billion a year to about $10,000 billion a year. Even allowing for inflation, these figures represent an enormous increase in real terms. It is an impressive record, though one must make obvious qualifications, notably the failure of the less-developed countries to share proportionately in this fantastic overall growth. (xvii)

Gerard Curzon, in his detailed study of the General Agreement, describes a similar outcome: "The phenomenal expansion of trade since the end of the Second World War, and hence a feeling that all was well, has probably been responsible for the decline in interest in the subject [of commercial policy]. A reawakening of this interest has typically taken place when it was recently realized that while world trade was increasing, the relative share of the underdeveloped countries in this trade was falling" (1965, 7). The plight of developing countries in the trading world was recognized early on in a GATT-commissioned study of 1958, entitled "Trends in International Trade," which ascribed the declining share of trade of developing countries to the trade policies of the developed countries.[7]

An emerging body of recent scholarship has found both support and controversy in this issue of the distributive divide between industrialized and developing countries. The landmark studies that provide the empirical analysis for this book include Rose (2004), which not only argues that the GATT/WTO regime has had little or no overall effect on expanding trade but also finds that significant differences exist between industrialized and developing countries' trade, differences that mitigate in favor

---

7. The report is better known as the Haberler Report, in honor of Professor Gottfried Haberler, the chairman of the panel of eminent economists appointed by the GATT members and joined by leading economists Meade, Tinbergen, and Campos.

of the former, following accession to the GATT. Subramanian and Wei (2007) have also found support for the distributive divide, again finding large trade-creation effects for industrialized countries relative to developing countries. Goldstein, Rivers, and Tomz (2007) and Tomz, Rivers, and Goldstein (2007) provide important points of debate in the literature through their conceptualization and measurement of de facto and provisional membership. In their empirical analysis, they find support for trade-creating effects of the GATT and the WTO across the board, with membership bestowing developing countries with significant gains in trade. It is to this emerging body of literature that the empirical analysis directs its main attention, engaging the existing studies and their findings through an examination of the distributive consequences of the GATT and the WTO for international trade.

Chapter 3 argues that the strategy that the United States pursued in the GATT divided its members into two groups. A product of an executive intent on stabilizing postwar Europe and a Congress wary of import competition, the strategy created a highly skewed distribution of GATT benefits. It also had an unintended consequence: it left the discriminatory trade blocs of the interwar era largely intact. Using data on bilateral trade flows both before and after World War II, the analyses show that the Commonwealth, Reichsmark, gold, and exchange-control blocs continued to exert a positive and significant effect on trade after 1945. The GATT also had a very strong and significant impact on the trade of only the small set of states U.S. strategy privileged—that is, Canada, France, Germany, the United Kingdom, and the United States. This skewed distribution of benefits is much more consistent with the distribution of state power and preferences within the GATT than with the general welfare enhancement some associate with what is perhaps the paradigmatic example of an international regime.

Chapter 4 analyzes the effects of the WTO on trade among its members in its first decade of existence, 1995 to 2004. The analysis focuses on a key variable: the timing of membership. The chapter examines how trade among WTO members has been affected by the regime's accession rules and the timing of members' entry into the WTO. In its theoretical framework, the chapter distinguishes among "standing members," or those who were members of the GATT as well as the WTO, the "early adopters," those who entered the regime during the Uruguay Round or in the first year of the WTO's creation, and the "later entrants," who gained membership via the lengthy and complex accession process after 1995. The empirical analysis evaluates how WTO member trade has fared under the regime, both among members of the same group and between members of different groups. The chapter assesses the effect of the WTO on trade creation, that is, the degree to which trade expanded after states entered into the regime. The results of the analysis show positive but divergent effects among the groups, demonstrating, first, that old and new members of the WTO have benefited in different ways from participation in the regime, and second, that the rift between industrial and nonindustrial countries persists, as the regime has been largely unsuccessful as yet at boosting trade between them.

The concluding chapter summarizes the book's main findings and their implications for global trade governance and for globalization and governance more broadly. The discussion relates the book's central findings—the power-based bargaining protocol for tariff reductions and the distributive consequences for international trade—to the existing literature calling for institutional reform of the global trading system. Particular attention is devoted to the tradeoffs among preservation of the interests of powerful countries, whose participation in any global trade regime is crucial; the pursuit of economic efficiency that lies at the heart of a liberal trade regime; and the emerging calls for economic justice to level the playing field for developing countries. The chapter concludes with implications of the book's findings for broader issues of institutional reform for the post–Cold War, post-9/11 globalization era, with reference to the major debates surrounding institutional reform of existing Cold War legacies such as the UN and the IMF/World Bank and calls for new institutions to reflect the political and economic landscape of the twenty-first century.

Part I
RULES

1

Who Designs? Power and the Design of the General Agreement

"GATT: *Vive le Provisoire!*"

Gardner (1956[1980])

Why does global trade governance today look the way it does? The rules of trade embodied in the GATT and the WTO can be traced back to the institutional arrangements installed in 1947, when representatives from the various nations gathered to negotiate the first round of tariff reductions for the post–World War II era.[1] In doing so, the twenty-three countries, or "Contracting Parties," established a set of practices for managing international trade that have exhibited remarkable persistence over the years. By the time the Truman administration withdrew, in December 1950, the International Trade Organization (ITO) charter for consideration and ratification by the U.S. Congress, the first round of tariff negotiations had already been concluded in Geneva in 1947, with the Protocol of Provisional Application of the General Agreement on Tariffs and Trade (General Agreement) entering into force in 1948. Thus, until the creation of the WTO, the General Agreement was the de facto institution embodying the rules of international trade.

The two chapters comprising the "Rules" part of this book are devoted to an analysis of the design and development of the GATT, focusing on the original institutional arrangements of 1947 and the evolution of established practices—"rules"—for negotiating the reduction of trade barriers. It offers a present-day reading of the GATT some six decades after its establishment,

---

1. *General Agreement on Tariffs and Trade,* signed in Geneva on 30 October 1947. Applied provisionally as from 1 January 1948 pursuant to the *Protocol of Provisional Application. United Nations Treaty Series* Volume 55, Registration number 814 (Registered *ex officio* on 30 May 1950).

focusing on the great power politics that drove its inception and development. The analysis has implications for how we can understand the role of power in the governance of today's global trading order, as the global trade regime faces critics portraying the WTO as the "rich man's club" that is "rigged" in their favor (Kapstein 2006) with only a semblance of sovereign equality (Steinberg 2002). An important question in the "power politics" story of the GATT is why the great powers chose an institution like the General Agreement but rejected the ITO, a formal international organization to govern trade. The answer lies in great part in the resolution of key bargaining points that the principal architect—the United States—brought to the fore in the negotiations over institutional arrangements.

Problematizing Power in Institutional Design: Who Designs?

The principal architects that bring an institution into existence, variously labeled the "enacting coalition" (Gruber 2000) or the "prime movers" (Moravcsik 1998), are invariably the great powers, states whose positions rank high on factors such as military capability and market size. Existing scholarship has yielded important insights into how the powerful influence institutional outcomes through their "compulsory power" (Barnett and Duvall 2005a, 13–15), the ability to directly control others' actions or circumstances, whether intentional or unintentional. Powerful countries can determine the outcome of distributive conflicts on the "Pareto frontier" (Krasner 1991), produce cooperation through coercion (Martin 1992a), or remove the status quo from the menu of institutional alternatives (Gruber 2000) as well as by keeping certain items on the agenda and leaving others off (Bachrach and Baratz 1962; see also Grieco 1993; Garrett and Weingast 1993; and Oatley and Nabors 1998). Less attention has been directed, however, to the identity and attributes of the principal actors themselves. The General Agreement was an American brainchild, an institutional manifestation of "*American* hegemony" (Ruggie 1992), a commonly accepted view of the trade regime and of little controversy. Such a view necessarily merges power with identity as the main determinants (Nau 2002, 2003) of U.S. leadership in the design of the global trade regime, and this approach frames this chapter's analysis of the regime's design.

The analysis focuses on power in terms of preferences and outcomes, utilizing Nagel's definition: "A power relation, actual or potential, is an actual or potential causal relation between the preferences of an actor regarding an outcome and the outcome itself" (1975, 29). Preferences are defined generally in this analysis, in terms of an actor's ranking of outcomes in a given environment (Frieden 1999, 41), here captured in U.S. preferences regarding the institutional arrangements of the General Agreement. Preferences and outcomes are variables that can be readily observed in the institutional design process, so it avoids making the analysis of power and institutional design contingent on other controversial and contested concepts such as interests, which are not easily observed (Dahl 1991, 31–32).[2] Power as an independent variable also implies the conceptualization of power as causation, applying a notion of influence and capacity attended by intent, the ability to "act on" others and "bring about" institutional outcomes (McFarland 1969, 6–7). It emphasizes the relational and dynamic aspects of *social* power, as contrasted with a more static conception of power as a property (Lasswell and Kaplan 1950, 75).

The focus on power and institutional design engages the existing literature in two main ways. First, it highlights institutions as "structures of power" as much as "structures of cooperation." It brings power back into the analysis in the study of institutions, in which the role of power has been marginalized due to the strong "logic of voluntarism" that emphasizes credible commitments, self-enforcing agreements, and cooperation for mutual benefit, relegating to power a peripheral role (Moe 2005). Indeed, one of the chief conclusions of the rational design project, which identified the major components of institutional design and yet did not include power among them, was the need to analyze "more fully and explicitly" the role of power (Koremenos, Lipson, and Snidal 2001b, 1054).

Second, the question of who designs also directs greater attention to the identity and attributes of the principal architects, which may include, among others, the value systems of the decision-makers involved (Burley 1993; Dahl 1991; Goldstein 1988). Cowhey (1993), for example, has argued that the particular structure of domestic political competition and the transparency of the system as a whole made U.S. commitment to multilateralism after World War II much more credible to the outside world. In this connection, it matters greatly whether it is the United States or Great Britain or China that is the principal architect, and this is more than a little consequential to what the institution will actually look like. The "national identity" (Nau 2002) that the United States sought to realize in Geneva in 1947 is perfectly evident in the words of Herbert Feis of the U.S. delegation: "The American government was eager to preserve in as much of the world as possible the *American* type of trading system; one shaped mainly to private initiative and calculation, ruled mainly by competition, nominally open to all on equal terms, unclamped by rigid controls. It was convinced that by preserving such a system of trade, all countries, and not merely the United States, would

---

2. This precludes, however, an examination of the "third face of power," or the broader social context in which power relations are imbricated (Lukes 1974).

benefit" (Feis 1948, 41; emphasis added). U.S. preferences in the Geneva negotiations of 1947, to the extent that they provided key bargaining points and gave rise to critical cooperation problems for the participants, demonstrated how "*American* hegemony," more than "American *hegemony*," played a defining role in the General Agreement's formation (Ruggie 1992).

The identity and attributes of the principal architects are important for understanding the relationship between power and institutional design, because *who* designs has a direct bearing on *how* the powerful exert their influence. The menu of choices available to those holding "compulsory power" (Barnett and Duvall 2005a) includes bargaining power (Fearon 1998; Krasner 1991), coercive power (Martin 1992a), or "go-it-alone power" (Gruber 2000), the latter involving virtually no coercion but rather the ability of the most powerful to create and derive benefits from a new and exclusive regime without the participation of less powerful actors. It includes agenda control, namely the ability both to put certain issues on the agenda and keep others off (Bachrach and Baratz 1962). Last but not least, there is strategic restraint, in which the leading actor seeks long-term returns to power through institutions rather than short-term gains through coercion alone (Lake 2008, 287; Deudney 2007; Ikenberry 2001).

Finally, it must also be noted that *who* designs and *how* they do so is contingent on *what* is being designed, a question that calls for defining the weight, scope, and domain of power in its effect on institutional design (Lasswell and Kaplan 1950, 77). The extent of the principal architect's participation, the matters over which a powerful actor has influence, and the degree of influence vis-à-vis other actors vary according to the particular issue area or the particular policy-contingency framework (Sprout and Sprout 1956, 49). Baldwin (1971, 1979) argues that political power resources have low levels of fungibility, so the specification of scope and domain—the particular issue area—is critical to gauging the effects of power. This may go far in explaining, for example, why the major post–World War II institutions—the UN, the IMF/IBRD, and the General Agreement—are very different in design despite the leadership of the same principal architect, the United States. Institutional preferences and cooperation problems are strongly framed by the different issue areas, whether they concern international security, monetary relations, or trade. In this sense, context matters as much as the contest among powerful participants in institutional design.

The Imprint of U.S. Leadership

The United States undoubtedly exerted the greatest influence economically, politically, and normatively on the design of the General Agreement as it was negotiated in Geneva in 1947. In the aftermath of World War II, the United States emerged as the leading creditor nation in the global economy. It accounted for approximately one-third of global production and produced 50 percent of the world's manufactured goods (Wilkinson 2006, 24). Clair Wilcox, vice chairman of the U.S. delegation to the Geneva negotiations, pointing out that in 1947 the United States accounted for a third of world exports but only a tenth of its imports, noted, "We [the United States] were in the position of selling everything to everybody... of being creditor to all and debtor to none" (Wilcox 1949, 11).

As table 1.1 shows, in 1946, the year preceding the tariff negotiations, the United States was the leading exporter among the Contracting Parties in Geneva, far ahead of its major ally the United Kingdom and the other major traders such as France and the Benelux countries. The United States also held a significant trade surplus due to the low level of imports relative to its exports. So the United States was in the strongest economic position to influence tariff negotiations, and given its substantial trade surplus, it was expected to offer concessions that would expand trade and aid in postwar reconstruction. Its leadership in the political arena, instrumental

Table 1.1. Exports and imports 1946/1947, GATT contracting parties

Country	Share of world exports (%)	Share of world imports (%)
United States	32.37	14.89
France	7.49	17.61
United Kingdom	12.20	15.60
Canada	7.39	5.30
Belgium	2.25	3.86
India	2.31	2.79
Brazil	3.22	2.01
Australia	2.09	1.69
Cuba	1.58	.89
Netherlands	1.02	2.65
South Africa	1.30	2.58
New Zealand	1.08	.68
Norway	.84	1.37
Pakistan	.55	.18
Czechoslovakia	.95	.61
Chile	.72	.59
China	.11	.37
Luxembourg	.23	.25
Syria	Less than .01	.27
Lebanon	Less than .01	.26

Notes: Data not available for Burma, Ceylon, and Southern Rhodesia. India and Pakistan figures from 1947; data not available for 1946. Data Source for percentage calculations: Barbieri, Keshk, and Pollins 2008.

in constructing the United Nations and the Bretton Woods institutions, afforded it equal influence in the Geneva negotiations. And finally, by virtue of its economic and political position, the United States commanded as well the normative foundations of the postwar peace.

Negotiations over the design of the General Agreement thus proceeded in the shadow of the preponderance of U.S. power (Crick 1951; Diebold 1952; Gardner 1956[1980], 369; Ikenberry 1992; Knorr 1948). Though the product of negotiations among the Allies, in particular the United States and its chief ally Great Britain, the General Agreement's institutional arrangements privileged U.S. preferences. As Wilkinson notes: "The other Allies were merely Greeks at the Rome Court. It was inevitable that the postwar economic institutions would reflect U.S. preponderance" (Wilkinson 2006, 23). The same held true for other countries, especially the developing countries as they tried to assert their preferences in the negotiations over the ITO Charter, the General Agreement's parent organization. India, the countries from South America and Asia, "the smaller countries which have little industry and small variety of natural resources" (Feis 1948, 51), were de facto excluded from the core of decision-making process, thus giving rise to a North-South divide at this early juncture. Indeed, the United States demanded specific nonnegotiable exceptions to be written into the ITO Charter and vetoed motions by China, India, and the Netherlands to amend them (Goldstein 1993, 218).[3]

U.S. Preferences on the General Agreement

The influence of U.S. leadership on the General Agreement's institutional design reflects the confluence of three main forces. First, multilateralism provided the foundational principle on which U.S. planners designed the postwar international order, and it influenced all the institutions that came into being at this time, including the General Agreement. It guided U.S. efforts in forging a "constitutionalist" order (Ikenberry 2001) built on layers of institutions that provide long-term returns to power in place of short-term gains achievable through coercion alone. The multilateralism guiding U.S. postwar planning for the trade regime can best be defined as an "architectural form" or a "deep organizing principle" (Caporaso 1992) characterized by generalized principles of conduct as exemplified through

---

3. These included (1) an escape clause; the exclusion of agricultural commodities from the prohibition of (2) quantitative restrictions; and (3) export subsidization; and (4) exceptions for national security reasons. The United States vetoed China's motion to extend exceptions on quantitative restrictions to manufactured goods and another by China, India, and the Netherlands to allow quantitative restrictions as part of domestic price stabilization policies.

the principle of nondiscrimination, indivisibility as to the collective benefits of free trade, and diffuse reciprocity emphasizing aggregate and indirect gains (Ruggie 1992).

Policymakers pursued multilateralism as a response to the bilateralism of the interwar years, identified with "Peekinese economics" (Culbertson 1937) after George Peek, the sometime special advisor to the president on foreign trade who unsuccessfully attempted to challenge Cordell Hull and his trade agreements program. This bilateralism involved efforts to balance trade on a case-by-case basis with each partner; selective bargaining through the use of the conditional most favored nation (MFN) provision, in which only states that had granted reciprocal concessions would receive MFN treatment for their goods; and extensive state intervention in foreign commerce. In Europe, where this type of bilateralism ran rampant, states deployed trade and exchange controls such as quotas, subsidies, clearing arrangements, and government monopolies that sought to balance trade among particular countries in an effort to limit hard currency exchanges because they were scarce or to gain political advantage, or both.[4] It was exemplified most prominently in the New Plan designed by Hitler's finance minister, Hjalmar Schacht, which sought to secure the dependence of southeastern European countries on the German export market in order to secure German access to raw materials in these countries (Hirschman 1945[1980]).[5]

After the end of World War II, some two hundred bilateral trade and payments agreements were in operation among European countries (Pollard 1985, 65).[6] Bilateralism denied European countries the opportunity

---

4. For a survey of trade and exchange rate policy tools employed in the interwar era of "bilateralism," see Culbertson (1937, chs. 2, 6), who regarded it as the "new mercantilism" designed to support autarchy and nationalism. Snyder, in a study of 510 commercial treaties between 1931 and 1939 comprising only half of those actually negotiated, pointed out that "after nearly a century of world trade on a multilateral basis, a new system has developed" (1940, 791). The vital element of this system was the trade within a pair of states, considered in isolation from trade with others. It relied far more on bilateral bargains, thus giving short shrift to the principle of equal treatment and the unconditional MFN provision that was the norm of the preceding era. Provisions for quotas and exchange controls became integral instruments for bilateral trade-balancing, reflecting stronger control by governments of foreign trade for political purposes. Such rules greatly hindered the expansion of trade in the interwar years as they defined precisely, in qualitative and quantitative terms, the trade between treaty participants (801).

5. During Schacht's short-lived appointment (1934–1937) as finance minister under Hitler, Germany had bilateral clearing arrangements with some twenty-five countries to ameliorate its debt position and increase political influence (Neal 1979, 391).

6. Patterson estimates a far larger number of bilateral exchange arrangements—over four hundred—to be in operation into the 1950s (1966, 54–60).

to buy or to sell goods on the most advantageous terms, kept the volume of intra-European trade below prewar levels, and discouraged long-term recovery (Oatley 2001). Such bilateral arrangements were greatly alarming to U.S. officials, who viewed them as significant obstacles to the recovery of international trade and political stability, and they understood the dismantling of these discriminatory trading arrangements to be a main goal of postwar planning.[7]

The multilateralism espoused by postwar planners also had a strong normative foundation, grounded in the belief of officials in the moral benefits of a liberal order, of which free trade multilateralism was its economic component. U.S. foreign policy took on an "Open Door" orientation, following precedents set by Secretary of State John Hay and the McKinley administration at the turn of the century in pursuing an international environment that afforded equal opportunities in trade and investment for all (Eckes and Zeiler 2003, 14). Adherence to multilateralism was also based on the firm belief that trade led to peace and prevented war, well captured in the slogan of the time that "if goods can't cross borders, soldiers will" (Gardner 1956[1980], 9). It was most strongly held and advocated by Secretary of State Cordell Hull, whose beliefs had a lasting imprint on the architecture of the postwar order. Postwar planners linked peace with prosperity, prosperity with free trade and also stable exchange rates and free capital movements. This normative dimension of U.S. multilateralism resonates strongly with Wendt's (2001, 1024–1029) emphasis on the "logic of appropriateness" as an alternative to the "logic of consequences" (March and Olsen 1998). As much as the U.S. influence on the General Agreement was strategic in the sense that it reflected core security interests in the economic realm, it was also very much driven by the normative concerns of the policymakers involved and by the involvement, to varying degrees, of these same officials in negotiating the establishment of all U.S.-led postwar institutions (Burley 1993).

Second, Cold War imperatives entailed gearing foreign policy toward the reconstruction of key U.S. allies, especially in Europe. Institutional choice surrounding the General Agreement had as much to do with U.S. security imperatives as with market and efficiency considerations. U.S. preferences

---

7. Though the currency depreciation and exchange controls attending these trading arrangements are roundly condemned as mechanisms that either caused or continued the Great Depression, this view is not without controversy. For example, Eichengreen and Sachs (1985) argue that currency depreciation in European countries promoted growth and caused a rise in real wages and exports, higher levels of competitiveness, and lower interest rates. More widespread adoption of such policies, they argue, would have benefited the global economy and brought countries out of the Great Depression.

were strongly driven by the "high" politics of national security. The British financial crisis in 1947, the result of a short-lived period of convertibility for the pound sterling, provided the final evidence of the decline of Great Britain as one of the three superpowers after World War II.[8] The withdrawal of British forces from Greece and Turkey, and America's filling of this political vacuum with the promulgation of the Truman Doctrine on 12 March 1947, officially marked the transition of the international system into bipolarity.

As the Cold War became the main focus of foreign policy, U.S. foreign policy under the Truman administration pursued the containment of Soviet power and influence through a combination of economic aid with political support to the "strongpoints" in Europe and Asia, namely Great Britain, France, Germany, and Japan (Pollard 1985, 240). The U.S. security agenda was directed toward strengthening its major allies, especially in Europe, reflecting the prevailing view of the importance of security dividends from a strong Western subsystem. This was reflected in the General Agreement as well, as tariff concessions frequently benefited the goods of major allies whose expansion of trade would have security dividends for the United States.[9] The case of the General Agreement demonstrates how security considerations among the great powers came to shape the governance of the global trading system.

Finally, U.S. preferences on the General Agreement's institutional design were shaped by domestic politics, reflecting the negotiating positions of U.S. policymakers as "transmission belts" (Moravcsik 1997, 518) for the preferences and social power of domestic actors. Domestic divisions over trade policy, in particular those surrounding the provisions of the Reciprocal Trade Agreements Act (RTAA), significantly curtailed the "win-set," or acceptable institutional arrangements (Putnam 1988) available to U.S. negotiators in Geneva. Cordell Hull's successful pursuit of the RTAA's passage

---

8. In accordance with the Anglo-American Financial Agreement of 1945, the British pound became convertible again on 15 July 1947. The subsequent weeks brought steep declines in Great Britain's dollar reserves: $106 million were drained in the week beginning 20 July, $126 million in the following week, $127 million in the week after that, reaching $184 million in the week ending on 16 August. To maintain its reserves at $2.5 billion, the British government took heavy drafts on the $3.75 billion loan from the United States, and by 16 August only $850 million remained in the line of credit (Gardner 1956[1980], 312). The British government suspended convertibility on 20 August 1947.

9. Cold War imperatives also entailed restricting trade with Communist countries. Truman invoked the escape clause in 1950 and withdrew concessions on fur felt hats and bodies, thus restricting imports from Czechoslovakia. Communist China withdrew from the General Agreement in 1950. Truman further restricted trade with the Soviet Union and its satellites by signing in August 1951 a proclamation that suspended trade agreement concessions to the Soviet bloc, including Czechoslovakia, the People's Republic of China, and Vietnam.

in 1934 had marked an institutional "turning point" (Haggard 1988), as for the first time in U.S. trade politics history, Congress granted effective authority to the executive for setting tariffs.[10] Nevertheless, the RTAA necessitated several practices that later became the bargaining protocol adopted under the General Agreement. It entailed adherence to item-by-item negotiations on tariffs, and the executive could not carry out, as the British would later argue for in the Geneva negotiations, unilateral or any form of across-the-board reductions in American tariff rates (Gardner 1956[1980], 22). Trade agreements were also concluded through bilateral accords in an effort to ensure reciprocity in the reduction of tariff barriers. The bilateral bargaining method was considered to impose the least disturbance to domestic producers and to secure for American exports concessions that reciprocated those made by the United States on its imports (Curzon 1965, 129).

Most important for the General Agreement, trade agreements adhered to the principal supplier rule, where the United States would offer concessions to the chief source of imports for a particular good and seek concessions on the main export of the United States to that particular country. The principal supplier rule was justified largely on economic grounds, both in its benefits to consumers in the form of lower prices (Taussig 1892) and in the U.S. bargaining position vis-à-vis trading partners (Culbertson 1937, 72).[11] It was thought to maximize bargaining leverage for the United States by concentrating on the partner country's largest export product. The United States would be able to secure the lowest tariff barriers through negotiations with the most important supplier of a good rather than with

10. For alternative views on how the RTAA was shaped by domestic forces and how this in turn affected trade liberalization in the United States, see Hiscox (1999), Schnietz (2000), and Destler (2005). Schnietz, in particular, argues that the RTAA was intended on the part of its supporters to protect the Democrats' low tariff policy from future reversals by Republicans. It "institutionalized" a low tariff policy and led to a durable low tariff policy, one that could not easily be turned over, as had been done in previous years, by a Republican-controlled Congress. On the other hand, Hiscox argues that the resilience of the RTAA is attributable more to exogenous changes, chiefly the postwar boom in U.S. trade, which shifted the support base of the Republican Party in favor of export-oriented constituencies of the South and the West. Combined with the long-term shift as well in U.S. comparative advantage toward capital intensive industries, such trends resulted in a wholesale shift in support of liberalization for the Republican Party.

11. "In the first place, there must be a sufficient field for tariff bargaining. This exists when the other country concerned is an important, usually the principal, supplier of one or more articles which might be made the subject of tariff commitments on our part. Tariff reductions on commodities of which the country concerned is not an important supplier are scarcely feasible since they would unduly diminish the basis for negotiation with the country which is the principal supplier." (Culbertson 1937, 72).

a smaller supplier (Butler 1998, 104). The bilateral approach to bargaining in trade agreements was reconciled with multilateralism by way of the unconditional MFN provision, included in all trade agreements negotiated under the RTAA.

Effect on the General Agreement:
Normative Foundations and Centralization

U.S. leadership in the Geneva negotiations influenced the design of the General Agreement in two main ways. First, the multilateralism espoused by the United States became enshrined in the General Agreement's guiding principle of nondiscrimination, provided for in the unconditional MFN provision.[12] As Curzon emphasizes, "Non-discrimination is probably the most important single concept that informs General Agreement" (1965, 57). Sir Eric Wyndham White, director general of the GATT for the first two decades of its existence, similarly referred to nondiscrimination as the "cornerstone" of the regime (Finlayson and Zacher 1981, 566). Article I of the General Agreement reads, "Any advantage, favour, privilege or immunity granted by any contracting party to any product originating in or destined for any other country shall be accorded immediately and unconditionally to the like product originating in or destined for the territories of all other contracting parties."

The normative basis of the unconditional MFN provision was, and continues to be, equality of treatment. It is synonymous with "generalized principles of conduct," a key property of multilateralism (Ruggie 1992). In his analysis of the unconditional MFN clause, Curzon (1965, 68) argues that the multilateral context of the unconditional MFN provision made it all the more significant. Unlike in bilateral agreements where the provisions secured the best possible treatment only for the two parties involved, the General Agreement's multilateralism clause contained the recognition that discrimination only leads to more discrimination and in the long run everyone would lose even if some may benefit temporarily. It thus secured, at least in principle, a commitment to the benefits of nondiscrimination in international trade.[13] Although significant exceptions allowing for flexibility would

12. Insertion of the unconditional MFN clause was part of the U.S. *Proposals for the Expansion of World Trade and Employment*, delineating the Roosevelt and later Truman administrations' plans for post–World War II reconstruction. It also received the support of Great Britain, which agreed with it as a basis of the post–World War II trading arrangement (Curzon 1965, 61).

13. The nondiscrimination principle is attended by the other "pillar" of the General Agreement: the principle of reciprocity (Bagwell and Staiger 1999: 217). Reciprocity involves the

follow in negotiating the General Agreement, its institutional arrangements were nevertheless framed by the central organizing principle of multilateralism that defined U.S. leadership, and the principle of nondiscrimination has endured as a longstanding norm to guide international economic activity after World War II.[14]

Second, U.S. leadership also led to centralization in the General Agreement. It centralized bargaining through "clustering" (Pahre 2001), bilateral negotiations taking place simultaneously among the nineteen negotiating units representing twenty-three countries.[15] The bilateral agreements that resulted from the negotiations were then combined, thus forming the General Agreement on Tariffs and Trade. More important, however, the General Agreement's institutional arrangements centralized bargaining *power* in the group of principal suppliers that made up the main negotiating parties. This was the result of applying U.S. practices in implementing the RTAA.

The principal suppliers among whom the negotiations were centralized were the large trading nations in the group of twenty-three Contracting Parties. The group included the great powers and the key European economies—the United States, the United Kingdom, France, Canada, and the Benelux countries as a group. Together they represented over three-quarters of the trade conducted by all twenty-three Contracting Parties in the Geneva Agreement.[16] They included the most important trading

---

exchange of "concessions," in which one country agrees to reduce its protection of trade in return for the same from a trading partner, thus resulting in a mutual exchange that is likely to lead to equal changes for both countries' imports. The General Agreement relies also on "first-difference" reciprocity, emphasizing equality in changes and reductions of tariffs from their initial levels. This is distinguishable from and arguably a piecemeal effort toward "full" reciprocity, which emphasizes reciprocity of overall market access and a "level playing field" in trade relations (Bhagwati and Irwin 1987, 117).

14. Aversion to discriminatory arrangements, especially those reminiscent of the interwar period, persisted in policy circles well into the post–World War II era. In his study of the collapse of the Bretton Woods system, for example, Gavin (2004) notes that the fear of abandoning the gold standard and adopting a floating exchange rate regime was in great part driven by the view of policymakers that this was to blame for the collapse of the world economy in the interwar years, pushing countries to promote autarchic economic policies and support dictatorships and, eventually, war. Gavin notes, "Any situation that remotely looked like a repeat of the 1930s was to be avoided at all costs" (25).

15. The final negotiating units included the first sixteen consisting of Australia, the Benelux Customs Union (Belgium, Luxembourg, and the Netherlands), Brazil, Canada, Chile, China, Cuba, Czechoslovakia, France, India and Pakistan, the Lebanon-Syrian Customs Union, New Zealand, Norway, South Africa, the United Kingdom, and the United States. Burma, Ceylon, and Southern Rhodesia signed the agreement separately from Great Britain, though Great Britain carried out the initial negotiations. Similarly, India conducted the initial negotiations, but Pakistan, which became newly independent during this time, signed the Agreement separately (USTC 1948, Part II, 19, 40).

16. *General Agreement on Tariffs and Trade* (1947), Annex H.

partners of the United States, as reported by the U.S. Tariff Commission (1948).[17] Moreover, the members of this group included the large economies that U.S. officials considered critical to European reconstruction and to the containment of the Soviet threat on the continent.[18] So in centralizing bargaining among the principal suppliers, U.S. leadership had the effect of centralizing bargaining power as well.

For the United States, the item-by-item approach to tariff cuts conformed to the requirements of the RTAA and at the same time enabled U.S. officials to concentrate concessions among the key beneficiaries of postwar planning, the large economies of Western Europe. Centralization in the General Agreement is closely related to its conceptualization in Oatley's (2001) study of the European Payments Union, of which the United States was the main source of capitalization (958–959). As the main creditor and the leading economy after the war, the United States was in the strongest position to affect the course of the trading system. It did so by concentrating its concessions on goods from countries critical to its postwar reconstruction goals. Over half of the dollar amount of U.S. concessions in Geneva—52 percent—was granted on goods from major allies and European economies: Canada, the United Kingdom, and France.[19] U.S. multilateralism was tempered by considerations of European security and especially British economic strength and recovery.[20]

17. These countries are included among the group (A) countries, with which the United States had trade agreements predating the General Agreement and which accounted for over half of U.S. imports and exports in 1939 (USTC 1948, Part III, 58). These agreements were superseded by the General Agreement following its signature.

18. Germany and Japan, as important U.S. Cold War allies, fared differently under the General Agreement regime. U.S. officials came to recognize that European reconstruction required Germany's participation and pursued its successful accession to the General Agreement in 1951. Japan's accession, however, did not occur until 1955, due to opposition from countries with strong textile interests, and was consistently the target of Article XXXV invocations, the "non-application" clause (Curzon 1965, 67). U.S. efforts to obtain membership for Japan failed in Annecy in 1949 due to opposition by Great Britain and other European countries (Lipson 1983, 250n58). Even in securing Japan's accession, the United States offered generous concessions to European countries in return for the latter's granting of concessions to Japan.

19. The figure is derived from the State Department's *Analysis of General Agreement on Tariffs on Trade* (1947, 136–137). Of the approximately $1.34 billion dollars' worth of concessions made by the United States in Geneva, including reductions in duties, tariff bindings, and duty-free items, approximately $691 million (52 percent) were granted on goods from these three major powers. Extended to include trade from Belgium, the Netherlands, and their respective colonies, the concessions to these five countries comprised just about two-thirds (66 percent, or $882 million) of total U.S. concessions. These figures were calculated on the basis of value of imports in 1939.

20. U.S. support to key Cold War allies within the General Agreement would extend as well to smaller economies such as Italy after its accession. In Annecy in 1950, for example, U.S.

The main effect of power, in the form of U.S. leadership, provided the normative foundations of the General Agreement's institutional design and led to centralization in its main task of bargaining over tariffs. The preferences of the United States were a product of the multilateralism of postwar planners, the security imperatives of the Cold War, and the constraints of domestic politics. Its role as the principal architect led to centralization in bargaining, in terms of who bargained—the principal suppliers—and on what goods—those from countries whose economic recovery through trade was critical to European reconstruction. In doing so, the General Agreement also centralized bargaining power among the major powers and key U.S. allies in the Cold War, thus embedding these power relations in the General Agreement's institutional design.

Distributional Conflict

Power in the General Agreement's institutional design also had significant interaction effects, as U.S. preferences clashed with those of other actors, giving rise to or intensifying cooperation problems during the Geneva negotiations. The most important of these were distribution and uncertainty problems.[21] First, the distribution problem in the General Agreement's design centered on the resolution of conflict between its two most powerful participants, Great Britain and the United States.[22] U.S. goals of dismantling discriminatory trading arrangements clashed most strongly with Great Britain's intention to retain Imperial Preference, and in this way the distribution problem was intensified by strong U.S. preferences on this particular issue. The Anglo-American conflict became the distribution problem most critical to the General Agreement's institutional establishment. Despite the

---

negotiators granted a concession on lemons, a key export for Italy, and cut its tariff by 50 percent. Truman, ignoring the peril point limits on lemon imports, supported the concession to aid in Italy's economic stability to prevent Communist insurgency in Sicily and to secure Italy's allegiance to NATO (Zeiler 1999, 177).

21. While the focus of this book is on the interaction of power with uncertainty and distribution problems in the General Agreement's design, these variables had individual main effects, or "lower order" effects, of their own, though they did not figure as prominently in determining institutional design outcomes. These included the distribution problem surrounding special treatment for developing countries, which was more prominent in negotiations over the ITO Charter, and uncertainty more generally among the Geneva negotiating parties. The flexibility provisions of the General Agreement partly reflected the resolution of these cooperation problems.

22. The positions of power held by the United States and the United Kingdom were evident as well in the construction of other postwar institutions, such as during the Bretton Woods conferences: "There were few instances in which countries other than the United States and United Kingdom were able to influence the final outcome" (Mikesell 1994, 3).

multilateral context of the Geneva negotiations, the importance of Anglo-American agreement had the result of rendering a strong bilateral aspect to the bargaining process (Diebold 1988, 12).

The distribution problem resolved by institutional arrangements involves choosing from among a known set of alternatives. Negotiations over the General Agreement centered on how and what form of cooperation was to be achieved through the General Agreement's institutional arrangements. Actors, especially the major powers, were already agreed on the need for cooperation in reducing tariff barriers. Conflict over institutional design occurred because actors could not agree on which cooperative arrangement to adopt as they negotiated on outcomes along the "Pareto frontier," the range of Pareto-improving institutional outcomes yielding benefits of varying degrees for all participants (Krasner 1991; Sebenius 1991).[23] In negotiations over the reduction of trade barriers, distributional conflicts arose over which countries would lower or eliminate how much of their tariffs or trade preferences. It was a "bargaining problem," with multiple possible arrangements that all parties prefer to no agreement, but where the parties disagree in their respective rankings of preferred arrangements (Fearon 1998, 274). Because early outcomes resolving distributional problems are subject to long-term consequences, institutional formation entails high contracting costs, demonstrating "Fearon's dynamic" (Rosendorff and Milner 2001, 850), in which the long shadow of the future makes it more difficult to strike the initial bargain.

The Anglo-American Distributional Conflict

The Anglo-American conflict over Imperial Preference, the tariff preferences negotiated among Great Britain and its dominions Canada, Australia, and New Zealand in the Ottawa Agreement of 1932, was the single most difficult obstacle to the conclusion of the General Agreement in Geneva (Gardner 1956[1980], 355).[24] At the heart of the disagreement were the

---

23. Morrow identifies four distinguishing characteristics of distribution problems: (1) several Pareto-improving solutions exist; (2) all are better off coordinating on one solution rather than individually different solutions; (3) there is uncertainty on the part of actors about their own preferences, though some information is available on what each may prefer; and (4) given this uncertainty, actors have divergent preferences in the ranking of the institutional arrangements (1994, 391–392). These problems are specific to the institutional design, or bargaining phase (Fearon 1998), and their resolution precedes issues of enforcement, that is, "There is nothing to enforce without an agreement" (Morrow 1994, 393).

24. On the provisions of the Ottawa Agreement and its impact on Dominion trade and especially U.S. trade with Great Britain, see Glickman (1947). Anglo-American conflict over Imperial Preference actually began during the war. In negotiating Article VII of the Lend-Lease Master Agreement with Britain, signed 23 February 1942, the United States in the end

differing positions on the nature and priorities of the postwar order. Postwar planners in the U.S. State Department were intent on the revival of an open global trading order, but the British wartime cabinet prioritized full employment and economic stability. The former entailed the dismantling of trade barriers, a main target of which included the system of Imperial Preference under the Ottawa Agreement, characterized by Secretary of State Cordell Hull as "the greatest injury, in a commercial way, that has been inflicted on this country since I have been in public life" (Pollard 1985, 12).[25] The latter, on the other hand, implied the maintenance of Imperial Preference and even bilateral arrangements to balance trade.

In the end, the negotiations in Geneva were saved by a compromise: the United States would agree to the continuation of Imperial Preference, and in return, Great Britain would agree not to increase them.[26] The onset of the Cold War had greatly privileged the position of Great Britain, the main ally of the United States in the superpower struggle and described by Speaker of the House Sam Rayburn as "our great natural ally" (Gardner 1956[1980], 251).[27] Britain was a key component of U.S. security, as a strong and prosperous Britain would lead, it was believed, to an equally prosperous and democratic Europe that would stand as a bulwark against Soviet expansionism. The emergence and resolution of distributional issues in the General Agreement negotiations were in this way fundamentally shaped by the great power politics of the Cold War and the need for solidarity within the Western alliance.

Related to the issue of Imperial Preference and also a significant source of distributional conflict was the formula for tariff reductions. British officials

---

did not compel Britain to relinquish trade preferences. Though Article VII did call for an end to trade discrimination and the reduction of trade barriers, the provision was qualified by the insertion of the phrase "mutually advantageous economic relations" as a condition for such goals (Zeiler 1999, 26). Similarly, in negotiations over the provisions of the Atlantic Charter, announced on 14 August 1941, shortly before negotiations resumed over the Lend-Lease Agreement, Point Four, which provided for commitment to liberalize postwar trade, included the phrase "with due regard for our present obligations," which Britain inserted in order maintain preferences for the Commonwealth (26).

25. Glickman argues, however, based on aggregate trade figures and an analysis of the changes in the composition of trade, that U.S. trade was "not greatly injured" (468) by the Imperial Preference system (1947, 468).

26. Zeiler (1999, 108–121) provides an excellent account of the drama surrounding the Anglo-American agreement, which did not conclude until 17 October 1945, two days past the official termination date, held up agreements with the dominions, and generally held the entire fate of the General Agreement hostage.

27. In the congressional debate on the Anglo-American Financial Agreement of 1945, for example, which provided a $3.75 billion line of credit for Great Britain to aid in its postwar recovery, supporters argued that approval of the loan agreement would greatly determine the future of the international order, between one with cooperation between British and American spheres and one with cooperation between British and Soviet spheres.

called for an across-the-board tariff reduction. This had been the central recommendation of the Overton Report, the British plan for the postwar economic order. It recommended tariff reductions on a sector-wide basis, so as to encourage more sweeping concessions from the United States in return for a "radical diminution of Imperial Preferences" from Great Britain (Zeiler 1999, 29). The sectoral approach to tariff cuts was also preferred by the Executive Committee on Foreign Policy in the United States, as it imposed a more precise obligation to participating countries. Nevertheless, U.S. officials recognized that such an approach would have difficulty finding support. Provisions placing a ceiling on tariff levels and an across-the-board formula for tariff reductions were beyond the authority granted by the RTAA. Instead, U.S. planners proposed an alternative method to tariff cuts that better suited its provisions. This alternative proposal called for simultaneous negotiations of bilateral accords between pairs of countries on a product-by-product basis, with concessions being generalized to a "nuclear" club of major nations (Zeiler 1999, 43). Such an approach was consistent with the RTAA, as it entailed tariff reductions on selected items among principal suppliers that were generalized through the unconditional MFN clause. This was the bargaining protocol, conforming to U.S. preferences, that would eventually be implemented in Geneva.

Effect on the General Agreement: Flexibility

The Anglo-American distributional conflict was resolved through flexibility in the General Agreement. This flexibility was adaptive, designed to take account of special circumstances, rather than transformative, which entails a more profound renegotiation of institutional arrangements (Koremenos, Lipson, and Snidal 2001b, 773). Flexibility provisions in the General Agreement as a whole took the form of "exceptions" to the principle of nondiscrimination and to the unconditional MFN clause. They resolved not only problems of distribution but also uncertainty problems, which figured prominently in the Geneva negotiations and are discussed in the next section. The Anglo-American distributional conflict was resolved through Article I, paragraph 2, which allowed for the continued application of existing preferences in accordance with the compromise between the United States and Great Britain. It was specifically designed to accommodate the existing system of Imperial Preference, but the United States was also able to grandfather preferences it had granted to Cuba in 1903 and to the Philippines in 1946 when it became independent.

The exception allowing the continued application of existing preferences immediately follows the unconditional MFN clause in Article I, paragraph 1. Its position in the General Agreement suggests that existing preferences, and in particular Great Britain's Imperial Preference, comprise the most important "exception" to the nondiscrimination principle, at least at the time it was instituted.[28] Nevertheless, it was qualified by the other half of the Anglo-American compromise, that preferences would not be increased. As specified in the London Suggested Charter for the International Trade Organization, the General Agreement's intended parent organization whose provisions would later be incorporated into the Agreement, there were three specific limitations on continued preferences. First, there would be no new goods on which preferences would be applied, and existing margins of preference would not be increased. Second, in the event of reductions in MFN rates, this would automatically reduce or eliminate the present margins of preference. Finally, existing international commitments would not stand in the way of agreements in reductions in preferences (Gardner 1956[1980], 348).[29]

Uncertainty about the State of the World

The second cooperation problem influencing the General Agreement's formation was uncertainty, which the rational design project proposes as a new variable to consider in the study of institutional design (Koremenos, Lipson, and Snidal 2001b, 774). The uncertainty problem most applicable to the Geneva negotiations is uncertainty about the "state of the world," an information problem addressing the lack of knowledge about future circumstances and the consequences of particular choices (Morrow 1994).[30] Of particular importance to this analysis is the conceptual development provided in Rosendorff and Milner (2001). Their study analyzes the role of domestic politics as an important source of uncertainty about the state of the world and how it affects the design of trade institutions. They argue that safeguards such as escape clauses are an "efficient equilibrium under conditions of

---

28. Curzon argues that preferences did not long continue to be the thorny issue that it was in 1947. By the 1960s, Curzon notes, "It hardly seems credible that the American negotiators' failure to dislodge Imperial Preferences in 1947 should have been one of the bigger stones thrown at the [ITO] Charter and the Agreement." (1965, 76).

29. *Havana Charter for an International Trade Organization* (U.S. Department of State 1948), Article 17.

30. The rational design project also distinguishes between uncertainty about preferences and uncertainty about behavior, but these figured less prominently in the General Agreement. Requests and offers for tariff concessions were circulated among all Contracting Parties before the start of negotiations, thus reducing uncertainty about these particular preferences. The tariff schedule, which specifically listed reduced or bound rates of duties on negotiated goods, lessened uncertainty about behavior and compliance with agreed tariff reductions, though nontariff barriers such as import controls and quantitative restriction still posed problems for assessing compliance.

domestic uncertainty" (831).[31] Where the future of domestic support for free trade or protection is difficult to predict, safeguards allowing for flexibility make trade-liberalizing agreements more politically viable. Along similar lines, this study also finds that uncertainty regarding domestic political support for free trade and trade liberalization in the United States shaped its institutional preferences and was a significant factor leading to flexibility in the design of the General Agreement.

Uncertainty in U.S. Politics

Uncertainty about the state of the world began essentially with the question of domestic support in the United States for its leadership in the overall postwar order. This uncertainty played a prominent role in postwar planning during the war. During the Roosevelt administration, officials of the Political Subcommittee noted that "one of the principal elements of *uncertainty* in our preparations for the peace was the question of how far public opinion in this country would be willing to go in international cooperation after the war" (Notter 1949, 195; emphasis added).[32] The experience after the First World War with the Treaty of Versailles and especially the League of Nations was still fresh in the public's mind. Any participation by the United States in a postwar system that involved a formal organization for international cooperation depended on congressional approval. The prospects for participation would be adversely affected by a negative or even indifferent public reaction to such participation. Officials involved in postwar planning recognized the possibility that any U.S. proposal, even if accepted by the Allies, may fail to be endorsed by the American people and the Congress, thus significantly weakening the U.S. position (Notter 1949, 195).

The fate of the RTAA came to be the focal point of the uncertainty problems plaguing the Geneva negotiations. The source of the uncertainty associated with the RTAA was its temporary nature, as it was subject to renewal and thus to the vagaries of congressional politics at each round. The politics surrounding its renewal heightened the uncertainty among postwar planners in the United States, who could not predict with confidence the level

---

31. Horn, Maggi, and Staiger similarly argue that where uncertainty concerns domestic demand or shocks in the volume of trade, the inclusion in trade agreements of escape clauses may be optimal and appealing to governments as they allow discretion over domestic policy instruments (2006, 4).

32. Harley Notter's documentation of postwar planning in the State Department between 1939 and 1945, undertaken at the request of President Truman, provides a detailed narrative prepared from "thousands of minutes of meetings, memoranda, reports, telegrams, drafts and revisions of studies, notes on personal ideas and suggestions, as well as matured papers containing recommendations and proposals" (1949, 3).

of congressional support for the reciprocal trade agreements program. For example, in the renewal of 1943, in the midst of the war, legislators were concerned about the "unpredictable economic conditions which would confront the United States when the hostilities ended" (USTC 1948, Part II, 13). So the RTAA was renewed, though in its original form, for a period of two rather than the three years accepted in the previous renewals of 1937 and 1940.

Congress renewed the RTAA in 1945 as World War II was drawing to a close, this time for a period of three years, until 1948. In the congressional hearings and debates that preceded the renewal, attention was focused "on the question of adequate safeguards for domestic producers in the event of further duty reductions, especially in view of the *uncertainties of the postwar period*" (USTC 1948, Part II, 15, emphasis added). It was at this renewal that Congress received assurance from the Truman administration of a comprehensive "escape clause," similar to the one included in the trade agreement with Mexico in 1942, that would be included in all future trade agreements.[33] This ensured that future trade agreements would go further "to avoid serious injury to domestic industries and to afford adequate safeguards" (15). The specific measures authorized by the escape clause included the withdrawal of previously granted concessions as well as their modification, through the imposition of quota limitations on imports or other such restrictions, when "found necessary to prevent or remedy serious injury to domestic producers" (15). On 25 February 1947, only a few months before negotiations began in Geneva, Truman issued Executive Order 9832, which required every agreement thereafter entered into under the authority of the RTAA to include an escape clause.[34]

Uncertainty and the Geneva Negotiations

The uncertainty of trade politics in the United States exerted a powerful impact on the position of many of Geneva's negotiating teams. Great

33. This was a compromise for the Truman administration, which had to contend with Republican leaders such as Senators Vandenberg and Millikin, who represented congressional skepticism regarding the economic benefits of the RTAA and especially the outcome of the Geneva negotiations that were about to begin. The senators wanted to limit future tariff concessions through the insertion of peril points for the next renewal of the RTAA. Although Truman rejected this proposal, he did accept the other proposal that escape clauses be inserted in all future trade agreements.

34. "There shall be included in every trade agreement hereafter entered into under the authority of the said act of 12 June 1934, as amended, a clause providing in effect that if, as a result of unforeseen developments and of the concession granted by the United States on any article in the trade agreement, such article is being imported in such increased quantities and under such conditions as to cause, or threaten, serious injury to domestic producers of like or similar articles, the United States shall be free to withdraw the concession, in whole or in part, or to modify it, to the extent and for such time as may be necessary to prevent such injury" (Executive Order, 9832, Part I, Article 1).

Britain, more than any other by virtue of its position as a major power and key player in the post–World War II order, was skeptical of U.S. commitment to trade multilateralism in the long term. Its domestic situation, marked by huge trade deficits late in the war, made the British reluctant to adopt American multilateralist programs. British officials also questioned the strength of U.S. commitment: "What assurance, they asked, did Britain have that American isolationism would not reemerge after the war, just as it had after World War I?" (Pollard 1985, 67). Following the American multilateralist trade program might in fact worsen Great Britain's balance of payments position and bring a halt to their efforts toward full employment.

Concerns about the renewal of the RTAA and, if renewed, what form it would take in the way of protectionist provisions such as peril points—maximum allowable tariff reductions, determined individually for each product under negotiation—compelled U.S. allies to seek even greater concessions from the United States. The uncertainty problem centered on the prospect that they might grant concessions only to have the United States, in the renewal of the RTAA, "defect" later on by putting up protectionist barriers (Zeiler 1999). Even during the negotiations, the leader of the British delegation, Sir Stafford Cripps, pointed out that Britain was at a disadvantage. Imperial Preference was bound against increases in a permanent way; however, U.S. tariff concessions were bound only for three-year periods, and even then they could be withdrawn at any time under the escape clause. He emphasized that concessions had to be "mutually advantageous... not just in terms of paper concessions, but in terms of trade likely to flow" (Gardner 1956[1980], 356).

The uncertainty problem also had the effect of intensifying the major distributional conflict at the Geneva negotiations. Events such as the Republican victory in the congressional elections of 1946, Executive Order 9832 mandating the escape clause, and the U.S.-Philippine trade agreement of 1946 that granted special preferences to the newly independent country heightened the uncertainty over the U.S. commitment to trade multilateralism in the long term and in turn intensified the distributional struggle among the major powers. For the British in particular, these developments served to indicate the lack of assurance in the U.S. commitment to multilateralism and to tariff reductions. As a consequence, the British side felt more urgently the need to hedge its bets and hold onto Imperial Preference.

Effect on the General Agreement: Flexibility

Institutional preferences originating in the uncertainty of postwar domestic politics in the United States heightened as well the general uncertainty faced by countries in the Geneva negotiations, and it led to greater flexibility in the General Agreement's design. This flexibility was adaptive rather than transformative, as was the case for addressing the distributional problem, allowing the institution to accommodate temporary "defections" due to special circumstances while retaining the institution itself.

Flexibility provisions to address problems of uncertainty in the General Agreement took three main forms. First, the escape clause in Article XIX provided for emergency action on imports as a result of unforeseen circumstances. It allowed Contracting Parties to suspend, withdraw, or modify a concession on a particular good if imports of the good "cause or threaten serious injury" to domestic producers of "like or directly competitive products" and for the time it takes to "prevent or remedy such injury."[35] This provision was a direct incorporation of U.S. preferences into the General Agreement.[36] It conformed to Executive Order 9832 under the Truman administration in 1946, which required the insertion of an escape clause in all future trade agreements and which Truman had promised earlier to address concerns of postwar uncertainty in the RTAA renewal of 1945.[37]

Second, the general uncertainty facing many of the General Agreement's Contracting Parties, chiefly the result of uncertainty in U.S. trade politics but also of domestic uncertainty in other countries, led to a host of "exceptions" to the unconditional MFN provision and to the nondiscrimination principle. As a group they make up the "compromise of embedded liberalism" that has characterized the post–World War II trading order (Ruggie 1982), reconciling the imperatives of a liberal international trading order with the exigencies of domestic economic priorities. In the language of the rational design project, they also functioned as mechanisms of adaptive flexibility and made room for institutional arrangements to make allowances for special circumstances affecting countries' capacities to conform fully to a multilateral trading order. From the long-term view, it provided mechanisms to increase the cost of exercising the "exit option" (Hirschman 1970) and also to minimize the cost of adhering to the institution should domestic opposition someday threaten the continuation of the institution.

Part II of the General Agreement, which incorporated the provisions of Chapter V of the ITO Charter that was never ratified, contains the major flexibility mechanisms. They include the provision allowing import restrictions

---

35. *General Agreement on Tariffs and Trade* (1947), Article XIX, subparagraphs (a) and (b).

36. As noted earlier, the escape clause was one of four exceptions in the General Agreement on which the U.S. position was non-negotiable (Goldstein 1993).

37. Though Truman would invoke the escape clause in December 1950 and withdraw U.S. concessions on fur felt hats and bodies (Zeiler 1999, 185), it would be invoked rarely in subsequent years (Goldstein 1988, 189). Rather, Contracting Parties relied more on antidumping and countervailing duties to respond to sudden surges in imports (Curzon 1965), and these later become important elements of flexibility in the evolution of the General Agreement.

for balance of payments reasons (Article XII). Article XIII requires non-discriminatory use of quantitative restrictions if such restrictions should be applied, but Article XIV permits departures from this rule if it allows the implementing country to obtain additional imports without "unduly depleting their monetary reserves."[38] Import restrictions were also permitted for economic development reasons (Article XVIII) and for reasons of national security (Article XXI).[39]

The most significant of these flexibility provisions are those that would have unexpected consequences for the global trade system, namely Article XXIV permitting customs unions and free trade areas, and Article XI, paragraph 2, which provided for exceptions in agriculture.[40] Though plagued by imprecision and ambiguities (Pomfret 1988, 62–64), the customs union provision allowed preferential arrangements directed toward the reduction of tariffs, so long as the margin of preference was "not on the whole higher" than those before the union and it was formed "within a reasonable amount of time."[41] It was under the aegis of the General Agreement's Article XXIV and the support of the United States that the European Community was subsequently formed. Equally important is the provision permitting import restrictions in agriculture that could be claimed under Article XI, paragraph 2(c), which allowed "import restrictions on any agricultural or fisheries product, imported in any form, necessary to the enforcement of governmental measures which operate." The only instance in the General Agreement in which agriculture is specifically mentioned (Curzon 1965, 167), this provision was another safeguard measure negotiated by the United States team, which needed to reconcile the General Agreement's prohibition on quantitative restrictions (Article XI, paragraph 1) with the production limits and import quotas implemented under the U.S.

---

38. *General Agreement on Tariffs and Trade* (1947), Article XIX, 1(a).

39. Article XXV may also qualify as a flexibility provision, as it allows a country to "waive an obligation" imposed by the Agreement. However, unlike the other exceptions that allow unilateral action that may be accompanied by consultation or followed up with information, this waiver is subject to prior approval, requiring a two-thirds majority vote where the majority constitutes more than half of all Contracting Parties.

40. Another important exception in subsequent years of the General Agreement is Article XXXV, added in 1955, which allowed the non-application of the Agreement among parties that had not entered into tariff negotiations or by a Contracting Party against another at the time of the latter's accession.

41. Chase (2006) argues that Article XXIV and its controversial provisions exempting free trade areas were inserted to accommodate a secret trade treaty between the United States and Canada. The trade treaty, it was hoped, would bolster North American cooperation and provide the impetus for a Western European customs union, thus strengthening the economic foundations of the Western alliance.

Agricultural Adjustment Act.[42] Such a provision set the precedent for excluding agriculture from trade liberalization agreements and led others, especially European countries through their Common Agricultural Policy, to raise their own barriers (Goldstein 1993).

Last but not least, and aptly captured in Gardner's telling depiction of the acceptance of the GATT over the ITO—"Vive le Provisoire!"—the General Agreement embraced its own impermanence and lack of structure, to the detriment of the permanent and formal International Trade Organization (ITO). The schedules of concessions, declared as an "integral part" of Part I of the Agreement containing the unconditional MFN clause, were, as of 1948, to be in effect for only three years, until 1 January 1951, when concessions may be subject to modification or removal.[43] The original agreement contained no specific provisions for additional rounds of negotiations, and the term "Contracting Parties" was purposefully used to imply that there were no such commitments for the future (Zeiler 1999, 122). Implicit also in this aspect of the General Agreement was the expectation that the ITO Charter would shortly subsume the General Agreement upon the Charter's ratification by member countries.[44]

As the fate of the ITO was sealed when its Charter was withdrawn from ratification proceedings in the United States, effectively making the organization unviable for the rest of the signatories, the General Agreement was able to take its place as the trade-governing mechanism because the first round had been concluded, with the Protocol of Provisional Application of the General Agreement on Tariffs and Trade entering into force in early 1948.[45] As the trade protocol to be attached to its intended parent

42. In 1955, the U.S. obtained a waiver to permit the use of import quotas regardless of whether production controls were employed, as required by the Agricultural Adjustment Act. This was a "grave blow to General Agreement's prestige" (Dam 1970, 260), the first major step to remove agriculture from General Agreement rules.

43. Article II, paragraph 7. In subsequent versions of the General Agreement, the phrase was changed to "On the first day of each three-year period" (GATT 1969[86]).

44. Article XXVI. The Geneva agreement was to enter into full force thirty days after signatory governments whose countries' trade accounted for 85 percent of the total external trade of all signatories had ratified the Agreement and deposited their instruments of acceptance with the Secretary General of the United Nations.

45. The Protocol of Provisional Application was signed before the General Agreement was ratified by the signatories' respective governments. It allowed signatories to the protocol to apply provisionally beginning 1 January 1948 Parts I and III of the General Agreement and, "to the fullest extent not inconsistent with existing legislation," Part II as well. It was signed before the end of 1947 by nine countries, including Australia, Belgium, Canada, Cuba, France, Luxembourg, the Netherlands, the United Kingdom, and the United States, which accounted for about 80 percent of world trade. Czechoslovakia was the tenth country to sign the Protocol on Provisional Application, on 21 March 1948, and it put the Geneva agreement into effect

organization, the ITO, the General Agreement was virtually devoid of formal institutional features. As Hudec points out, the General Agreement "was a temporary side affair meant to serve the particular interests of the major commercial powers who wanted a prompt reduction of tariffs among themselves" (1975, 30). Furthermore, given its temporary and supplementary status, its legal standing was unclear, and it contained no provisions for a budget or a formal secretariat. "In short, the General Agreement was permeated by an atmosphere of impermanence," yet in paradoxical fashion, this dimension of flexibility secured its installation as the trade-governing mechanism of the post–World War II period (Gardner 1956[1980], 380).

What Could Have Been: The International Trade Organization

While the United States as principal architect yielded the particular institutional arrangements we know as the General Agreement, the argument about the importance of the designers suggests that under different leadership, global trade governance may well have taken on a different face, giving more priority to economic issues other than those espoused by the American postwar planners. The conflicting visions of the postwar order are already evidenced in the foregoing discussion of the Anglo-American negotiations, which pitted Great Britain's emphasis on attaining full employment against the U.S. vision of unfettered free trade but nevertheless yielded compromises between these two key actors. Going beyond these key players, however, the question still remains as to what global trade governance might have looked like had a different set of principal architects held sway.

In this connection, the initiatives and efforts of developing countries in fashioning global trade governance under the ill-fated ITO, the General Agreement's intended parent organization, provide a compelling way to consider alternative institutional arrangements at this critical juncture. While the ITO failed to assume its position as the global trade governance body for the post–World War II world, the course of the debate as the terms of the ITO Charter were negotiated by member countries strongly suggests how trade would have been managed had the less powerful countries had a stronger hand in fashioning these governance mechanisms. It further illustrates and sharpens the analytical lens on the importance of the principal architect, by contrasting U.S. positions on contentious issues with institutional alternatives advanced by other actors that, had they been the main

---

provisionally on 21 April 1948, at which time U.S. concessions negotiated with that country also became effective (USTC 1948, Part I, 7).

institutional drivers, would have fashioned a different set of governance mechanisms for managing trade in the post–World War II world.

This section thus turns to the major issues of contention during the negotiations on the ITO Charter. The discussion focuses in particular on the institutional initiatives of developing countries, which advanced positions divergent from the developed and powerful countries and reflected the developmental divide that emerged at this time.[46] The discussion also focuses on records of the Havana meeting of the International Conference on Trade and Employment, where representatives of participating countries debated on the final draft of the ITO charter. Though many contentious issues arose over the course of the ITO charter's preparation, it was this final meeting that led to the signing of the charter that exemplifies and highlights the issues dividing the developed and developing worlds at the time. Moreover, as Herbert Feis, member of the U.S. delegation, observed, it was at the Havana conference that the developing countries were "most assertive" in their efforts to secure terms that benefited their objectives of industrial development (1948, 51).

Efforts toward the establishment of the ITO began with two sessions of the Preparatory Committee of the International Conference on Trade and Employment. They were held under the auspices of the Economic and Social Council of the United Nations, which had earlier passed a resolution authorizing the U.N. Secretary General to call the conference of nations. The first session of the Preparatory Committee was held in London from 15 October to 26 November 1946, in which nineteen invited countries gathered to consider the *Suggested Charter for an International Trade Organization of the United Nations,* submitted by the U.S. State Department in September 1946 and outlining plans for the removal of trade barriers and the integration of national trade policies to expand global trade. An interim drafting committee was established, which met in Lake Success, New York, in January and February of 1947 to fulfill its task of drafting the ITO charter on the basis of the *Suggested Charter,* in particular providing alternative texts on those issues for which agreement could not be reached, such as charter provisions on state monopolies, policies vis-à-vis nonmembers, operational rules, and indirect trade policy restrictions as well as, most importantly, two articles addressing the issue of whether the ITO should adopt a weighted voting scheme, giving greater power to the largest traders, and whether or not certain members should hold permanent seats on the ITO's Executive Board.

46. The discussion in this section relies on verbatim and summary records of committee meetings held during the work of the Preparatory Committee of the International Conference on Trade and Development. These documents are available through the GATT Digital Library at Stanford University, available at http://gatt.stanford.edu/page/home.

The second session of the Preparatory Committee of the International Conference on Trade and Employment was held in Geneva from 10 April to 30 October 1947. The meeting was devoted to two main tasks: first, the completion of the draft of the charter for an international trade organization and second, the conduct of detailed bilateral negotiations among the eighteen participating countries toward a general agreement on tariffs and trade. It was at the second session of the Preparatory Committee meeting in Geneva on 10 April 1947 that participants agreed to consider a "General Agreement on Tariffs and Trade," drafted at the first session of the Preparatory Committee in London in October and November 1946. The draft of the General Agreement drawn up by the Interim Drafting Committee was designed to embody the foundational principles of the *Suggested Charter* and in particular its section on general commercial policy. The agreement among member states reflected their view that the most important prerequisite for trade liberalization, reducing tariffs and trade barriers, was to adopt the charter's fundamental principles, which were not yet in force. The General Agreement was intended to uphold and fulfill as much as possible article 17 of the draft ITO charter, in which members were to "enter into and carry out... negotiations directed to the substantial reduction of tariffs and other charges on imports and exports and to the elimination of preferences... on a reciprocal and mutually advantageous basis" (Wilcox 1949, 246).

Six main committees were established to organize their work on the Geneva draft charter that was submitted for consideration: Committee I on Economic and Employment Activity; Committee II on Economic Development; Committee III on Commercial Policy; Committee IV on Restrictive Business Practices; Committee V on Intergovernmental Commodity Agreements; and Committee VI on Organization.[47] Many subcommittees, working parties, and joint subcommittees were later established to study and debate the six hundred amendments that were proposed and to forge compromises on the many disputes that arose during the meetings.

In negotiating the terms of the ITO Charter, the first of the institutional initiatives advanced on behalf of developing countries was an amendment to the provisional agenda to include the issue of an international agreement on industrial development.[48] During an executive session of the Preparatory Committee, Australia's delegation head H. C. Coombs proposed that "a new topic relating to industrial development be inserted [into the

---

47. E/CONF.2/1, October 1947; E/CONF.2/10, 25 November 1947; E/CONF.2/SR.3, 26 November 1947.

48. See E/PC/T/1 for the provisional agenda. General remarks by heads of delegations during the plenary sessions can be found in E/PC/T/PV/1, E/PC/T/PV/2, E/PC/T/PV/3, and E/PC/T/PV/4.

agenda], designed to provide for positive aid in such development, to establish qualitative standards by which prospective development can be judged, to recognize the legitimacy of reasonable protection as an instrument of development."[49] He also proposed that the scope of work of Committee I, charged with formulating charter provisions for full employment, be expanded to include the issue of industrial development.

The Australian proposal was widely supported, especially by the delegations of developing countries such as India, Brazil, Chile, China, and Lebanon. Clair Wilcox, who led the U.S. delegation, supported the Australian proposal while pointing out that the *Suggested Charter* already included provisions on industrialization. Discussion then took place over whether to widen the scope of currently assigned committees to consider industrial development, specifically Committee I on Employment and Economic Activity and Committee II on General Commercial Policy, or to establish a special committee for the issue. Following a meeting of these two committees, a sixth Committee on industrial development was established, as a joint committee composed of Committee I and II members.

The Preparatory Committee's work on the charter was completed on 22 August 1947, and delegations from over sixty countries met in Havana for the opening of the United Nations Conference on Trade and Employment, where the draft charter was presented for consideration. The conference elected the head of the Cuban delegation, Sergio I. Clark, to preside over the meeting. The main task of the conference was to debate and to adopt the draft ITO charter.[50] The ITO charter contained three main objectives, namely to state the objectives of international trade, to define the rules of trading and commercial practices, and to establish a formal international trade organization to administer the rules of trade specified in the charter.

Every chapter of the draft charter was subjected to extensive and heated debate. However, the major cleavage dividing the delegations was along developmental lines, much of the time pitting the industrialized against the less developed countries. The most contentious areas of disagreement involved the issue of prior ITO approval with respect to the adoption of quantitative restrictions on trade and the formation of new preferential tariff arrangements.

In Committee II, which was the locus of the debate on Article 15 regarding the formation of preferential trade arrangements, South American country representatives (save Brazil) argued in favor of preferential tariff

49. E/PC/T/EC/3.
50. E/CONF.2/INF.8, 21 November 1947, on an Informal Summary of the ITO Charter.

arrangements without prior ITO approval.[51] In particular, Representative Oldini of Chile noted that countries in Latin America had long favored a preferential arrangement for the region, which they regarded as a homogenous economic entity. The United States, Canada, New Zealand, Norway, and Sweden argued for permitting preferential arrangements with ITO approval, provided they were more helpful than injurious. Representatives of Norway and Sweden stated that though preferential arrangements were undesirable, their governments would nevertheless take steps in forming them if there should be a worldwide movement in this direction. Delegates were also divided along developmental lines on the formation of new preferential tariff systems in regions. Eight countries of the Middle East—Afghanistan, Egypt, Greece, Iran, Iraq, Lebanon, Syria, and Turkey—proposed an amendment that would permit the formation of regional preferential trading arrangements. The amendment was opposed, again by the United States, Great Britain, and the western European countries, thus defending the draft charter's prohibition of new preferential agreements.

Committee III on Commercial Policy saw a heated debate among the delegates on the use of protective measures.[52] The dividing line in the major issue of contention—protective measures—was drawn along developmental lines, separating the industrialized countries from the developing world. Representatives from Greece and Mexico noted their apprehensions regarding the prohibition of such protective measures, which they argued could destroy small and infant industries. Representative Parra of Mexico contended that international trade was hampered by lack of purchasing power rather than by high tariffs, quantitative restrictions, or exchange controls. He argued that the reduction of tariffs might well lead to a further decline in the purchasing power of developing countries and greatly hinder their economic development. Representative Colocotronis of Greece, speaking for countries dependent on trade in commodities that were not considered basic necessities, argued that it was necessary to protect such fragile economies, even at the cost of permitting the use of quantitative restrictions.

Representatives of the developing world proposed doing away with the "prior approval" provision in the draft ITO charter to govern protective measures such as subsidies, tariffs, and import quotas. The United States led the group advocating the "prior approval" clause and argued that

51. E/CONF.2/C.2/SR.10, 20 December 1947; E/CONF.2/C.2/45, 15 March 1948; E/CONF.2/69, 18 March 1948.
52. E/CONF.2/C.3/SR.3, 2 December 1947; E/CONF.2/C.3/SR.4, 3 December 1947; E/CONF.2/C.3/SR.5, 4 December 1947; E/CONF.2/C.3/SR.6, 7 December 1947.

removal of this provision would render ineffective the charter's objective of reducing trade barriers. The U.S. delegation, led by Will Clayton, responded with a statement on 27 November urging the attending delegations to adopt the draft charter without overloading it with escape clauses and exceptions. Herbert Feis, writing about the controversy over quantitative restrictions, noted:

> They [the nations of Latin America, the Middle East and Asia] want to use quantitative restrictions as we used tariffs in the past; and besides, they wish to use them as a bargaining weapon. In the Geneva draft, this wish was recognized to the extent of permitting Members to use quantitative restrictions for development purposes on condition that they obtain prior approval of the ITO. At Havana (where more "undeveloped" countries are present) greater freedom in this matter has been most strongly advocated. Thus, the Conference is faced with a most difficult decision: whether to accord such freedom at the risk of depriving the Charter of some of its significance, or whether to resist the urgent advocacy at the risk of losing the future participation of some undeveloped countries in the ITO. (1948, 47)

Drafting of the charter continued in the early days of 1948 in spite of the deadlock on key issues such as quantitative restrictions and the demands of the less developed countries. As of January 1948, over 600 amendments had been debated in subcommittees and 150 meetings held over various issues of contention (ITO 1948, 136). The United Nations Conference on Trade and Employment concluded on 24 March 1948. Representatives of fifty-three countries signed the Final Act, which included the charter of the ITO and committed them to submit it to their governments for ratification.[53] The ITO charter was to go into effect sixty days after ratification was completed in a majority of the signatories, or twenty-seven countries. The Final Act also provided that in the event that the majority requirement had not been fulfilled in one year's time, by 24 March 1949, then twenty ratifications would suffice to put the charter into effect. If the ratification requirement was not met by 30 September 1949, the U.N. Secretary General was to call a meeting of the governments that had ratified the charter to determine the conditions under which the charter could be brought into effect at that time. Withdrawal of the Charter from ratification proceedings in the United States, however, no longer made the Charter politically feasible for the rest of the signatories, so the ill-fated ITO was cast aside while the General Agree-

---

53. Of the fifty-six countries eligible to vote, Argentina and Poland had expressed their intention to abstain, and the delegation from Turkey announced that its instructions were delayed.

ment came to assume its position as the global trade governance body of the post–World War II world.

Conclusion

The formation of the General Agreement and the failure of the International Trade Organization to come into being illustrate how the institutional preferences of the principal architect—who designs—determine the particular institutional arrangements that result and the form that global trade governance still takes six decades later. In fashioning the General Agreement, the distinct leadership of the United States exerted a defining influence on the regime's institutional identity as a multilateral institution founded on the principle of nondiscrimination. In institutional design, it led to centralization in the General Agreement's main task of bargaining over tariff barriers. The United States determined in great part the rules of bargaining in the General Agreement: simultaneous negotiations of bilateral accords among principal suppliers on a product-by-product basis. The most centralizing aspect of the General Agreement's bargaining protocol is its principal supplier rule, in which a country (a Contracting Party) offers tariff concessions to the principal source of imports of a good and requests concessions on its own main exports to the partner country. This limited negotiations to the major trading nations, the "democratic industrial powers" (Ikenberry 2001) critical to the reconstruction of Europe and the containment of communism. The bargaining protocol as a whole also closely resembled the practice followed in the United States in negotiating trade agreements under the Reciprocal Trade Agreements Act, to the extent that the General Agreement was widely labeled "the Trade Agreements Program writ large" (Diebold 1988, 11).

The effect of power on institutional design is also demonstrated in combination with the cooperation problems that emerged in Geneva. The U.S. goal of dismantling preferential trading arrangements increased the severity of the distributional conflict with Great Britain, which sought to hold on to its system of Imperial Preference. Indeed, the successful conclusion of this first round of trade negotiations hinged on the resolution of the Anglo-American distributional conflict. The Geneva round effectively ended only after the conclusion of the Anglo-American agreement, whose negotiations over Imperial Preference had dragged on longer than others, and whose conflict over the U.S. wool tariff had threatened to scuttle the General Agreement's talks completely and held up additional agreements with the British dominions and colonies (Zeiler 1999, 94–103, 121).

Negotiations on the General Agreement were also shaped by U.S. institutional preferences originating in uncertainty regarding long-term domestic support for trade liberalization. Officials in the United States and Great Britain as well as other allies confronted a high level of "uncertainty about the state of the world," the lack of knowledge about the consequences of specific institutional arrangements. In particular, the General Agreement's institutional design was shaped by conditions of domestic uncertainty, in which it was difficult to predict with much confidence the level of support for trade multilateralism in the United States. Legislators were mindful of this uncertainty in their deliberations on the renewal of the RTAA, and in Geneva this led to a higher level of uncertainty on the part of negotiating parties. Officials from other countries viewed with skepticism the viability of a long-term U.S. commitment to trade multilateralism and sought institutional provisions to counter this uncertainty.

The problems of distribution and uncertainty led to several provisions for flexibility in the General Agreement's institutional design. It sanctioned the continuation of existing preferences. It also provided an escape clause and a host of exceptions to the unconditional MFN provision as a means to address the uncertainty issues facing the negotiating teams. Finally, the three-year time delimitation in the tariff schedules rendered the General Agreement a temporary institution. That the ITO was rejected and the developing country initiatives were "lost" at this time in favor of the temporary General Agreement further symbolized the importance of flexibility in this institution borne of uncertainty.

2

Critical Moments and Institutional Resilience

The rules of the global trading system that originated in the General Agreement of 1947 evolved over eight rounds of trade negotiations spanning almost half a century until the establishment of the WTO. The regime followed a historical trajectory that is markedly resilient, such that even the shift from the GATT to the WTO is notable more for continuity rather than change in the trade regime (Barton, Goldstein, Josling, and Steinberg 2006). As the first agreement among its participants, the institutional arrangements produced by the General Agreement of 1947 embodied "early outcomes" that generated positive feedback processes in the GATT's institutional development, forming "deep equilibria" in which key bargaining practices continued to prevail amidst calls for reform (Pierson 2004, 157–160).

This chapter focuses on three of the most important "deep equilibria" or sources of institutional resilience that followed after the first General Agreement in 1947: the power-based bargaining protocol privileging principal suppliers and item-by-item bargaining; approval of the U.S. request for a waiver of its GATT obligations in connection with Section 22 of the U.S. Agricultural Adjustment Act (AAA); and the GATT members' somewhat tacit acceptance of the European Economic Community (EEC) under Article XXIV of the General Agreement. These cases illustrate how "institutional power" derived from the rules of trade governance continue to enhance the "compulsory power" of its most privileged participants, who created them.

The persistence of the principal supplier rule and item-by-item bargaining in trade negotiations and the renewal of tariff schedules demonstrates how the world's larger trading nations have retained their bargaining position in trade negotiations. The U.S. waiver in connection with Section 22 of the U.S. AAA, approved by the GATT in 1955, not only brought U.S. trade politics to the center of the GATT regime's attention but also effectively wrote in, unconditionally and permanently, a key piece of U.S. trade legislation into the GATT's history. It is a key case for understanding how the domestic politics of the leading country came to shape the evolution of the trade regime's flexibility mechanisms, as a means for the original creators of the regime to provide mechanisms that ensure institutional survival.

Flexibility arrangements in the GATT also included provisions for customs unions and free trade areas, which provided the political rationale for accepting, in practical terms, the EEC under Article XXIV. The EEC case was a key precedent for sanctioning such departures from the nondiscrimination principle and proceeded to engender a wide network of preferential trade agreements.[1] The exceptions brought about by the U.S. and EEC cases became permanent installations of the global trading order but were largely unanticipated consequences of these flexibility provisions (Pomfret 1988, 67). By building up institutional tolerance to exceptions that effectively went against the nondiscrimination principle, they also contributed to the GATT's institutional resilience.

Power Politics in Time

Adding time to the mix of power and institutions highlights the dynamic role of power in the process of institutional development. Studying power in the institutional design stage provides a momentary and static view of its importance, on its own and relative to other explanatory factors. However, that "institutional design creates and reproduces political power," as Wendt points out (2001, 1035), suggests that institutional evolution is an endogenous process in which compulsory power and institutional power are mutually constitutive. As much as power determines the initial design of institutions, powerful actors are in turn shaped by the institution over time.

1. The United States endorsed, within the GATT, the Schuman Plan and the formation of the European Coal and Steel Community (ECSC) in spite of its discriminatory qualities, as the prospect of Franco-German cooperation in these industries had major security dividends, notably eventual French acceptance of West German rearmament and membership in NATO. The United States also supported European integration through the formation of the EEC in 1957 for the same reasons, tolerating its discriminatory trade practices against the United States and other countries (Patterson 1966, 156–157).

This approach is especially applicable to the GATT as part of the "constitutional order" that the United States created (Ikenberry 2001), committing the victor to institutional arrangements with expectations of future gains even when lesser states grow stronger. This analysis examines the dynamic role of power in the GATT's development as a sequence in which the rules of the GATT—the earliest institutional choices of the leading actors— subsequently served to preserve their privileged positions within the regime.[2]

This chapter also directs greater attention to the "path-dependent" aspect of institutional development, in which outcomes over time reproduce the power relations established in the earliest "rules" of the institution. Where endogeneity captures *what* form institutional development takes, path dependence describes *how* and *why* institutional resilience is such a prominent feature of this process.[3] "Path dependence" describes the self-reinforcing nature of institutional arrangements and the positive feedback process that operates over time (Arthur 1994; David 2000; Pierson 2004).[4] It is distinguishable from inevitability and emphasizes instead the importance

2. This approach avoids the potential pitfalls associated with a causal framework in which two variables—power relations between the two sets of actors and institutional outcomes—are endogenous, that is, affect one another as each operates as both cause and effect. The endogenous nature of their causal relation implies a feedback process, but one in which "determining causality then becomes impossible" (Büthe 2002, 485). Introducing a temporal component transforms this causal feedback loop instead into a causal sequence, which makes it possible to look at each of these variables—power relations and institutional outcomes—both as cause and effect but at different points in time.

3. Pierson (2004), for example, identifies four main sources of institutional resilience: coordination problems among the actors regarding different equilibria and their distributive consequences (Krasner 1991; Knight 1992) that render existing institutional equilibria "sticky" (Hardin 1989; Calvert 1995; Cox 1997; Carey 2000); "self-referencing" veto points (Miller 2000, 539) nested in institutional rules; asset specificity (Alt, Frieden, Gilligan, Rodrik, and Rogowski 1996; Lake 1999) that highlights the importance of investments made by actors in a set of "relationships, expectations, privileges, knowledge of procedures" (Gourevitch 1999, 144–145) that are specific to an institution; and positive feedback through such mechanisms as "interconnected rules" (March and Olsen 1989, 1970) that provide greater increasing returns (North 1990, 95), thus reinforcing the constituent institutions.

4. Classic illustrations of path dependence include the Pólya urn process (Arthur 1994; David 1985, 1994, 2001; Pierson 2004), which begins with a single draw from an urn containing one red ball and one black ball. The ball that is drawn is returned to the urn and an additional one of the same color is added to the collection of balls, and this process is repeated until the urn is full. The distribution of balls at the end of this process demonstrates the importance of the early draw, which occurs by chance, and how this affects the final proportion of red and black balls in the urn. Other prominent examples of path dependence include the story of the QWERTY keyboard (David 2001) and how the VHS format in videocassette recorders came to dominate the market (Arthur 1995, 1–12). These examples demonstrate the importance of "early outcomes" and the moment of institutional choice that is characterized by "openness" and "permissiveness" (Mahoney 2000; Abbott 1997), in which more than one outcome is possible but is followed by the consolidation of the initial institutional arrangements that effectively closes off alternative institutional choices.

of early outcomes in delimiting the "choice set" in subsequent institutional decision-making (North 1990, 98–99). At the individual level, the structural elements of the institution—its rules and procedures—are taken as given, which "enables, motivates, and guides" actors' actions in such a way as to recreate the structure itself (Greif 2006, 53). Path dependence may be variously used to describe the "lock-in" effects of institutional rules and procedures once they are put in place and the "stickiness" of institutions that give rise to punctuated equilibria in institutional evolution (Baumgartner and Jones 1993). Actors, especially the principal architects, receive "increasing returns" from participation in and commitment to the regime, thus also contributing to its resilience (Arthur 1994).

The General Agreement exhibited strong path-dependent features in the politics that pervaded its development over time. Created to govern trade, the GATT as a political institution overwhelms its status as a market institution in which "competition and learning" contributes to institutional change (Pierson 2004, 40–41; Moe 1984). As is characteristic of political institutions, the GATT carried with it an inherent bias toward the status quo, as demonstrated in the persistence of its power-based bargaining protocol for negotiating reductions in trade barriers.[5]

Finally, the endogenous process of institutional development that privileges powerful countries and the path-dependent outcomes that contribute to institutional resilience is marked by *when* significant opportunities for institutional change present themselves. "Critical moments" are pivotal points in time at which institutional change emerges as a possibility through bargaining among the actors (Bulmer and Birch 1998, 605).[6] These "critical moments" present opportunities for significant change, and they arise from exogenous forces from within as well as outside the institution.

For the General Agreement, two critical moments yielded key turning points in its institutional development. The first involved the granting of a U.S. request for waiver of its GATT obligations insofar as they conflicted with Section 22 of the U.S. Agricultural Adjustment Act (AAA). The second

---

5. Nested within the broader network of postwar institutions such as the United Nations and the International Monetary Fund/World Bank, the General Agreement as well exhibited strong resistance to institutional unraveling, even "after hegemony" (Keohane 1984) and power shifts among the major actors, due arguably to factors such as institutional inertia over time, sunk costs (Stinchcombe 1968, 108–118) from time and effort invested in the institution, the benefits of services provided by the institution, and common goals among the actors (Ruggie 1992).

6. "Critical moments" are distinguishable from the "critical juncture" that defines the moment of institutional choice, in which the collapse of existing institutions due to an exogenous event such as war provides a unique opportunity for the construction of new institutions.

was the formation of the European Economic Community (EEC) and its subsequent acceptance by GATT members under Article XXIV governing the formation of free trade areas. Together with the persistence of the power-based bargaining protocol, these features of the GATT have had longstanding consequences for the regime's evolution and the governance of international trade. The following sections examine each of these mechanisms in turn, as well as the "critical moments" that they produced for the GATT.

Centralization of Bargaining Power and Institutional Resilience

Centralization, as introduced in the previous chapter on the design of the General Agreement, is the extent to which the important tasks of an institution, including but not limited to information dissemination, the reduction of bargaining and transaction costs, and enforcement, are performed by a focal member or group (Koremenos, Lipson, and Snidal 2001b, 11). In the General Agreement, it refers to the concentration of bargaining power, in which the main task of the institution—bargaining to reduce trade barriers—is concentrated among key players, in particular the major economies of the industrialized world. Centralization of the institution's main tasks protects the powerful actors that establish institutional rules and their position in the institution, which makes the rules themselves resistant to change.

In the General Agreement, centralization is represented by the main bargaining protocol for tariff negotiations, namely the principal supplier rule, which is attended as well by bilateral negotiations on an item-by-item basis and the renewal of tariff schedules. The principal supplier rule is the main pillar of the U.S. Reciprocal Trade Agreements Act, in which trade negotiations were to be conducted with the main source of imports for a particular good. It is combined with item-by-item bargaining over tariff reductions, in which Contracting Parties conduct bilateral negotiations on specific items. This bargaining method can be contrasted with the alternative proposed by Great Britain at the time of the General Agreement's formation. The British negotiating team had argued for linear cuts in tariffs, which involved across-the-board tariff cuts by sector. Because American officials considered this method to be inconsistent with the provisions of the U.S. Reciprocal Trade Agreements Act and also politically infeasible, it was the item-by-item negotiation option that prevailed as the General Agreement's bargaining protocol. The resulting tariff schedules from the trade negotiations also contributed to the resilience of the General Agreement, as members eventually agreed that they would be renewed automatically if no objections were raised.

Principal Supplier Rule

The principal supplier rule, also called the "major interests norm," is an informal but key practice adopted by negotiating parties since the inception of the General Agreement (Finlayson and Zacher 1981, 590). There is no formal provision mandating the principal supplier rule as the bargaining method for tariff negotiations. However, it is mentioned in the provisions for tariff *re*negotiations. Article XXVIII of the Agreement stipulates that when a Contracting Party wishes to modify or withdraw a previously granted concession, it is required to negotiate compensation with (1) Contracting Parties with whom the concessions were originally negotiated; and (2) Contracting Parties with a *substantial interest or principal supplying interest,* namely those with a market share for the good that is greater than that for any other party with whom the concessions were originally negotiated.[7]

Given that the principal supplier rule is an informal practice adopted by the GATT and later the WTO regime as well, there is no set criterion for determining *substantial supplying interest* or *principal supplying interest.* Indeed, Article XXVIII 1:7 notes that "substantial interest" does not lend itself to a precise definition (GATT 1969[86]). Nevertheless, over time GATT members have adopted several consistent practices to determine who the principal suppliers may be. The practice has been to recognize principal suppliers as those with a significant share of the market in a particular good, usually 10 percent or more of the total trade share in that good. The GATT formally provides for the Contracting Parties to determine principal supplier status. Principal suppliers may be identified simply by the Contracting Parties' recognition of a member who claims a principally supplying interest or substantial interest in tariff renegotiations over a particular concession.[8] Article XXVIII 1:4 specifies that a party with a market share larger than any other member with whom the concessions were originally negotiated has a principal supplying interest. Later, in the GATT of 1994 negotiated in the Uruguay Round, another category of principal suppliers was added, namely those whose exports would be the most severely affected by the modification or withdrawal of a particular concession (Hoda 2001, 13–14).

---

7. The term *substantial interest* appears in the original General Agreement of 1947. However, the term *principal supplying interest* was added and put into effect in 1952. GATT 1986, 38 UNTS 336.

8. GATT BISD, Twenty-seventh Supplement, 26–28.

The first bargaining round in 1947, which produced 123 agreements covering about fifty thousand tariff items (Srinivasan 1998, 10), had established the precedent that tariff concessions would be negotiated bilaterally on a product-by-product basis. A GATT document noted that the "principal supplier rule" was to govern the exchange of tariff concessions and that this "rule" dictated a manifestly bilateral bargaining procedure: "the importing country negotiates its tariff rate with its principal supplier and not with all suppliers of the same product." This was to prevent "an unnecessary multiplicity of negotiations on the same product." The "rule" would ensure that an importing country would only offer a tariff concession to a principal supplier, which, as the primary beneficiary of the concession, would be more willing than secondary suppliers to pay for it (Finlayson and Zacher 1981, 590).

The principal supplier rule can be defended on several counts, most having to do with efficiency gains in trade negotiations. That the practice allows for bargaining by the largest exporter or group of exporters, defined according to market share, "is an optimal response to the MFN free rider problem" addressing the problem of free riding typically associated with trade negotiations accompanied by unconditional most favored nation treatment for all parties (Ludema and Mayda 2005, 8). It allows for the lowest tariffs to be negotiated, as the parties involved are the largest exporters of the goods involved, thus minimizing the MFN externality, making it an optimal mechanism. Moreover, the bilateral nature of these negotiations among principal suppliers effectively limits bargaining to those who have a "genuine interest" (Curzon and Curzon 1976). It prevents overloading the GATT's workload by avoiding multilateral negotiations on matters that may more effectively and efficiently be resolved bilaterally or in a limited multilateral context (Finlayson and Zacher 1981, 590).

The bilateral negotiating method and the principal supplier rule reflected a fine balance between the two pillars of the General Agreement: reciprocity and the unconditional MFN principle, respectively. It addressed the potential free rider problem, in which secondary suppliers of a good may enjoy the tariff reductions negotiated among principal suppliers without offering any equivalent concessions themselves, by keeping concessions provisional until all bilateral negotiations on all goods were completed and the full tariff schedule was signed by all parties. This maintained the multilateral and nondiscriminatory foundations of the GATT. At the same time, the negotiations also ensured reciprocity through bilateral negotiations that maximized internalization, the extent to which tariff reductions actually benefited the principal suppliers who negotiated them (Finger 1979). According to Winters, by the Dillon Round (1960–1961), the internalization for U.S. trade was 96 percent multilaterally and an "amazing" 69 percent bilaterally (1989, 1291). Thus the method of bilateral negotiations among principal suppliers maintained a fine balance between nondiscrimination through the unconditional MFN principle and reciprocity.

On the down side, however, the principal supplier rule has also effectively excluded many of the GATT's members from participation and influence in trade negotiations. It biased negotiations in favor of goods from large economies—the major traders, which tended to be the principal suppliers of goods more than other smaller countries. Hence the trade negotiations among the large economies were widely characterized as a "*petit sommet*" of the principal suppliers (Finlayson and Zacher 1981, 590). Over the years, labels such as the "big three" during the Tokyo Round for the United States, the European Economic Community, and Japan, or "the Quad," referring to the United States, the European Union, Canada, and Japan, have followed the major actors in the GATT and the WTO, often not only principal suppliers of many goods but also prominent players in the accession proceedings for prospective members. Developing countries are marginalized, both because they are not principal suppliers and hence do not take a place on the negotiating table for most items but also because their development goals are not given priority as part of the "rules" of international trade (Zeiler 1999, 128). The disenfranchisement in the GATT of the developing countries, or what is now known as the Global South, was arguably a result of power asymmetries that were reproduced over the negotiating rounds. These are countries that are regularly excluded from the infamous "Green Room" negotiations, referring to meetings held in the director general's conference room that include only a select group of members and whose decision-making process remains largely opaque to those outside of it.

Item-by-Item Bargaining

The principal supplier rule entailed not only bilateral negotiations but also adherence to the item-by-item bargaining method prevalent in GATT negotiations. Originating in the negotiating practices followed at the time of the General Agreement's formation in 1947, tariff reductions were negotiated bilaterally and separately for individual goods, on a product-by-product basis. It was a practice consistent with the U.S. Reciprocal Trade Agreements Act, which posed strict conditions of reciprocity in tariff negotiations. The item-by-item bargaining method was followed in the first five rounds of multilateral trade negotiations: Geneva in 1947, Annecy in 1949, Torquay in 1951, Geneva in 1955–1956, and the Dillon Round in 1960–1962. A critical moment for institutional change occurred after the conclusion of the Geneva Round in 1956, the results of which were labeled modest at best and, more important, were thought to be the last round of negotiations to be conducted on an item-by-item basis. Countries were frustrated by the lack of negotiating leeway as a result of item-by-item bargaining. Although the United States granted concessions on imports valued at approximately $900 million and received approximately $400 million in concessions, with tariff reductions averaging 15 percent, the round was regarded as unsuccessful, as many countries left the negotiating table or offered few concessions (Curzon 1965, 94–95). The prevailing attitude of frustrated negotiators was that "if there was to be another tariff conference, they would insist on the use of new rules" (Curzon 1965, 95).

By the beginning of the Dillon Round, GATT members, with the exception of the United States, actively pursued the option of abandoning the item-by-item method in favor of automatic and across-the-board reductions. According to Curzon, the negotiations demonstrated the "absurdity of the time-honored practice of item-by-item type negotiation," leading to a call for change. The United States resisted the calls for change in the item-by-item bargaining method, arguing that it had few alternatives in dealing with the tariff barriers going up around the European Economic Community at the time. Nevertheless, the calls for change in the bargaining method that had been an integral part of the U.S. Reciprocal Trade Agreements Act of 1934, which had been renewed regularly over the years, showed that the machinery of the bargaining protocol "was creaking. It had been designed for a different world" (Curzon 1965, 100). Perhaps as a consequence, the results of the Dillon Round were less than successful, as neither the 20 percent tariff reductions offered by the European Economic Community nor the equivalent concessions offered by other industrial countries in response was fully implemented.

The U.S. Trade Expansion Act of 1962 under the Kennedy administration, however, considerably expanded executive authority to negotiate tariff reductions. First, for goods with tariffs at 50 percent or higher, the legislation allowed for cuts of up to 50 percent of their levels at the time the Act came into effect. Additionally, it allowed for the complete elimination of duties on goods with tariffs below 50 percent. It further provided for the elimination of duties on goods comprising 80 percent of world trade accounted for by the United States and the EEC. It did away as well with peril points, which placed floors below which tariff rates could not be reduced and extended the president's trade-negotiating authority to five years. Most important for the GATT negotiations, however, the Act allowed the executive to negotiate linear tariff reductions across broad sectors of goods and did not require continued adherence to the item-by-item method of bargaining.

Nevertheless, the Act did not completely alleviate the constraints of U.S. trade politics. While the Trade Expansion Act allowed the executive to negotiate tariff reductions, it was empowered to do so only on the basis of reciprocity, thus limiting the president's maneuverability. U.S. preferences on the bargaining method, strongly constrained by its domestic politics, provided key veto points (Pierson 2004) and limited the win-set (Putnam 1988) necessary to affect change in regime's rules. In May 1963, when the GATT members' trade ministers met in Geneva, the differing U.S. and European positions on the item-by-item versus linear methods of tariff reductions posed a significant obstacle to setting the date for the next round of trade negotiations. A compromise was finally reached, in which across-the-board, linear tariff reductions would be negotiated for the majority of goods allowable under the Trade Expansion Act. This applied to the bulk of tariff concessions. Tariffs on goods in which there was great disparity in tariff rates between the United States and the European Common Market would be negotiated separately, "based upon special rules," that is, according to the item-by-item bargaining method (Curzon 1965, 105). This method of tariff reduction was officially adopted and enabled the Kennedy Round of negotiations to be launched in 1964.

This linear method, with exceptions, characterized the Kennedy Round (1964–1967) and the Tokyo Round (1973–1979) of trade negotiations under the GATT. This method is also referred to as the formula approach, in which members negotiate to reduce tariffs across the board based on a formula to which members agree from the start. Nevertheless, for many goods, especially those on the exceptions list and thus eligible for item-by-item bargaining, countries deviated widely from the formula-based cuts or "ignored the formula entirely" (Hoda 2001, 30–32). Item-by-item negotiations still took place bilaterally among principal suppliers. So rather than simplifying and lending greater efficiency to multilateral negotiations, the linear approach adopted for the Kennedy and Tokyo Rounds still relied on heavy bilateral bargaining and merely provided yet another tool for countries to bring to the negotiating table (Hoda 2001, 47; Ludema and Mayda 2005, 8n7). By the Uruguay Round, negotiations reverted to the item-by-item method, as this was the method the United States preferred. Thus while the critical moments provided by the active calls for change in the item-by-item bargaining during the Dillon Round led to the introduction of the linear method for the Kennedy and Tokyo Rounds, the item-by-item method of bargaining in the GATT's negotiating protocol proved to be very resilient.

Renewal of Tariff Schedules

A third and equally important source of institutional resilience that preserved the centralization of bargaining power in the GATT is the renewal of tariff schedules. The Agreement included "provisions for stability" regarding the tariff schedules, as their modifications or withdrawals were subject to strict rules (Curzon 1965, 108–109).[9] Should negotiations for modifications or withdrawal be held, Article XXVIII (1) urged members to "endeavor to maintain" tariff levels "not less favorable" than those already provided in the General Agreement. The schedules detailing each country's tariff concessions are the direct and most tangible product of the bilateral negotiations among principal suppliers on an item-by-item basis, as they outlined the goods on which tariffs were reduced, bound, or eliminated. Although the tariff schedules were made an integral part of the General Agreement, as provided in Article II, the schedules themselves were originally valid only for three years, until 1951, after which time tariff concessions were subject to modification or withdrawal as members retained the right to negotiate them under Article XXVIII. Preserving these early tariff reductions was an important task for the members of the regime.

The first of several critical moments for the tariff schedules occurred with the end of the first three-year period, coinciding with the conclusion of the Torquay Round of negotiations. At this time it was decided that an amended date for Article XXVIII would be inserted into the Torquay Protocol (1950), binding the schedules until the end of 1953. The amendment, as part of the protocol of the Torquay negotiations, would go into effect with the signature of two-thirds of the Contracting Parties. Curzon argues that delegates chose this since it was easier than the alternative, which was to draft a separate protocol to extend the original Article XXVIII, thus subjecting it to its own ratification debate in each Contracting Party. Indeed, many of the discussions over the renewal were held with minimum publicity so as to avoid pressures from interest groups to renegotiate tariffs, as "a post-GATT decision change ... is more difficult than an ante-GATT-decision obstruction" and delegates were eager to bring home something of a *fait accompli* that would then be presented for discussion at home but would be difficult to reverse (Curzon 1965, 111). The amendment, as part of the Torquay Protocol, did bind the tariff schedules until 1953, at which time the Contracting Parties once again faced the issue of their extension.

In 1953 the Contracting Parties agreed not to invoke the provisions of Article XXVIII for a period of eighteen months, until June 1955. As in the previous instance, this was a convenient alternative and bound the tariff schedules without making the provision formal and thus subject to national ratification. Another option at this time was to amend Article XXVIII to

9. Curzon (1965) provides a detailed account of events, summarized in this section, leading up to the installation of the new version of Article XXVIII, which provided for the automatic renewal of tariff schedules and was put into effect in December 1957.

extend the tariff schedules formally; however, this would require national ratification from each member. Instead, agreement not to invoke Article XXVIII allowed delegates once again to avoid public debate and retain existing tariff reductions. They also considered not extending the schedules at all, thus allowing modifications for or withdrawals from any country that desired them. However, this was the least desirable course of action, as it would be the most likely to threaten the existing structure of tariff concessions. Moreover, as it was now clear that the United States would not ratify the ITO Charter and the GATT was to remain as the only trade governance mechanism, providing greater stability in the Agreement and preventing the unraveling of tariff reductions became even greater considerations for the Contracting Parties.

Nevertheless, difficult negotiations continued over the binding of tariff schedules and the renegotiation provision. With a revised draft of Article XXVIII pending acceptance by the Contracting Parties, the agreement in 1953 not to invoke Article XXVIII was renewed for another eighteen months, until December 1957, when the revised Article XXVIII would come into force. This revised version of Article XXVIII did away with time limits on the tariff schedules, as it now read, "On the first day of each three-year period" rather than "On or after January 195–." The textual change was minor, but it now made permanent the validation of the original tariff schedules. The revised Article XXVIII was still a renegotiation provision, as it dealt with modifications in and withdrawals of concessions. However, the revision introduced "administrative and psychological barriers [to renegotiation], which are of the greatest value in securing the permanency of the results achieved" (Curzon 1965, 115).

Irwin characterizes the agreement among members to forego the right to invoke the renegotiation provision in Article XXVIII, beginning in 1953, as "a crucial achievement," as they successfully preserved the "sanctity" of these early tariff cuts. It provided for a powerful "lock-in feature" for the original tariff cuts (Irwin 1995, 325, 326). They contributed to the resilience of the regime as they prevented the unraveling of the bilateral agreements that comprised the GATT. Even a single country's move to withdraw or renegotiate concessions could have wide ramifications for the GATT, bringing on retaliatory withdrawals from others in a chain reaction. The erosion of tariff cuts in one agreement would most likely lead to the nullification of other bilateral agreements as well, as the countries negatively affected by a given renegotiation would seek redress by withdrawing concessions on other goods, which often were included in a separate bilateral agreement with other countries. This could well threaten to unravel the GATT's multilateral web of arrangements and return the global trading order to the protectionist chaos of the interwar years. Instead, tariff stabilization significantly lessened the uncertainty surrounding long-term prospects of market access for exports (Black 1959) as well as maintaining the early tariff reductions and making them difficult to change.

Critical Moments, Flexibility, and Unexpected Consequences

The second key source of institutional resilience in the General Agreement is flexibility, the rules and procedures in institutional arrangements that enable the institution to adapt to new and changing circumstances. According to the rational design project, flexibility mechanisms in institutional arrangements are often the result of resolving cooperation problems surrounding uncertainty, whether about behavior, compliance, the preferences of other parties, or the state of the world. The prevailing source of uncertainty at the time of the General Agreement's adoption was uncertainty about the state of the world, that is, the lack of knowledge on the part of involved parties about the consequences of their choices (Koremenos, Lipson, and Snidal 2001b, 13, 18).[10] In particular, it was the uncertainty over the tide of trade politics in participating countries and especially in the United States that led to the installation of flexibility mechanisms in the General Agreement.

Flexibility is argued to be an important means by which the principal architects of an institution ensure institutional continuity and survival in the face of changing domestic political conditions (Gruber 2000, 2005). That is, governmental actors of the leading countries, anticipating the possibility that the regime may one day face political heirs that are now opposed to the regime, have incentives to construct flexible institutional mechanisms to provide avenues for change that do not threaten the existence of the institution itself. This approach brings greater attention to the domestic politics of the leading countries, in particular whether the political opponents and heirs of these governments are likely to support or oppose the current government's commitment to the institution (Gruber 2005, 117). Rosendorff and Milner have argued that flexibility mechanisms such as escape clauses

---

10. An illustrative example is provided by the authors on the Spratly Islands dispute, which involves a group of islands in the South China Sea claimed by at least five states (China, Vietnam, Thailand, Taiwan, and the Philippines). Although it is believed that the waters around these islands are rich in oil and natural gas deposits, it is as yet unknown just how extensive these deposits are and their present and future value. Thus any institutional arrangement that resolves the dispute among involved parties will have to take account of the "uncertainty about the state of the world," or the lack of knowledge regarding the value of the resources purportedly associated with these islands and the consequences of agreeing to institutional arrangements that divide these potential resources.

are an "efficient equilibrium under conditions of domestic uncertainty" (2001, 71). Such "safeguards" are effective in allowing countries to suspend temporarily their obligations to comply with institutional arrangements. In the face of domestic uncertainty, flexibility mechanisms allow governments to have greater discretion in setting policy. Horn, Maggi, and Staiger (2006) have similarly argued that as incomplete contracts, trade agreements with escape clauses enable governments to retain autonomy over domestic instruments in trade policy and to take steps that will aid governments in addressing uncertainty in demand for imports. More important, however, because flexibility mechanisms allow a member of an institution to suspend obligations without exiting the institution, it contributes to the continued viability of the institution itself.

The design of the General Agreement included several flexibility mechanisms, among them safeguard measures added at the insistence of the United States. They included an escape clause, Article XIX, that allowed for the suspension, withdrawal, or modification of a concession when particular imports caused or threatened "serious injury" to domestic producers. It was consistent with the requirements of the renewal of the RTAA in 1945 and the subsequent Executive Order 9832 that all trade agreements contain such an escape clause.[11] The United States also insisted on several exceptions for agriculture to make it consistent with its domestic programs (Hathaway 1997). Indeed, in the earliest negotiations in Geneva in 1947, negotiators made U.S. participation in the regime contingent on the inclusion of specific provisions for agriculture (Goldstein 1993, 218).[12] Other exceptions listed in Part II of the General Agreement incorporating Chapter V of the ITO Charter include provisions permitting import restrictions for balance of payments reasons (Article XII), suspension of Article XIII's obligations on nondiscriminatory use of quantitative restrictions for the purpose of obtaining additional imports as long they do not result in "unduly depleting their monetary reserves" (Article XIV), and exceptions for reasons of economic development (Article XVIII) and national security (Article XXI).

---

11. *General Agreement on Tariffs and Trade* (1947), Article XIX, (a) and (b).

12. First, under specified conditions protection of agricultural commodities were to be exempted from the prohibition on quantitative restrictions; and second, agricultural goods were also to be exempted from any commitment to the prohibition on export subsidies. These provisions were nonnegotiable from the vantage point of the United States. Indeed, the U.S. negotiating team vetoed China's proposal to extend the exception to cover manufactured goods and another by China, India, and the Netherlands to exempt domestic price stabilization measures from the prohibition on quantitative restrictions. These twin exceptions, in subsidies and quantitative restrictions, served to make complete the exclusion of agriculture from the rules of the GATT.

These provisions provided the "compromise of embedded liberalism," at least from the perspective of the principal architect, which reconciled the demands of domestic economic exigencies within the United States with the need to construct and maintain a multilateral trading system based on liberal trade principles.

The GATT and the AAA: U.S. Waiver, 1955

The changing winds of U.S. domestic politics came to take center stage once again in the GATT in January 1955, when the United States submitted to the Contracting Parties of the General Agreement a request for a waiver of its obligations, for reasons having to do with the newly amended terms of Section 22 of the U.S. Agricultural Adjustment Act (AAA).[13] The system of price supports in place since 1933 had been sanctioned under the General Agreement of 1947 as an exception, in Article XI. However, because Section 22 now did not limit the range of products to be restricted, the United States requested a permanent waiver of its obligations insofar as they involved import restrictions undertaken under the terms of Section 22. In submitting its request, the communication from the United States read: "The United States wishes to *regularize* this situation and therefore desires to request the contracting parties to grant it a waiver of its obligations under the Agreement to the extent necessary to prevent a conflict with the Agreement in the case of action required to be taken by the United States Government under the terms of Section 22."[14]

In effect, the U.S. request was for a permanent waiver of its GATT obligations insofar as they conflicted with Section 22 of the AAA. The U.S. Congress had recently enacted the amended Section 22 of the AAA to provide that whenever the president finds, based on recommendations from the secretary of agriculture and investigation by the U.S. Tariff Commission, that imports of certain products render ineffective or materially interfere with an agricultural support program, action must be taken to prevent imports from having that effect. The procedure for identifying such imports was to be initiated by the secretary of agriculture following a preliminary investigation. If particular imports were found to have the effects for which the use of Section 22 action would be required, the secretary of agriculture was to request that the president direct the U.S. Tariff Commission to make

13. The two case studies in this chapter on the U.S. waiver and on the Treaty of Rome and Article XXIV application utilize archival materials, recently made public by the WTO, from the GATT Digital Library, 1947–1994, Stanford University, available at http://gatt.stanford.edu/page/home.

14. L/315, 28 January 1955, p. 2, emphasis added.

a study of the case. Following its study, the Tariff Commission was to make recommendations regarding the obligations imposed upon the president under Section 22, namely whether and what kind of action should be taken along with the basis for its findings and recommendations. (Section 22 also permits immediate action by the president where required, which would be in effect until the president acts on the report of the Tariff Commission.) The terms of Section 22 provide for the use of quotas and fees as necessary to remove the effects of the imports on the domestic market. In setting quotas, the president was not allowed to set quotas below 50 percent of the total imports of a particular good in a representative period. In the case of fees, the president was allowed no more than 50 percent ad valorem on the imported product. Embargos were not permitted.

This legislation is important in two key respects. First, the action to be taken by the president is "mandatory," obligating the executive to impose import restrictions in cases so defined by the U.S. Tariff Commission. Second, and more important for the GATT, in 1951 Congress added a paragraph to the law that explicitly established the priority of national law over international law. That is, the new paragraph provided that "no international agreement heretofore or hereafter entered into shall be applied in a manner inconsistent with the provisions of this Section," thus effectively subordinating GATT obligations to the requirements of U.S. trade law.[15]

The particular nature of Section 22 legislation was also intertwined with another development in U.S. trade politics, namely the submission of the GATT's Organizational Agreement to Congress for approval. The Agreement was the GATT Contracting Parties' attempt, following the failure of the ITO, to formalize the trade regime rather than maintain its informal status. In this little-known and ultimately unsuccessful attempt, GATT members sought to establish a more official presence for the regime through the formation of an Organization for Trade Cooperation to manage the General Agreement. The submission of this Agreement to Congress coincided with the debate over the U.S. waiver request to the GATT.

The U.S. waiver was placed on the agenda for the Ninth Session of the GATT Contracting Parties, as requested by the United States, and the Contracting Parties agreed that it be discussed at an early meeting of the session. In presenting the waiver request to the GATT members at the Ninth Session, the U.S. delegation emphasized that the United States was not seeking an amendment of the General Agreement and that the issue was over the Agreement in its existing form, arising out of the "particular circumstances of the United States." Moreover, the issue of the waiver was linked to the GATT's

---

15. Ibid., p. 1.

Organizational Agreement that was to be presented to Congress for approval, and the delegation noted that the U.S. government was "anxious" to have a decision on the waiver before the Agreement's presentation, as the U.S. Congress would likely wish to know the position of the Contracting Parties on the waiver request in considering the Organizational Agreement.[16]

In presenting its case to the Ninth Session, the U.S. delegation sought to assure other GATT members by pointing out that in the past U.S. Government actions under Section 22 were "relatively limited" and that it was "unlikely" that the actions mandated by the trade legislation would be extensively used in the future. Approval of the waiver was explicitly linked to the fate of the Agreement on the Organization for Trade Cooperation (OTC), which was the GATT's renewed attempt at forging a formal organization for trade governance following the failure of the ITO. As the Organizational Agreement for the OTC was shortly to be submitted to Congress, the U.S. delegation noted that in asking Congress for legislative authority to participate in the Organization, it expected Congress to be especially concerned with the relationship between any new organization entered into by the United States and the provisions of Section 22 of the AAA. The U.S. representative noted, "In order to ensure the full participation of the United States [in the new Organization], it was therefore essential that any possible inconsistency between United States commitments under the GATT and Section 22 be removed," so the United States was requesting a general waiver of its GATT obligations to this end.[17]

The U.S. waiver request was a "critical moment" for the GATT, as noted by several members during the meeting. Representative Rattigan of Australia, for example, noted that the issue "inevitably raised the question of whether the Agreement could remain one to which all of its members continued to subscribe." Representative White of New Zealand, pointing out that his country had already suffered "direct injury" as a result of U.S. restrictions on agricultural imports, questioned whether granting of a general and permanent waiver would merely provide an "escape clause for the continuation of an inequitable situation." It urged that in the event of a waiver, the terms explicitly provide for the United States to give an indication of the conditions under which the restrictions would be lifted in the future. The Italian delegation pointed out that the U.S. waiver request related to Article XI, one of the most important principles of the GATT. The delegation voiced its concern that the general, or permanent, waiver was

16. SR.9/33, 7 February 1955, p. 8.
17. Ibid., p. 1.

a dispensation so broad in nature that it "threatened the very foundations of the GATT."[18]

The most vociferous opposition to the U.S. waiver came from the Canadian delegation, whose remarks during the Ninth Session were circulated separately at its request. The statement reiterated Canada's strong opposition to the U.S. waiver, emphasizing that it would oppose any arrangement that, in effect, would write Section 22 "unqualified and unsupervised" into the GATT.[19] The Danish delegation, noting that Denmark, along with Australia, Canada, and New Zealand, had been the countries most directly affected by Section 22, pointed out the "damaging implications of the proposed waiver on future cooperation under the Agreement" and stressed that granting of the waiver to resolve the conflict between U.S. trade legislation and the GATT would be "a very bitter solution for his country to accept."[20]

Perhaps the view that best reflected the outcome of this case was voiced by representative Vassiliou of Greece, who at once noted the two arguments of principle that made the U.S. waiver request so controversial. One was the issue of whether international law should supersede national law, a view that was increasingly gaining currency in Europe. Though such a principle was essentially a domestic matter to resolve, the representative expressed concern over the "mandatory" character of the U.S. legislation and that it was coming from the "country undertaking leadership of the free world." Second, he noted that there was no question that the U.S. waiver request was "in complete contradiction to the spirit of the [General] Agreement, whose rule would thereby be completely set aside," making it unacceptable from a legal standpoint.[21] Nevertheless, the Greek delegate argued, the U.S. waiver request went beyond the technical details of the debate; he stated that "in a political spirit," Greece would support the U.S. waiver request. Delegates from South Africa and the Netherlands noted as well the political necessity of granting the U.S. waiver request, as it was recognized that the waiver was necessary in order to submit the Agreement for the Organization for Trade Cooperation to Congress.

The U.S. waiver request was referred to a Working Party at the close of this plenary session, which consisted of seventeen members including the United States, with Max Suetens of Belgium assuming the role of chairman.[22]

---

18. Ibid., pp. 3, 4, 7.
19. L/319, 10 February 1955.
20. SR.9/33, 7 February 1955, p. 6.
21. Ibid., p. 7.
22. Other Working Party members included Australia, Germany, Pakistan, Canada, India, Turkey, Cuba, Italy, the Union of South Africa, Denmark, the Netherlands, the United Kingdom, France, New Zealand, and Uruguay.

The United States delegation submitted a draft waiver to the Working Party, which used it as the basis for their deliberations.[23] Amendments and memoranda on the terms of the waiver were proposed by Australia, Cuba, Canada, the United Kingdom, and Pakistan.[24] Among these, the Working Party noted in its report to the Contracting Parties, amendments of "major importance" were not included, specifically as they would conflict with the terms of the amended Section 22 of the U.S. Agricultural Adjustment Act.[25] These failed amendments sought to define the parameters of the waiver in several ways. They argued, as in the amendment proposed by Cuba, for a "defined scope" for the waiver and product limitations, applying the waiver only to products actually and currently falling under the restrictions. Several members suggested a limited timeframe for the waiver or that it be accompanied by conditions that would provide for the lifting of restrictions under Section 22 by a specified date. The proposals also included the inclusion of a special review mechanism for the waiver, to be applied after a specified period.

These proposed amendments, however, were wholly defeated, as they conflicted directly with the terms of Section 22.[26] The U.S. delegation emphasized that these amendments, were they incorporated into the waiver, would not sufficiently meet the terms of Section 22 and would thus not remove the inconsistency between the GATT and the U.S. trade legislation. Thus the United States came to obtain a general waiver, unconditional and indefinite, for its agricultural restrictions. The official text of the waiver read that the Contracting Parties

decide, pursuant to paragraph 5(a) of Article XXV of the General Agreement and in consideration of the assurances above, that subject to the conditions and procedures set out hereunder the obligations of the United States under the provisions of Articles II and XI of the General Agreement are waived to the extent necessary to prevent a conflict with such provisions of the General Agreement in the case of action required to be taken by the Government of the United States under Section 22.[27]

23. W.9/170, 3 February 1955.
24. W.9/183, 8 February 1955 on amendments suggested by Australian delegation; W.9/195, 9 February 1955 on suggestions by Cuban delegation; W.9/186, 9 February 1955 note by Canadian delegation; W.9/187, 10 February 1955 memorandum by United Kingdom delegation; W.9/192, 11 February 1955 Pakistan views on U.S. waiver.
25. L/339, 3 March 1955.
26. The terms of the waiver did include, however, a provision for an annual review by the Contracting Parties, under which the United States would be obligated to provide a report of current restrictions.
27. L/339, 3 March 1955, p. 6.

The draft decision granting the waiver specified that the "restrictions" imposed under Section 22 would include both fees and quantitative limitations. Hence, the waiver applied to U.S. obligations under Articles II and XI of the General Agreement. The scope of the waiver, covering fees in particular, reflected the intention of the U.S. government to maintain the general stability of tariff bindings already under implementation under the GATT. Rather than modify or withdraw tariff concessions as circumstances dictate, the United States sought an exception in the form of a waiver so as not to disturb existing tariff concessions. The United States also sought to maintain the general integrity of the General Agreement with a provision that allowed any interested Contracting Party the "fullest notice and opportunity for…representations and consultations," thus explicitly placing no limitations on GATT members' recourse to provisions in Articles XXII and XXIII. The draft decision further emphasized that the waiver "does not affect the obligations of the United States under any other provisions of the Agreement," and the United States would in no way by virtue of the waiver obtain additionally the right to deviate from the rule of nondiscrimination provided in Article XIII.[28]

The vote to adopt the decision granting the U.S. waiver was taken by roll call, and the decision was adopted with 23 in favor and 5 against.[29] In the discussion preceding the vote, delegates largely reiterated their remarks from the earlier plenary session that led to the establishment of the Working Party. Opposing the decision to approve the waiver, representative Couillard of Canada reemphasized that approval of the waiver meant that the "the whole Section 22 of the [U.S.] Agricultural Adjustment Act would be written into the General Agreement unqualified and virtually unsupervised."[30] In his remarks following the vote approving the waiver, Representative Couillard noted once again that Canada was affected more than any other country by the waiver, as two-thirds of its trade was conducted with the United States, a large part of which was in agricultural goods.[31] The Canadian position was echoed by representative Press of New Zealand, who pointed out that the approval would mean "an important piece of United States domestic legislation would be written into the General Agreement"

28. Ibid., p. 3.
29. SR.9/44, 15 March 1955. Countries voting in favor of the U.S. waiver included: Australia, Austria, Belgium, Chile, the Dominican Republic, Finland, France, Germany, Greece, India, Indonesia, Italy, Luxembourg, Nicaragua, Norway, Pakistan, Peru, the Federation of Rhodesia and Nyasaland, Sweden, Turkey, the United Kingdom, Uruguay, and Japan as well as the United States. Canada, Cuba, Denmark, the Netherlands, and New Zealand voted against the wavier. Brazil, Burma, Ceylon, Czechoslovakia, and the Union of South Africa abstained.
30. SR.9/44, 15 March 1955, p. 10.
31. SR.9/45, 18 March 1955, p. 2.

and afford no checks on U.S. actions in this respect. Those supporting the approval of the waiver did so largely for "political" reasons that sidestepped the issue of legality or conformity with the General Agreement. Perhaps the most significant of these was that approval of the waiver was directly tied to the fate of the GATT's Organizational Agreement for the Organization for Trade Cooperation, which was at the time under consideration before the U.S. Congress. Representative Finnmark of Sweden pointed out that the "paramount importance of securing the full cooperation of the U.S. Government in the activities of the Organization [for Trade Cooperation] was the decisive factor in his Government's acceptance of the Decision." Representative Crawford of Australia voiced his government's support of the waiver as a means for the "United States Administration...to persuade Congress that the world looked to the United States for effective economic leadership in the free world."[32]

Thus in 1955, the United States obtained from the GATT Contracting Parties an unconditional and indefinite waiver of its obligations under Articles II and XI, thus effectively writing Section 22 of the Agricultural Adjustment Act into the General Agreement. This waiver was to remain in place for the life of the General Agreement and more important, it determined the place of agriculture in global trade negotiations.[33] The waiver allowed the United States to restrict imports of agricultural goods such as sugar, peanuts, and dairy products (Hathaway 1997). While the approval of the U.S. waiver demonstrates just how U.S. trade politics came to dominate the politics of the GATT, it set a major precedent for the management of trade in agriculture under the regime, especially among the leading economies (Coleman 1998). The unexpected consequence of the GATT's exception for agriculture, spearheaded by the United States, is that it set an important precedent for restricting imports under the European Economic Community's Common Agricultural Policy (CAP) adopted in January 1962. Aside from centralizing policymaking on trade restrictions, subsidies, and local usage regulations, the CAP provided for direct market intervention for setting prices on agricultural goods and for imposing subsidies on exports and consumption to address problems of excessive supply. The higher level of protection under the CAP was reconciled with GATT obligations with legal arguments that pointed to the absence of any provision in the General Agreement prohibiting a comprehensive program on agricultural

32. SR.9/44, 15 March 1955, pp. 10, 14, 16.
33. The Uruguay Round agreement required the United States to convert restrictions on Section 22 items to tariff-equivalents and tariff-rate quotas, the latter of which would impose one rate of duty for imports within the quota limit and another, substantially higher rate for out-of-quota imports.

production and, more important, to the precedent set by the United States to exclude agriculture (Goldstein 1993, 221; Hill 1984).

The preferences of the United States continued to function as a key veto point in any GATT attempts at reform in this area. Over the course of the GATT's development, the United States obstructed efforts by GATT members to address the problem of excluding agricultural goods from the purview of the regime. It derailed any new commodity trade agreements by vetoing all proposals within the GATT for separate commodity agreements covering trade in agricultural goods and refused to participate in any new commodity trade agreements (Goldstein 1993, 222), leading to "disarray" in the world's agriculture market as market-distorting policies left prices unstable and artificially low (Johnson 1973; Tyers and Anderson 1992). These exceptions for agriculture have been the most enduring, in no small part due to the insistence of the United States and later the European Economic Community (Josling, Tangerman, and Warley 1996).

Article XXIV, Preferential Trade Agreements, and the Formation of the European Community

Another mechanism of flexibility installed in the General Agreement was Article XXIV, which allows the formation of customs unions and free trade areas, a provision that has had lasting and unexpected effects on the development not only of the GATT but also of the global trade system as a whole (Mathis 2002). Though imprecise and ambiguous in many respects (Pomfret 1988, 62–64), Article XXIV allowed the formation of customs unions provided that the margin of preference was "not on the whole higher" than those before the union and that it was formed "within a reasonable amount of time." A "critical moment" for the GATT regime arose with the formation of the European Economic Community, which applied for sanction of the regime through the provisions of article XXIV.

The GATT Contracting Parties received their first communication from the Council of Europe in July 1956, which submitted to the GATT members for study a proposal for the establishment of a free trade zone among the six members—the Benelux countries, France, Germany, and Italy, collectively referred to as the "European Six"—that would eventually lead to a European customs union.[34] The GATT's Intersessional Committee, meeting

---

34. L/500, 27 July 1956. The communication to the GATT followed the famous conference at Messina, at which time the drive toward European integration gained as member countries developed plans for the Common Market and, for common management of nuclear energy, Euratom. For an account of this formative period of postwar Europe, see Camps (1964).

in September 1956, was asked to consider whether the issue should be included in the Provisional Agenda for the Eleventh Session of the GATT Contracting Parties, to be held in the following year.[35] The Committee agreed to the inclusion of an item entitled "Proposals for Closer Economic Integration of Europe by the Formation of a Customs Union and/or Free-Trade Area" for Contracting Parties to consider both the European customs union and parallel plans for a free trade area under study by the Organization for European Economic Cooperation (OEEC).[36] The OEEC Council had appointed a Working Party to study possible methods of association (including the creation of a free trade area) between the proposed customs union and other member countries. Both plans were to be considered under the broader subject of "Plans for Tariff Reduction."[37]

At the Eleventh Session, GATT members charged the Intersessional Committee, meeting in between plenary sessions, with following the developments in the plans of the European Six. The Treaty of Rome establishing the European Economic Community (EEC), signed on 25 March 1957, was officially transmitted to the GATT on 18 April, approximately one month after its signing, for consideration in accordance with Article XXIV provisions on free trade areas and customs unions.[38] The Intersessional Committee's deliberations, held 24–27 April 1957, were focused on the terms of the treaty and the procedures that were to be followed within the GATT for its examination under Article XXIV.[39] At the request of the Intersessional Committee, the Interim Committee for the Common Market submitted a memorandum on the key provisions of the Treaty of Rome.[40] This was followed by questions from other Contracting Parties on the treaty's provisions and replies from the Interim Committee for the Common Market.[41] These exchanges were accompanied as well by the submission of a "specimen tariff" from the Interim Committee for the Common Market, which showed the rate of duty to be applied to a lengthy list of products considered most "representative" of the trade between the European Six and

---

35. IC/SR.27, 26 September 1956; L/535, 28 September 1956.
36. The OEEC was founded in 1948 to assist in administering the U.S. Marshall Plan for the reconstruction of Europe after World War II. The OEEC originally had eighteen members, including the six members of the EEC and Austria, Denmark, Greece, Iceland, Ireland, Norway, Portugal, Sweden, Switzerland, Turkey, and the United Kingdom. The OEEC was superseded by the Organization for Economic Cooperation and Development, which was established in 1961 and extended membership to non-European countries.
37. L/550, 12 October 1956.
38. L/626, 24 April 1957.
39. IC/SR.30, 3 May 1957.
40. L/637, 11 June 1957; L/637/Rev.1, 22 August 1957.
41. L/639, 19 June 1957; L/656, 2 August 1957.

other GATT members.[42] As the Intersessional Committee recommended, the GATT Secretariat also submitted its own statistical documentation. The Secretariat report documented the value of trade, exports, and imports in the aggregate and in product categories, distinguishing between trade among Common Market countries and trade with GATT members outside the European Economic Community.[43]

At the Ministerial Meeting during the Twelfth Session following the report of the Intersessional Committee, the GATT members adopted a decision to establish a committee to examine the treaty.[44] The terms of reference for the Committee on the Treaty Establishing the European Economic Community were threefold:

A. To examine, in the light of the provisions of the General Agreement on Tariffs and Trade, the relevant provisions of the Treaty of Rome and the problems likely to arise in their practical application. Such examination would include, inter alia, the arrangements provided for in the Treaty with respect to tariffs, the use of quantitative restrictions, trade in agricultural products and the association of overseas countries and territories with the European Common Market.
B. To recommend, in the light of the conclusions which result from the examination provided for above, such action as may be appropriate and desirable, including a determination of the means of establishing effective and continuing co-operation between the CONTRACTING PARTIES and the European Economic Community.
C. To report to the CONTRACTING PARTIES, and make such recommendations as maybe appropriate with respect to the continuation of the work of the Committee.[45]

The Committee, including in its membership all GATT members and headed by Dana Wilgress of Canada, appointed subcommittees for each of the four major issues of concern to the Contracting Parties and included in the Committee's terms of reference: Sub-Group A on Plan and Schedule, and Tariffs, namely the common external tariff of the Community; Sub-Group B on Quantitative Restrictions; Sub-Group C on Trade in Agricultural Products; and Sub-Group 4 on the Association of Overseas Territories.[46]

42. L/684, 26 September 1957; L/684/Add.1, 14 November 1957.
43. L/709, 18 October 1957; L/709/ADD.1, 22 October 1957; L/709/ADD.2, 26 October 1957; L/709/ADD.3, 5 November 1957; L/709/ADD.4, 20 November 1957; L/709/ADD.5, 22 November 1957; L/709/ADD.6, 25 November 1957.
44. L/696, 4 October 1957; SR.12/2, 24 October 1957; SR.12/10, 2 November 1957.
45. W.12/14, 1 November 1957.
46. Summary Record of Meetings of the Committee on each issue: CRT/SR.1, 8 November 1957 on Plan and Schedule, and Tariffs; CRT/SR.2, 9 November 1957 on Quantitative Restrictions; CRT/SR.3, 12 November 1957 on Trade in Agricultural Products; CRT/SR.4, 12 November 1957 on Association of Overseas Territories.

Sub-Group A on Tariffs and Plan and Schedule was charged chiefly with evaluating the European Community's common external tariff and the elimination of import and export duties among Community members vis-à-vis provisions of the GATT's Article XXIV. In reporting its work to the Committee, Sub-Group A concluded that "it was not possible at this time to determine whether the Common Tariff would be consistent with the provisions of paragraph 5(a) of Article XXIV," as the rates of duty were not yet known for a large part of the common external tariff.[47]

The work of Sub-Group B was devoted to examining the provisions for quantitative restrictions in the Treaty of Rome. Sub-Group B noted that the Treaty's provisions on quantitative restrictions "were not mandatory and imposed on the members of the Community no obligation to take action which would be inconsistent with the General Agreement."[48] Like Sub-Group A, however, Sub-Group B also had little to offer in the way of a definite conclusion on the consistency of the Treaty's provisions and the General Agreement. Its report stated that "in view of the uncertainties about the way in which the provisions of the Rome Treaty would be implemented the members of the Sub-Group other than the Six considered that at this stage it was not possible to make a judgment that that application of the provisions of the Rome Treaty concerning the use of quantitative restrictions would or would not be compatible with the relevant provisions of the General Agreement."[49] Sub-Group B did, however, agree that no special machinery was needed within the regime to address issues arising from the use of quantitative restrictions by the European Six, and that such issues, should they arise, could be resolved through consultations under the provisions of the General Agreement.

Sub-Group C, in its report on Trade in Agricultural Products, noted the large amount of discretion left to the European Six and their institutions due to the lack of precision in the Treaty of Rome regarding how agriculture provisions would apply to trade with countries outside the European Community and the removal of barriers within it. The majority of the members of Sub-Group C noted a "strong presumption" that the Treaty would result in increased external barriers vis-à-vis third countries and new internal barriers to substitute those in existence.[50] Nevertheless, Sub-Group C in its report declined to take a strong stand on the Treaty's consistency with Article XXIV and "decided that it was not able determine at this time either

47. W.12/57, 28 November 1957; CRT/SR.5, 9 December 1957.

48. L/778, 20 December 1957, p. 12. Also W.12/51, 28 November 1957; CRT/SR.5, 9 December 1957.

49. W.12/51, 28 November 1957, p. 4.

50. L/778, 20 December 1957, p. 19. Also W.12/56, 28 November 1957; CRT/SR.5, 9 December 1957.

that the agricultural provisions of the Rome Treaty or their implementation would be consistent with the provisions of the General Agreement."[51] It did, however, recommend the establishment of special machinery within the GATT to serve as liaison to the European Community's institutions, a recommendation the Six vehemently opposed and instead argued for consultations under Article XXII.

Perhaps the most controversial of the provisions in the Treaty of Rome was the Association of the European Economic Community with Overseas Territories, which would grant present and former colonies of the European Six preferential access to their markets. This provision created a legal question for the GATT, as the formulation of Article XXIV contained no mention of the simultaneous formation of a customs union and a free trade area, the latter of which would result from the granting of preferential access in the Six's colonial trade. The report from Sub-Group D on Association of Overseas Territories explicitly noted that the provisions of the Rome Treaty on this matter were "incompatible" with Article XXIV. The report also pointed out that the beneficiaries of preferential access in the Six's colonial trade included those not originally entitled to the preferences authorized under Article 1, paragraph 2 of the General Agreement, which only allowed for the continuation of existing preferences and thus precluded such new preferences as stipulated by the Treaty of Rome. Nevertheless, as was the case with the others, Sub-Group D could provide "no definite conclusions" on the matter of Association with Overseas Territories but also recommended the establishment of a special body to deal with the questions emerging from discussions in the four sub-groups.[52]

In his address to the Twelfth Session of the Contracting Parties in December 1957, Wilgress noted that the reports from the sub-groups contained "no definite conclusions," either due to time constraints or lack of information.[53] They were being submitted to the Contracting Parties as reports of an interim nature but were expected to figure importantly in the future consideration of problems arising from Treaty of Rome. Nevertheless, the Contracting Parties adopted the report of the Committee, with continued consideration to the questions regarding the Rome Treaty to be deferred to the Intersessional Committee. In view of the importance of the questions that the Rome Treaty had raised for the trade regime, the Intersessional

51. CRT/SR.5, 9 December 1957, p. 57.
52. W.12/59, 28 November 1957. This sub-group continued its work following its report to the Committee on the Treaty of Rome and the Twelfth Session. It reconstituted itself as the Working Party on the Association of Overseas Territories, as part of the arrangements for further and continuing consideration of the Treaty of Rome. IC/SR.36, 5 December 1957.
53. SR.12/20, 11 December 1957, p. 1; L/778, 20 December 1957, p. 1.

Committee was to consist of representatives of all GATT members, as the Committee chairman's report had recommended.[54]

Following the adoption of the report from the Committee on the Treaty Establishing the European Economic Community, the Intersessional Committee continued, as charged by the Contracting Parties at their Twelfth Session in 1957, to continue to consider the issues related to the Rome Treaty in its meeting in May 1958.[55] The Committee agreed on the procedures to be followed in dealing with the specific and procedural problems that might arise from the creation of the European Economic Community.

The two most important features of the case involving the European Community and the GATT are that first, it set the precedent for leaving aside the "questions of law and debates about the compatibility of the Rome Treaty with Article XXIV of the General Agreement" in favor of directing greater attention to "specific and practical problems." European Economic Community representative Baron Snoy et d'Oppuers, in addressing the Intersessional Committee, noted in particular the report of Sub-Group B on Quantitative Restrictions, which stated that the provisions of the Treaty of Rome "imposed on the Members of the [European] Community *no obligation to take action which would be inconsistent with the General Agreement*," whatever the scope and interpretation that were to be attached to the interpretation of Article XXIV of the General Agreement, and that "any particular problems that might arise in the actual application of import restrictions by the individual members of the community would be examined through consultations under the provisions of the General Agreement."[56]

Second, the European Community, strongly supported by the United States, expressed their desire to remain within the GATT system and its existing institutional mechanisms for managing and negotiating trade. The European Economic Community representative echoed the words of the U.S. delegation in bringing the Community within the broader multilateral framework of the General Agreement rather than to create a specialized mechanism for accommodating this new trading entity: "We do not envisage a new kind of machinery, established primarily or exclusively for this purpose. Rather, we have in mind the normal procedures for exchanging information and views along lines which are in keeping with the best traditions of the GATT."[57]

Indeed, the Intersessional Committee concluded that the "normal procedure of the General Agreement and the techniques and traditions of the

---

54. L/766, 29 November 1957. L/778, 20 December 1957, p. 2.
55. IC/SR.38, 19 May 1958.
56. Ibid., pp. 20, 27, emphasis added.
57. Ibid., p. 28.

Contracting Parties in applying them, were well adapted to the handling of such problems," where such problems arose as a result of the European Community's trade practices.[58] Of particular interest was the utility of Article XXII, which enables any Contracting Party to seek arrangements with any other Contracting Party on any matter of relevance to the operation of the General Agreement.

The European Economic Community sought practical integration within the GATT, deferring, as did the GATT report, the legal questions of compatibility with the regime. Moreover, it emphasized working within the existing machinery of the GATT, with Baron Snoy noting that to do otherwise by establishment of special procedures would be an implicit acknowledgement of the Community's legal conflict with the General Agreement and weaken the regime at a time when what was needed was to strengthen the GATT to combat world recession and the (re)turn to the bilateralism of the interwar years. The European Economic Community emphasized the importance of maintaining the multilateral negotiating procedures within the GATT. Finally, in responding to the remark from the South African delegation regarding the sheer size of the economic entity that would now be formed through the Treaty of Rome and the implications for the smaller countries whose interests might now be affected, Baron Snoy was prescient in acknowledging the influential position of the European Community in the years to come, acknowledging that the "great trading nations have responsibilities which are considerably greater than those of countries whose interests are more limited." Indeed, speaking for the European Community, Baron Snoy emphasized, "We are prepared to assume such responsibilities."[59]

The GATT provision allowing customs unions and free trade areas had a paradoxical effect on the development of the GATT and the global trade system as a whole. On the one hand, it figured as an important source of institutional resilience, as such agreements were subject to review and sanction by GATT members. The tacit acceptance under Article XXIV of the Treaty of Rome and its provisions for the formation of the European Economic Community set an important precedent by introducing a weakness of interpretation, maintaining the imprecision and ambiguity of Article XXIV. Without a clear legal interpretation of its provisions when the opportunity to do so presented itself, the case of the European Economic Community customs union led to the de facto acknowledgement that Article XXIV provisions were in effect inapplicable. Furthermore, subsequent notifications of agreements for customs unions and for free trade areas also failed to

58. Ibid., p. 20.
59. Ibid., p. 29.

yield any clear assessments of their compatibility with Article XXIV, and any conflicts among members on this issue were dealt with on a case-by-case basis. The Understanding on the Interpretation of Article XXIV of the GATT of 1994, concluded during the Uruguay Round, clarified some procedural issues; nonetheless, there was no substantive clarification or interpretation of the article's essential requirements (Fiorentino, Verdeja, and Toqueboeuf 2007, 27).

At the same time, as Gardner Patterson noted in his analysis of the formation of the European Economic Community, "It was only the beginning of a worldwide movement," as by mid-1965 half of the GATT's seventy-nine members were already participants in such preferential trade agreements at various stages of formation (1966, 139–140). Moving forward four decades, as of December 2006, a total of 367 preferential trade agreements, or Regional Trade Agreements (RTAs), have been notified to the GATT/WTO, and 214 are in force (Fiorentino, Verdeja, and Toqueboeuf 2007), leading scholars to point to the "proliferation" of such agreements in recent years (Mansfield 1998).[60] The WTO reports that, given current agreements that have been proposed, are under negotiation, or have been signed but not yet implemented, close to 400 RTAs are expected to be in force by 2010.[61]

Conclusion

This chapter has examined components of the General Agreement's institutional evolution, namely the persistence of power-based bargaining in tariff negotiations and the flexibility mechanisms that allowed the regime to adapt to the changing circumstances presented by U.S. domestic politics and economic integration efforts in Europe. The theoretical framework emphasized the endogeneity of power and institutional development, path-dependence in terms of the reproduction of power relations as seen through the persistence of the regime's power-based bargaining protocol, and the critical moments marked by changes in U.S. trade politics and the formation of the European Economic Community.

The analysis focuses on two particular features of institutional continuity in the GATT: centralization and flexibility. Even though there was a three-year limit on the General Agreement's tariff schedule, subsequent

---

60. These include notifications made under the General Agreement's Article XXIV, the General Agreement on Trade in Services (GATS) under the WTO, the Enabling Clause, and accessions to existing RTAs.

61. Available at www.wto.org/english/tratop_e/region_e/region_e.htm, accessed 10 December 2008.

rounds of the General Agreement's negotiations demonstrated a remarkable stability and persistence in the rules of bargaining established in Geneva. Negotiations continued to take place bilaterally among principal suppliers even with amendments to the Agreement allowing for multilateral procedures, due largely to continued U.S. adherence to bilateral accords.[62] Negotiating parties reverted to this practice after variously and half-heartedly experimenting with others in previous rounds. Indeed, even though the previous Kennedy and Tokyo Rounds officially adopted multilateral and sectoral approaches to tariff cuts, many deviated from, if not completely ignored, these alternatives (Hoda 2001, 30–32), choosing instead to follow these longstanding early practices. The item-by-item approach to tariff bargaining persisted even with significant changes in U.S. trade legislation allowing for a sectoral approach. The tariff schedule itself was installed as an integral part of the Agreement and was made difficult to change in subsequent rounds through automatic renewals (Curzon 1965, 115). Thus the rules set in Geneva continued to privilege the large economies and major powers, and negotiations under the General Agreement largely took place among the United States, Canada, Great Britain, France, and later Germany after its accession.

The GATT's flexibility was tested at two critical moments in its evolution. First, U.S. domestic politics came to take center stage at the GATT, when it requested, and eventually obtained, a permanent and unconditional waiver of its GATT obligations in trade in agriculture, which resolved the conflict between GATT obligations and the provisions of the U.S. Agricultural Adjustment Act but allowed the United States to impose import restrictions for agricultural goods. Second, the signing of the Treaty of Rome, its subsequent notification to the GATT under Article XXIV provisions allowing the formation of a customs union, and the GATT members' tacit acceptance of the EEC set a key precedent with unexpected consequences for the global trading system.

---

62. *General Agreement on Tariffs and Trade,* Article XXVIII (bis), 2(a) (General Agreement 1969). Effective 24 September 1952.

Part II
CONSEQUENCES

3

Power and Politics in the GATT

The Effects on Trade, 1950–1994 (with Joanne Gowa)

The GATT yielded a definite and significant "distributive divide" that divided the regime's participants into "winners" and "losers." The General Agreement set precedents on what kind of trade should be governed by the multilateral trade regime, and it also determined how trade should be governed. Though these rules of trade governance provided an important and effective means to manage the global trading system in the post–World War II period, not all members benefited from them; some did, others did not.

The next two chapters, comprising the second part of this study, on "Consequences," are devoted to assessing the distributive consequences of the regime, to identifying its beneficiaries and contrasting them with other members that did not fare as well, and to explicating the link between this distributional consequence and the rules that preceded them. Chapter 3 examines closely the consequences of the GATT's bargaining protocol—the principal supplier rule and the item-by-item bargaining method. The analysis also uncovers an important but unintended consequence of the General Agreement's bargaining protocol, namely the persistence of discriminatory and trade-distorting interwar trade blocs whose dissolution was an important objective of the U.S. postwar planners. Chapter 4 analyzes the

This chapter is based on Gowa and Kim (2005) and an earlier version of the manuscript. Original article: Joanne Gowa and Soo Yeon Kim, "An Exclusive Country Club: The Effects of the GATT on Trade, 1950–94," *World Politics* 57, no. 4 (July 2005).

impact of accession rules in the WTO, the GATT's successor regime that heralded a new era for global trade governance.

The chapters utilize quantitative methods to analyze the extent to which countries that have joined the regime have experienced an increase in trade with their GATT/WTO trade partners. The results of the analysis reported here strongly suggest that the GATT and the WTO have produced an uneven allocation of benefits from participation in the regime. Most important, the results of the analyses provide evidence of a significant distributive divide as a result of the GATT/WTO's governance of trade among its members, specifically between the industrialized countries of the North and the nonindustrialized countries of the South.

Using data from the interwar and postwar periods, the analysis in Chapter 3 finds that the GATT had a large, positive, and significant impact on trade for *only five* of its member states: Great Britain, Canada, France, Germany, and the United States. This finding differs markedly from the conclusions of recent path-breaking studies of the GATT/WTO regime.[1] Moreover, the results show that the postwar system coexisted with, rather than supplanted, several interwar blocs: the Commonwealth, Reichsmark, gold, and exchange-control blocs continued to exert positive and significant effects on post-1945 trade. These outcomes are attributable to the protocol that governed tariff negotiations under the auspices of the GATT. The analysis in Chapter 4 finds that the WTO era has brought little change to this long-standing distributive divide between the developed and developing worlds. The results speak to the urgency of a successful conclusion to the Doha Development Round.

Background: Interwar Trade

The distributive impact of the GATT is well framed by the background of the interwar period, in which World War I reinforced a trend toward protection that had begun in the late nineteenth century (see, for example, O'Rourke and Williamson 1999, 35; Sachs and Warner 1995, 7). The advent of the Great Depression and the collapse of the gold standard destroyed whatever had remained of the prewar system of liberal trade (Irwin 1993, 106). In 1930, with the passage of the Smoot-Hawley Tariff Act, the United States increased its average tariff rate from 38 to 52 percent, its highest level since 1820 (Hiscox 1999, 671–672). Average tariffs in the major European powers rose to about the same level (Bagwell and Staiger 2002, 43). Between

---

1. Rose (2004, 2007); Subramanian and Wei (2007); Goldstein, Rivers and Tomz (2007); and Tomz, Goldstein, and Rivers (2007).

1929 and 1932, real world output declined by 20 percent, while trade volume fell by 40 percent (Irwin 1993, 112).

Several attempts to agree on a cooperative international response to the Great Depression failed. The decentralized actions that ensued established "each of the major industrial and financial powers" as "the center of a currency and trading bloc of its own" (Feinstein, Temin, and Toniolo 1997, 150). Great Britain, France, and Germany believed that the blocs would help to expand domestic output and employment. Sometimes built on preexisting networks of trade produced by political preference and economic dependence, the blocs had a satellite or hub-and-spoke structure that linked one large country to several relatively small states (Ritschl and Wolf 2003, 11).

The Imperial Preference system that the 1932 Ottawa Agreements established, for example, joined Britain to several smaller states that produced primary products, for the most part. While more than 50 percent of British exports were industrial goods, over 90 percent of Australia's and New Zealand's exports were foodstuffs and raw materials. A similar structure characterized the Reichsmark bloc, which joined Austria, Bulgaria, Germany, Greece, Hungary, Rumania, Turkey, and Yugoslavia. Germany exported manufactured goods, while at least 75 percent of East European exports consisted of foodstuffs and raw materials (Aldcroft 1981, 220).[2]

Although the interwar currency blocs were originally designed to fix exchange rates among their members, efforts to do so transformed them into preferential trading zones. The sterling bloc tied Australia, Denmark, Finland, Ireland, New Zealand, Norway, Portugal, and Sweden to Britain, which devalued after it abandoned the gold standard. In contrast, members of the gold bloc—France, Belgium, Switzerland, the Netherlands, and Poland—sought to maintain their currencies at par. Doing so led them to impose tariffs, quotas, and a surtax or "exchange dumping" duty on imports from countries that had devalued (Ritschl and Wolf 2003, 13; Eichengreen and Irwin 1995, 7).[3] Members of the exchange-control bloc relied on controls on foreign-currency transactions and bilateral clearing arrangements. They included most of the Reichsmark bloc states as well as Denmark, Finland, Italy, the Netherlands, Norway, Spain, Sweden, and Turkey (Ritschl and Wolf 2003, 14).

---

2. Of the successor states of the Austro-Hungarian Empire that joined the German bloc, only Austria was a predominantly industrialized state (Kaiser 1980, 19).

3. Several gold bloc members also shifted an increasing portion of trade to their colonies during the 1930s. Thus, for example, the percentage of French imports that came from its colonies rose from 16 percent in the 1920s to 29 percent in 1936. The corresponding statistics for French exports are 19 percent and 33 percent, respectively (Pomfret 1988, 47).

The development of these blocs seemed to have an all-too-predictable impact on U.S. trade. Between 1929 and 1933, the U.S. share of world exports declined from 15.6 percent to 10.3 percent (USTC 1958, 93). In response, President Franklin D. Roosevelt sought congressional authority to negotiate trade agreements with other countries. The 1934 Reciprocal Trade Agreements Act (RTAA) granted him that authority, but Congress made it very clear that it intended him to use it to expand market access abroad while protecting domestic industry.

The Distributive Impact of the GATT

Despite the crucial role that the GATT assumed in the reconstruction of world trade following World War II, it remained "relatively innocent of institutional provisions" (Dam 1970, 336). Indeed, it never acquired the organizational capacity that would have allowed it to resolve the market-failure problem that is often cited as its raison d'être: the need to monitor whether states comply with the agreements they sign. Instead, the trade regime operated largely as a bargaining forum. The protocol that governed the tariff bargains its members struck is therefore crucial to understanding the distribution of the regime's benefits. Under the GATT protocol, tariff bargaining adhered to the principal supplier rule. Trade barriers were reduced on the basis of concessions on particular goods exchanged between principal suppliers—that is, the nations that were the main source of these goods to each other's markets. As such, it privileged trade expansion among the major trading nations.

The small subset of signatories privileged by the GATT's bargaining protocol included Great Britain, Canada, France, Germany, and the United States. This group included the largest "natural" trading partners of the two states that dominated the creation of the GATT—that is, the principal trading partners of Britain and the United States in the period before the Great Depression, the Smoot-Hawley tariff, and the interwar trade blocs distorted international commerce.[4] It also included Canada's top four trading partners and the three largest trading partners of France and Germany.

More surprising than the country composition of the privileged group is the omission from it of two states that might seem to have been equally plausible candidates for membership: Japan, the second-largest trading partner of the United States before 1929, and Italy. Their export profiles help to explain their exclusion. When Japan acceded to the GATT in 1955,

---

4. We identified the rankings of trading partners we report here using 1928 data, described below.

more than 40 percent of the membership denied it MFN treatment in order to protect their markets against a flood of textiles and other labor-intensive products in which Japan held a comparative advantage (Pomfret 1988, 53; Tussie 1987, 15).[5] Italy's exports were also heavily weighted toward textiles, clothing, leather goods, and shoes (Zamagni 1993, 31, 368). In addition, almost 25 percent of Italy's exports in 1949 were agricultural goods, as compared with, for example, 10 percent of British and German exports (Milward 2000, 441). Thus, both countries specialized in precisely those products that privileged group members succeeded in exempting from GATT rules.

The principal supplier rule represented the divergent trade policy goals that characterized the U.S. government as it began planning for postwar reconstruction. Officials of the Roosevelt administration sought to destroy the interwar trade blocs and promote European and transatlantic trade. This would help to stabilize Europe and contribute to the creation of a Western bloc strong enough to deter Soviet expansion (Gardner 1956[1980], 8). Congress, however, had less ambitious goals, resembling those it had spelled out in the 1934 Reciprocal Trade Agreements Act (RTAA). While the RTAA authorized the president to negotiate trade agreements, it also instructed him to maximize market access abroad without jeopardizing domestic industry. It thus directed him to lower tariffs only as necessary to promote exports and only in accord with the "needs of various branches of American production."[6] It also demanded "reasonable public notice" of impending trade talks, prompting the administration to identify both prospective treaty partners and the products on which it intended to offer and request concessions (Goldstein 1993).[7]

The RTAA also included a most favored nation (MFN) clause, which required the signatories to a trade agreement to extend to each other any

---

5. Even after the Article XXXV exemption was lifted, member countries "sought to isolate" Japan, leaving it "at the periphery" of the GATT even as late as the Tokyo Round (Hart 1998, 126). Patterson agrees, noting that the MFN obligations nations assumed with respect to Japan "were qualified and the principle of 'orderly marketing' was endorsed" (1966, 295).

6. The source of the quotations in this paragraph is ch. 474 U.S. code, Sec. 354, 12 June 1934, 945.

7. The Interdepartmental Committee on Foreign Trade Agreements and the Committee on Reciprocity Information were "responsible for identifying likely negotiating partners, designating concessions to be offered and demanded during negotiations, and supervising the negotiations as they were undertaken by the Department of State" (Butler 1998, 104). Thus, before negotiations began, "the public is given notice of the Government's intention to negotiate, is advised of the list of articles on which the grant of import concessions will be considered, and is invited to supply the Government with any information that might be useful to it in the conduct of the negotiations" (USTC 1948, Part II, 53).

concession that either might later offer to a third country.[8] To respect this clause and expand exports while protecting domestic industry, administration officials developed "the so-called chief-source, or 'Principal Supplier,' rule" (Hawkins 1951, 81). Harry C. Hawkins, then head of the Trade Agreements Division, suggested that the United States "grant concessions on particular products to the country that...supplied the greatest proportion of our imports" of those products. This would enable the administration to defend itself against complaints that "other countries were getting something for nothing."[9]

Thus, the United States would offer to cut a tariff on a particular good only if the country receiving the benefit was the principal supplier of that product to the U.S. market.[10] Canada, for example, supplied 96 percent of the agricultural goods and 99 percent of the fish and lumber products on which the United States cut tariffs in the 1935 U.S.-Canadian trade accord (Butler 1998, 135). In negotiations with Argentina and Uruguay, the United States reduced tariffs on coarse and medium wools only. Had it cut the tariff on wool in general, it would have made an unreciprocated concession to Australia, which exported fine wools (Hawkins 1951, 92). Tariff specialization—that is, the "separating or 'ex-ing out' of portions of a tariff item for negotiating purposes"—served the same end (Pomfret 1988, 6). When the United States cut its tariff on British goods in 1939, for example, it revived a "separate classification for bone china" to restrict the exploitation of the lower rate to "the English manufacturers who were practically the sole exporters of chinaware containing calcified bone" (Bidwell 1956, 52–54).

Although little opposition existed within Congress to using the principal supplier rule after the war, the prospect evoked controversy within the administration. Members of the Executive Committee on Foreign Economic Policy, a group of high-level officials brought together to centralize trade policy planning, preferred a linear approach (Gardner 1956[1980], 150; Goldstein 1993, 209). That is, they preferred reducing tariffs equally across all product lines and trade partners to the item-by-item, country-by-country approach that the principal supplier rule required. In their view, the traditional approach insulated the products of powerful industries and the

8. Kenneth A. Oye argues that this was in the self-interest of the United States, given the way interwar trade agreements were structured (1992, 95–96).

9. Oral History, John M. Leddy, Staff member of the Trade Agreements Division, Department of State, Harry S. Truman Library, available at http://trumanlibrary.org/oral hist/leddyj, 8–9. Quotation is in Hawkins (1951, 81n16).

10. Hull believed that "if the United States signed [a treaty] with the low-cost producer, no industry would be hurt" by imports from other producers (Goldstein 1993, 208n14).

goods that more than one nation exported, while conforming to the letter rather than to the spirit of the MFN principle (Hoekman and Kostecki 2001, 128).

It was precisely these attributes of the traditional approach that appealed to Congress, however.[11] And Roosevelt proved unwilling to force the issue because it could endanger the renewal of the RTAA.[12] Moreover, as multilateral trade negotiations under the GATT proceeded in the shadow of the Cold War, the principal supplier rule was also consistent with the subsequent Truman administration's goal of stabilizing Western Europe. Indeed, because it targeted trade between the United States and its major postwar allies, the rule would tighten ties between the very countries the U.S. government considered key to deterring Soviet expansion. Thus, the United States would continue to negotiate item-by-item tariff cuts under the GATT as it had done since the passage of the RTAA (Gardner 1956[1980]; Zeiler 1999, 45).[13]

The Effects of the GATT on International Trade

The decision to do so was not cost-free, however. It would compromise the U.S. effort to dismantle the discriminatory interwar trade system. Britain had made it clear that it would not abandon Imperial Preference unless the United States agreed to a linear approach (Pomfret 1988, 30; Ruggie 1982).[14] As John Leddy, a State Department official at the time, recalled, the British argued that "if the imperial preference system was to be junked the scope of the action on the tariff…had to be very, very substantial, and very deep, and across the board. No piecemeal operation like the previous bilateral trade agreements program would work."[15] Congressional constraints, however, mandated adherence to the principal supplier rule. Thus,

11. Republican Party preferences were similar. Its 1944 platform asserted that because "the domestic market is American's greatest market," the tariff "which protects it against foreign competition should be modified only by reciprocal bilateral trade agreements" (Goldstein 1993, 227).

12. Oral History, John M. Leddy, op. cit., 37. A heated debate exists about the RTAA and the trade preferences of presidents relative to Congress. See, for instance, Lohmann and O'Halloran (1994); Hiscox (1999); and Weingast, Goldstein, and Bailey (1997). We do not engage this debate here, since we are concerned about only this one instance of executive-congressional interaction.

13. An attractive by-product of the approach was that it gave exporters an interest in lowering tariffs abroad. See also Bagwell and Staiger (2002); Gilligan (1997); and Irwin and Kroszner (1999).

14. Preserving its bargaining power and maintaining the Commonwealth also, of course, motivated British efforts to preserve Imperial Preference (Milward 2000, 351).

15. Oral History, John M. Leddy, op. cit., 21.

the United States would ultimately agree to grandfather the Commonwealth system, covering about one-third of world trade, into the GATT. Inevitably, this meant abandoning nondiscrimination more broadly: the GATT also grandfathered the colonial preferences of France, Belgium, and the Netherlands and preferential agreements between the United States and both the Philippines and Cuba.[16]

The compromise on existing preference systems, as it turned out, was only one among several ways in which the principal supplier rule impeded the destruction of the interwar system. Each of the trade blocs that had developed in the wake of the Great Depression linked one large state and several smaller countries. As such, dismantling the blocs would have required sustained attention to liberalizing trade between large and small countries. The principal supplier approach ruled this out, however. It also enhanced prospects for bloc survival because privileged group members preferred to reduce tariffs on intra-industry trade rather than on cross-industry trade. Focusing on differentiated products biased trade expansion toward country pairs with relatively similar factor endowments. As such, it had little effect on trade between members of the same interwar bloc, which, because it tended to exploit differences rather than similarities in relative factor endowments, favored cross-industry trade and trade in primary products.

The principal supplier rule might seem irrelevant to the distributional effects of the GATT, given that Article 1 of the General Agreement required that any tariff cut apply to all members. Because group members shared relatively similar factor endowments, however, their concessions were unlikely to benefit countries with very different endowments. Yet precisely for this reason, it might seem to make little sense for members of the group to engage in bilateral rather than multilateral bargaining. As in the interwar era, however, the products on which tariffs were cut were defined as narrowly as possible in an effort to restrict their benefits to a single country (USTC 1957, 140, 125; Verdier 1994, 196).[17] In 1948, for example, when the United States reduced its tariff on feldspar china, it simultaneously added "value brackets" to its tariff schedule, making the new rate applicable "only to plates, cups, saucers and other items *valued at more than specified amounts*" (Bidwell 1956, 54; emphasis in original). This precluded their application to the bulk of Japanese imports.[18]

---

16. More generally, Article XXIV sanctioned preferential trading agreements (PTAs) as long as they were not "more restrictive" than they had been previously.

17. Of the 1,014 tariff reductions that the United States agreed to between the wars, almost half involved tariff reclassifications (Verdier 1994, 196).

18. The growth of the U.S. tariff code attests to the effort to specialize tariffs. In 1963, it included 6,421 lines and by 2000, it had grown to 10,175 lines. Though as a whole the U.S. trade-weighted average tariff rate fell from 11.9 percent to 7.4 percent ad valorem in the interim,

That very few products appear on the concessions list of more than one pair of countries also attests to efforts to privatize tariff cuts. During the Geneva Round (1955–1956), for example, the United States cut its tariffs on a total of fifty-nine imports from Great Britain, Canada, France, and Germany. With one exception, no concession seems to have applied to a good produced by more than one of these countries. Thus, for example, the sets of products on which Great Britain and France received concessions from the United States were discrete. The British products included

certain chemicals, certain pigments, soaps, China clay, tiles, various iron and steel products, manufactures of brass and bronze, silver-plated ware, electric motors, automobiles, airplanes, office machinery, tobacco machinery, biscuits, wafers, puddings, Scotch and Irish whiskies, mustard, cotton yarn, various linen products, wool wearing apparel, tissue paper, coated paper, filtering paper, golf and lawn tennis balls, leather, shoes, and certain jellies, jam, and marmalades.

On the French list were fishing reels and parts, Angora yarn, velvet and tapestry carpets, razor pile ribbons, carbons and electrodes for producing electric arc lights, velvet ribbons of silk or rayon, and ornamented rayon (Bidwell 1956, 125).

As Bernard M. Hoekman and Michael M. Kostecki observe, postwar attempts to ensure reciprocity were "quite successful." One measure of the success of efforts to privatize the benefits of tariff cuts is the internalization ratio—that is, the ratio of the sum of all imports that originate in countries with which the importing country exchanged concessions to the sum of total imports on which concessions are made. This ratio was about 90 percent for the United States in both the Dillon and the Kennedy Rounds (Hoekman and Kostecki 2001, 31).[19] Indeed, some observers believe that the "ability of judicious product selection to internalize the benefits of concessions" explains postwar trade expansion (Hoekman and Kostecki 2001, 42).

That the principal supplier rule governed postwar tariff bargaining suggests that its benefits were unlikely to be distributed uniformly across its members. It suggests instead that the primary, if not exclusive, beneficiaries of the GATT would be the five states privileged by the principal supplier rule. It also suggests that the postwar regime was more likely to have coexisted with the interwar blocs than to have replaced them. Below we test whether the evidence is consistent with these hypotheses.

---

tariffs also became increasingly specialized as narrower product categories were defined to direct tariff cuts to specific trading partners (USTC 2000).

19. For the internalization ratios for each GATT round though 1967, see Finger (1979, 424).

Quantitative Analysis

We employ quantitative analysis to test our hypotheses on the consequences of the principal supplier rule. We begin by describing the data we use, distinguishing them from the data employed in current studies. To ensure that the differences in our data do not account for our findings, we initially estimate the models that generate the results these studies report. We first examine the effects of the trade regime on its members as a whole. Next, we disaggregate its members, estimating the effects of the GATT on trade between industrialized and nonindustrialized countries. The results of the baseline analyses we report below are generally consistent with the findings of the existing literature. We then go on to test our hypotheses about the effects of the principal supplier rule on the trade of the "privileged group" of five major states and the interwar trade blocs. We focus our discussion on the substantive implications of our findings and relegate technical information to the Methodological Appendix, which can be found at the end of the book. The appendix provides the baseline model, a description of the variables, and the countries included in the analysis.

Our unit of analysis is the dyad-year, or pairs of countries observed annually. Our sample consists of dyads that were members of the interstate system between 1950 and 1994. The end date is dictated by the fact that the WTO formally replaced the GATT in 1995. Because our hypotheses are specific to the structure of the GATT, we use data only through 1994. Our sample consists of dyads composed of members of the international system and thus excludes non-independent political entities such as Hong Kong, for example, which is included in Rose (2004). This is because our analyses include political variables, namely democracy, alliance, and militarized interstate disputes, and data on these political variables exist only for system members. We use the Correlates of War 2 Project (COW2) to identify system members.[20] The Methodological Appendix lists the 145 countries used in our analysis.

The dependent variable used in our analyses is trade, specifically bilateral trade in a given year, consistent with the dyad-year, the unit of analysis. Our trade data come from the IMF's *Direction of Trade Statistics* (DOTs), which we convert to constant dollars using the consumer price index (CPI).[21] We use

---

20. That is, a state is a system member if it is a UN member or its population exceeds 500,000 and it receives diplomatic missions from at least two major powers. Correlates of War 2 Project. 2003. State System Membership List, v2002.1. Available at http://cow2.la.psu.edu. The appendix lists the 145 countries that are in our analysis, subject to system membership and data availability.

21. CPI for Urban Consumers, all items; 1982–1984=100; available at www.economy.com/freelunch.

bilateral import data because they are generally considered to be the most accurate measure of trade.[22] As in Goldstein, Rivers, and Tomz (2007, 48), our data are in the form of directed-dyads—that is, there are two observations per country pair for each year: imports of country a from country b and imports of country b from country a.

For our independent variable of interest—GATT membership—we define more states as GATT members than do either Rose (2004) or Subramanian and Wei (2007), because we do not restrict membership status to those states that concluded the formal accession process. According to Tomz, Goldstein, and Rivers, the GATT also extended "rights and obligations" to other countries and territories, among them colonies, de facto members, and provisional members (2007, p. 2005; also Goldstein, Rivers and Tomz 2007).[23] This set of "non-member participants," according to Tomz, Goldstein and Rivers, includes certain colonies and overseas territories of the Contracting Parties, newly independent territories that chose not to accede formally to the GATT for a period of time but maintained their de facto status, and some countries that had begun but not completed the accession process and to which certain members chose to apply the terms of the GATT on a provisional basis. We code these cases as GATT members as long as they are also system members; that is, we include former colonies as of their year of independence. States with provisional member status are also included as of the year in which their provisional membership begins.[24]

Baseline Model

As in Rose (2004), Subramanian and Wei (2007), and Tomz, Goldstein, and Rivers (2007), we first measure the impact of the postwar regime on the trade of its members as a whole. We find, as Rose puts it, that trade "cannot be dependably linked" to GATT membership (2004, 112). Next, as in Rose and Subramanian and Wei, we disaggregate GATT members into

---

22. Rose (2004), for example, uses the average of four trade measures, specifically the average across exports and imports reported by each member of the country-pair.

23. See also Rose's (2007) reply to Tomz, Rivers, and Goldstein.

24. This chapter and the article on which it is based relied on earlier versions of Tomz, Rivers, and Goldstein (2007) and Goldstein, Rivers, and Tomz (2007), at which time Tomz et al. had not responded to our request to allow us to use their data. To construct their roster of "nonmember participants," Tomz, Goldstein, and Rivers use GATT archival material that is not yet publicly available. Our roster of nonmember participants thus does not exactly replicate theirs. This is so, because, for example, while they note that "the maximum allowable duration of de facto status changed over time," they do not define exactly how it did so. Similarly, they state that not all members accorded provisional members MFN treatment, but, with one exception, they do not identify these countries.

industrialized and nonindustrialized countries. Our results are consistent with theirs: we find that the GATT has had a positive and significant effect only on trade between industrialized countries. This finding can be attributed to, inter alia, the exclusion of agriculture, the creation of special rules for labor-intensive industries such as textiles and apparel, and the import-substituting industrialization policies of developing countries.

We employ a gravity model of international trade, consistent with the studies cited above and our specification of bilateral trade as the dependent variable. In our analysis, we specify bilateral trade in terms of the volume of imports, specifically the (natural) log of each country's imports from the other in each year calculated in constant U.S. dollars. As the outcome of interest in assessing the distributional consequences of the GATT, the volume of trade is a strong indicator of the regime's key objectives, namely the expansion of trade for those that subscribe to the rules of the regime.

The independent variable of primary interest in our analyses is GATT membership, which we operationalize using a dichotomous indicator that takes on a value of one if both countries in the dyad are GATT members in a given year and zero otherwise. The estimate on this variable reflects the extent to which the regime had trade-creation effects for its participants. Where the estimate is positive, it would indicate that trade between the two countries increased—the trade-creation effect—after their entry into the regime, controlling for the effects of other explanatory factors. Conversely, if the estimate is negative, it would show that trade between the two countries fell after their accession to the GATT. The model also includes a dichotomous indicator that equals one if only one of the countries in the dyad is a GATT member in a given year and zero otherwise. This variable measures the extent of trade-diversion (Viner 1950), or the degree to which trade between two countries was affected when one of the two countries became a GATT member. Where the estimate is negative, it would show that trade between the two countries in the dyad decreased, or was diverted, when one country became a GATT member and the other remained outside the regime.

Our analysis controls for the effects of other independent variables, explanatory factors that have also been found to affect trade flows. Among these are economic factors such as GDP and GDP per capita, as well as geographic variables such as distance between the two countries comprising the dyad, whether the two countries share a land border, the number of countries—0, 1, or 2—within the dyad that are landlocked or island countries, and land areas. The model includes as well a dichotomous measure that equals one if the two countries in the dyad share a common language.

Our control variables also include dummy variables to measure different aspects of colonial relationships, which take on a value of one (and zero otherwise) if the two countries in the dyad were former colonies of the same country after 1945 or if either country was ever a colony of the other. To account for the effects of economic institutional arrangements other than the GATT, the model includes a dichotomous measure that equals one (and zero otherwise) if two countries are members of the same regional trade agreement (RTA) and another that indicates whether they share a common currency in a given year. Also included is an indicator variable that equals one (and zero otherwise) if one country grants preferences to the other under the Generalized System of Preferences (GSP), agreements that were negotiated under the auspices of the United Nations Conference on Trade and Development (UNCTAD). Our data on these variables come from Rose (2004).[25] Last but not least, we also include year fixed effects, that is, dummy variables for each year (except one) in the sample. They capture all unmeasured factors that are expected to exert similar effects on the trade of all countries, including, for example, the oil price shocks of the 1970s and 1980s.

In the first and second columns of table 3.1, we report the results of our analysis of the baseline model. Although we include all control variables in each analysis, in the interests of clarity we report in the table only the results on the variables of interest in this study. In the first column are the results obtained from an ordinary least squares (OLS) analysis including year fixed effects. The second column shows the results of estimating a model that includes dyadic (that is, country-pair) and year fixed effects. The inclusion of dyadic fixed effects, as we discuss in greater detail below, controls for unobservable characteristics that are intrinsic to a given pair of countries, which are correlated with other independent variables and also affect trade flows. It also has the effect of incorporating a temporal dimension in the analysis to evaluate the effect of GATT membership over time, specifically by comparing trade flows between members before and after accession to the regime.

As in earlier studies, the results in the first two columns show that the GATT cannot be "dependably" related to its members' trade, as both the size and significance of its effect vary between them. Column 1 of table 3.1 shows that the GATT had a large, positive, and statistically significant effect on trade: that is, its members traded about 29 percent more with each other than did countries in the base group.[26] As the table makes clear, however,

25. For details, see www.faculty.haas.berkeley.edu/arose.

26. P-value=0. Percentages were calculated using the semi-elasticity equation in Wooldridge (2006, 198): 100*(exp(b)−1). The base group, the major comparison category for assessing the impact of GATT membership, includes dyads in which neither country is a GATT member in a given year.

Table 3.1. The effects of the GATT on bilateral trade, 1950–1994

	(1)[a]	(2)[b]	(3)[b]	(4)[b]
Both GATT	0.254*	0.019	0.034	0.012
members	(0.033)	(0.028)	(0.028)	(0.029)
One GATT	0.110*	−0.015	−0.011	0.007
member	(0.030)	(0.024)	(0.024)	(0.024)
			0.167*	0.151*
Joint democracy			(0.018)	(0.018)
			−0.031	−0.040
Alliance			(0.047)	(0.047)
			−0.019	−0.023
MID			(0.056)	(0.055)
Both GATT and				0.758*
industrial dyad				(0.068)
Observations	267970	267970	267970	267970
R-squared	0.638	0.860	0.860	0.861

Notes: *significant at 1 percent. Dependent variable: log of imports.
[a] OLS with gravity-model variables and year fixed effects included but not reported.
[b] Fixed effects analysis using areg in STATA 9.0, with observations clustered by directed-dyad and corresponding dyadic fixed effects absorbed into the intercept; gravity model variables and year effects included in estimation but not reported. Newey-West standard errors in parentheses.

this result is not robust to the inclusion of dyadic fixed effects: the second column of table 3.1 shows that trade among GATT members is statistically indistinguishable from trade among countries in the base group.[27]

We believe that including dyadic fixed effects produces a more accurate estimate of the effects of the trade regime. Before we explain why, it is important to note that the questions addressed by OLS and fixed-effects analyses differ. An OLS analysis asks about cross-sectional variation: does trade vary between members of country pairs that join the GATT and those that do not? A fixed-effects analysis addresses a time-series question: what is the effect of joining the GATT on trade between members of a country pair; that is, how is trade between two countries affected as they accede to the GATT? We address the second or "within" question here, because fixed-effects analyses avoid the problems that unobserved heterogeneity can create. If dyadic effects are correlated with the included regressors—that is, independent variables and the error term—omitting them will generate

27. To be more specific, the GATT coefficient in Rose's (2004) OLS analysis is a statistically insignificant −0.04. Including country fixed effects produces a statistically significant estimate of 0.15 (2004, 104). We used Rose's data and variable definitions to estimate the GATT's impact between 1950 and 1994, the years we analyze here. An OLS analysis with year fixed effects produces a coefficient on the GATT of 0.116 (p-value=0.004). An analysis with dyadic and year fixed effects produces a coefficient on the GATT of 0.046 (p-value=0.150).

biased and inconsistent parameter estimates (see Green, Kim, and Yoon 2001).

It seems plausible that the data used here are so correlated. The political relationship between countries, for example, is likely to affect both trade between them and their decisions about whether to join the postwar trade regime. Thus, omitting a control for political relations risks generating inaccurate coefficient estimates. Dyadic fixed effects, however, control for these relations, as well as for all other unobservable characteristics of country pairs that might be correlated with variables we include in our analysis and correlate also with trade between their members.

Some studies advocate using country fixed effects or a separate intercept for each country in a dyad to capture a "multilateral resistance term" that reflects a country's trade costs or its attributes as an exporter or importer (Anderson and van Wincoop 2003, 2004; Mátyás 1997). We use dyadic rather than country fixed effects for two reasons.[28] First, country fixed effects do not control for country-pair attributes that can vary in consequential ways and that are quite difficult to measure with any accuracy. They may include, for example, the historical relationship between two countries and their relative factor endowments. Second, comparisons of different ways of controlling for heterogeneity find that virtually no difference exists between the estimates that analyses using country fixed effects and those using dyadic fixed effects produce. The latter, however, yields more efficient estimates.[29]

In table 3.1, column 3, we report the results of adding to the fixed-effects model three military-political variables: regime type, alliances, and militarized interstate disputes (MIDs). Studies have shown that these variables affect bilateral trade.[30] Recent studies of the GATT do not include them, even though omitting them can bias the parameter estimates. The results show that only joint democracy exerts a significant effect on bilateral trade. When both members of a country pair become democracies, their trade increases by about 18 percent.[31] Neither alliances nor militarized disputes have a significant effect

---

28. The results in table 3.1 are robust to the inclusion of country fixed effects, however.

29. Since the data are in the form of directed dyads, dyadic fixed effects are specified separately for each direction. Based on a likelihood ratio test, Cheng and Wall (2004) find that a symmetry restriction on the dyadic fixed effects rejects the null (that is, that fixed effects do not differ significantly between the dyad that reflects the imports of *a* from *b* and the dyad reflecting imports of *b* from *a*). Thus, they argue for including a separate term for each direction of the dyad.

30. See, for example, Barbieri and Levy (1999); Gowa and Mansfield (1993); Li and Sacko (1999); Polacheck (1978); and Pollins (1989).

31. P-value=0.

on trade.[32] Including these variables does not produce any notable change in the effects of the GATT: its coefficient remains statistically insignificant.

Next, as in Rose and Subramanian and Wei, we estimate the effects of the postwar regime on industrial and nonindustrial country pairs separately. Conventional wisdom holds that the industrial countries have been the major beneficiaries of the postwar regime, a belief that is consistent with the findings of Rose and Subramanian and Wei. To replicate their analyses, we construct a dummy variable that equals unity if a dyad is composed of two industrial countries and zero otherwise. Following WTO practice, we code as industrial countries these states: Australia, Austria, Belgium, Canada, Denmark, Finland, France, Germany, Greece, Iceland, Ireland, Italy, Japan, Luxembourg, the Netherlands, New Zealand, Norway, Portugal, Spain, Sweden, Switzerland, the United Kingdom, and the United States.[33] We also construct an interaction term that indicates whether both states in an industrial country pair are also GATT members. In table 3.1, column 4, therefore, the (omitted) base group, that is, the comparison group, consists of nonindustrial country pairs that are not GATT members.[34]

The results of our analysis are consistent with conventional wisdom and existing empirical analyses.[35] The results reported in table 3.1, column 4, show that the GATT had a significant effect only on trade among its industrial country members. Their trade is about 113 percent higher than is trade among members of the base group.[36] In contrast, no significant difference exists between the trade of nonindustrial country pairs in which both states are GATT members and the trade of dyads in the base group.[37]

Table 3.1 shows that the changes we made to the data produce results that are generally consistent with previously reported findings about the impact of the postwar trade regime. It also makes clear that the estimated impact of the GATT is sensitive to the method of analysis used. Analyses that include dyadic fixed effects, which we believe to be appropriate here, show that the GATT had no significant effect on trade among its members

32. In comparing these results to those in the existing literature, however, it is important to note that our analyses do not include former Soviet bloc members.

33. As reported in Subramanian and Wei (2003, 9). Belgium and Luxembourg are not in our analysis, however, because the IMF reports their trade separately only in 1997.

34. These include dyads where both members are nonindustrial countries or where one is an industrial country and the other a nonindustrial country.

35. The coefficient on industrial-country trade that Rose reports is a statistically significant 0.47 (2004, 108). The corresponding statistic in Subramanian and Wei is 0.322, a result that is statistically significant at less than the 0.05 level (2003, 29).

36. P-value=0.

37. P-value=0.663. We report Newey West (1987) standard errors applied to panel data, which are robust to heteroscedasticity and autocorrelation.

as a whole. It did, however, exert a positive and significant impact on trade among industrial states.

For reasons we have already explained, however, we believe that the industrial-country finding understates the skew in the distribution of the GATT's benefits, as it does not take account of the impact of the principal supplier rule. Moreover, no existing study considers whether the postwar regime actually succeeded in replacing the preceding system of discriminatory trade blocs.

Analysis

To test the effects of the GATT's principal supplier rule and the regime's impact on the interwar trade blocs, we take a somewhat different approach. In a fixed-effects analysis, only observations that experience a change in the value of an independent variable contribute to its parameter estimate. Thus, the coefficient on the impact of industrial-country GATT membership in table 3.1 estimates the impact of the GATT *only* in cases in which at least one member of an industrial-country pair joined the GATT after its inception.[38] As such, it does not capture the effect of the GATT on trade among its industrial-country founding members—that is, Australia, Belgium, Great Britain, Canada, France, Luxembourg, the Netherlands, New Zealand, Norway, and the United States.[39] Yet this group includes four of the five members of the "privileged" group, as well as two of the three anchor countries of the interwar blocs and many of their members.

Moreover, as the composition of the industrial-country group is also time-invariant, the analysis also precludes an estimation of its main effect, or the GATT's impact on this particular group. That is, since industrial country status is constant throughout the 1950–1994 period, a fixed-effects approach does not allow us to estimate its effect on trade. The coefficient on the industrial country variable in table 3.1 thus captures the combined effect on trade of the GATT *and* of industrial-country status relative to the base group, and only for those industrial countries that joined the GATT after its establishment. It does not distinguish between the impact of industrial-country status and that of GATT membership among industrial countries.

In order to distinguish and obtain reliable estimates on the impact of GATT membership on the trade of all of the industrial countries, including,

38. This is also true, of course, of members of other dyads that both joined the GATT at its inception or were allies or democracies throughout the sample period.

39. The thirteen remaining industrial countries—Austria, Denmark, Finland, Germany, Greece, Iceland, Ireland, Italy, Japan, Portugal, Spain, Sweden, and Switzerland—acceded to the GATT between 1951 and 1967.

in particular, the members of the privileged group and the interwar blocs, we extend our data backward in time. We add data on dyadic interwar trade collected by Albrecht Ritschl and Nikolaus Wolf.[40] Their data include information on the standard-gravity model variables for thirty countries in 1928, 1935, and 1938, including twenty of the twenty-one countries in our industrial-country sample. We add to these data information about joint democracy, alliances, and MIDs in each of the three interwar years.

Together, the interwar and postwar data enable us to address the issues of primary importance to this inquiry. We can test whether the trade the GATT fostered was skewed toward the small subset of industrial states that the principal supplier approach privileged, and we can determine whether the postwar regime succeeded in destroying the system of trade blocs that preceded it.

These data do not allow us to use a standard fixed-effects approach, however, because the dummy variables for privileged-group and interwar-bloc membership and for GATT founding members remain time-invariant.[41] Thus, we use a "treatment-effect" approach, following several recent studies of the impact of currency unions on trade (Ritschl and Wolf 2003; Nitsch 2002; Persson 2001). In pure experimental settings, a treatment-effect approach would randomize individuals into control or treatment groups. For non-experimental data, analysts of labor markets have developed methods to isolate "the effect of the treatment on the treated" (Blundell and Dias 2000).

The Ritschl and Wolf approach that we adopt here is one such method. To make this approach clear, we briefly describe their application of it. Using a pooled data set for the years 1928, 1935, and 1938, they examine whether the formation of the interwar blocs was endogenous to trade patterns that preceded the Great Depression. To do so, they first specify the "control" groups by constructing dummy variables to indicate the interwar blocs—that is, the gold, sterling, Commonwealth, Reichsmark, and exchange-control blocs.

---

40. We are grateful to Albrecht Ritschl and Nikolaus Wolf for making the data available to us. Iceland is not included in the Ritschl and Wolf (2003) data, so we exclude it from the analysis. Also, the following states are in the Ritschl-Wolf dataset but not in ours: Argentina, Belgium, Turkey, and several members of the former Eastern bloc, that is, Bulgaria, Czechoslovakia, Hungary, Poland, Romania, the Soviet Union, and Yugoslavia.

41. Panel data analysis can accommodate time-invariant variables using a technique that Hausman and Taylor (1981) developed. However, their method assumes that not all explanatory variables are correlated with the individual-level effects, an assumption that is not tenable here. The time-invariant nature of these variables also precludes an estimation based on first-differencing the data to account for the possible endogeneity of the GATT regime. See Baier and Bergstrand (2007).

Ritschl and Wolf set the values of each group dummy to unity for all years in the sample. This variable captures trade levels before currency arrangements are operative or after they expire. Next, they specify the "treatment" by constructing a dummy variable that is unity for the 1930s, the period in which the various blocs were in effect, and zero otherwise. They interact each group dummy variable with the dummy variable for the 1930s, which creates a structural break for the years in which the currency arrangements were in force. It is the coefficient on this interaction term, when the dummy variable for the 1930s shifts from zero to one beginning in 1930, that measures the effect of the treatment—that is, the effect of bloc formation on interwar trade. Thus, a bloc affects trade among its members only if the estimate on this interaction term is statistically significant.

Following the Ritschl and Wolf approach, we pool our data across the years 1928, 1935, 1938, and the years between 1950 and 1994, generating a maximum of forty-eight observations per directed-dyad. The dummy variables that serve as our "control" groups indicate whether the members of a country pair were (1) members of the privileged group; (2) "founding" members—that is, countries that joined the GATT at its inception; or (3) members of one of the five interwar blocs.[42] Values on these variables are set to unity for each group for all years. They are "control" groups in the sense that they capture the time-invariant characteristics of each group. As such, they are essentially the "fixed effects" for the country pairs in each group; Ritschl and Wolf argue that this allows for an unbiased estimation of the model (2003, 9n69).

To specify the "treatment," we create another dummy variable, *GATT years*, that is set to unity for the years in which the GATT existed (that is, 1950–1994).[43] To measure the "treatment effect," or the effect of GATT membership, we interact each of the group dummy variables with the variable *GATT years*. A significant difference can be said to exist between trade under the GATT regime and interwar trade only if the coefficient on the relevant interaction term is statistically significant, controlling for all other standard gravity-model variables.

With three exceptions, we do not interact the dummy variable for *GATT years* with either the gravity model or standard political variables, because

42. The privileged group and the founding-member group are mutually exclusive. The former consists of pairs of privileged-group members (Britain, Canada, France, Germany, and the United States). The latter consists of country-pairs formed among founding members that were not in the privileged group as well as founding members paired with each member of the privileged group.
43. Our post–World War II data begin in 1950; hence, we use this as the first of the GATT years.

we have no ex ante reason to believe that the effects of these variables differed after World War II. We do apply the structural break—the interaction term—to each of the two GDP terms, as the interwar period depressed the effects of increasing income on trade. We also apply the structural break to the alliance term, as previous studies suggest that the impact of these coalitions varies between the interwar and postwar periods.

Table 3.2 reports the results of an analysis of bilateral trade that includes data from the interwar and postwar periods. It presents estimates for the control groups and treatment effects, the latter represented by the interaction terms.[44] As before, we do not report results, but we do control for the impact of the standard gravity-model variables[45] Controlling for all the variables noted above, trade among members of the privileged group was about three times higher after World War II than it was in the period between the wars.[46] In contrast, GATT membership exerts no significant effect on the trade of other members of the founding group relative to their pre-1945 trade.[47] These results are robust to an analysis that excludes the interwar blocs as well as to an analysis that includes the six founding members of the European Community.[48]

Table 3.2 also shows that the GATT did not eliminate the interwar trade patterns that constituted a large part of its raison d'être.[49] Ex ante, the effects of the Commonwealth bloc would seem most likely to endure after 1945, because, as noted, the GATT protected Imperial Preference. Table 3.2 shows, however, that trade among members of the Commonwealth decreased after World War II relative to the interwar years.[50] As we report below, however,

44. Dependent variable: log of imports. Not reported: GDP, GDPPC and their interaction terms; distance; common language; island; landlocked status; land area; border; democracy; MIDs; and decade dummies for the 1960s, 1970s, 1980s, and 1990s. *significant at 5 percent; **significant at 1 percent.

45. These results are robust to the inclusion of country or dyadic fixed effects for countries that are not members of any of the groups in the analysis. In our sample, these countries are Greece and Japan.

46. P-value=0.000.

47. P-value=0.366.

48. We did not include the European Community in this analysis, because its membership did not remain stable over the postwar period and because it did not come into existence until 1958. We have, however, tested whether our results are robust to the inclusion of the EC6, since it formed relatively early in the postwar period. We find that the EC had a large positive (0.84) and significant (p-value=0.000) impact on its members' trade. Our results are robust to including the EC with these exceptions: the treatment effect for the gold bloc becomes insignificant (p-value=0.772); the coefficient on the interwar alliance term becomes significant (p-value=0.008), while its treatment effect becomes insignificant.

49. Eichengreen and Irwin (1995) used interwar and early postwar trade to predict trade in 1949, 1954, and 1964. See also Eichengreen and Irwin (1998).

50. P-value=0.000.

Table 3.2. GATT and industrial country trade:
1928, 1935, 1938, 1950–1994

GATT founding member dyad	0.042
	(0.112)
GATT years & founding member	−0.105
	(0.117)
Privileged group	−0.421**
	(0.159)
GATT years & privileged group	1.365**
	(0.182)
Exchange-control group	−0.233**
	(0.070)
GATT years & exchange-control group	0.233**
	(0.073)
Gold bloc	−0.215
	(0.160)
GATT Years & gold bloc	0.388*
	(0.162)
Commonwealth group	1.549**
	(0.227)
GATT Years & Commonwealth group	−1.040**
	(0.234)
Sterling bloc	0.385**
	(0.096)
GATT Years & Sterling bloc	−0.726**
	(0.108)
Reichsmark bloc	0.780**
	(0.167)
GATT years & Reichsmark bloc	−0.061
	(0.180)
Alliance	0.164
	(0.139)
GATT years & alliance	0.305*
	(0.142)
GATT years	−7.463**
	(1.618)
Observations	17390
R-squared	0.74

Notes: *significant at 5 percent, **significant at 1 percent.

their trade remained significantly higher than did trade among members of the base group under the GATT regime. In contrast, the interwar and post-war trade of Reichsmark members is statistically indistinguishable.[51] The exchange-control and gold blocs exerted positive and significant effects on trade among their respective members after the war.[52] Indeed, the sterling

51. P-value=0.735. Our sample includes, however, only two Reichsmark bloc members (Austria and Germany).
52. P-values=0.001 and 0.016, respectively.

bloc was the only trading bloc that experienced a significant net decrease in trade relative to its interwar counterpart. While its members traded about 38 percent more than members of the base group before 1939, their trade thereafter fell by 73 percent. Thus, the postwar trade regime incorporated rather than replaced elements of the interwar trade system.

Based on the estimates in table 3.2, table 3.3 reports for each treatment variable its net effect on postwar trade relative to the base group and the corresponding significance level.[53] It shows that trade among privileged-group members is about 94 percent higher than the trade of the base group after World War II.[54] In contrast, postwar trade among other founding-group members of the GATT is about 6 percent lower than trade among members of the base group, but it is a statistically insignificant difference.[55]

During the same period, Commonwealth members continue to trade about 51 percent more with each other than do base-group members.[56] The corresponding statistics for Reichsmark and gold bloc members are about 72 percent and 17 percent, respectively.[57] Relative to the base group, sterling bloc members trade about 34 percent less after the war, and trade among members of the exchange-control bloc is 0.01 percent lower under the GATT regime.[58]

That several interwar blocs continued to exert an effect on trade under the GATT is, as we have argued, related to the principal supplier protocol. It is also due, we believe, to the nonrandom process in which states originally entered the blocs. Some blocs were endogenous—that is, they linked states that had traded at unusually high levels with each other even before the Great Depression. In such cases, the blocs institutionalized rather than caused high levels of trade. According to Ritschl and Wolf, this applies to

53. To calculate these values, we sum the coefficients of the control and treatment effect variables (that is, the group dummy and its corresponding interaction term). The corresponding significance level is based on F-tests for the joint significance of each group's control and treatment effect estimates. They are statistically significant for all groups, except for founding members: $F(2,17356)=1.85$ (Prob>F=0.152); privileged group: $F(2,17356)=121.52$ (Prob>F=0.000); exchange-control bloc: $F(2,17356)=5.78$ (Prob>F=0.003); gold bloc: $F(2,17356)=11.85$ (Prob>F=0.000); Commonwealth bloc: $F(2,17356)=62.00$ (Prob>F=0.000); sterling bloc: $F(2,17356)=35.71$ (Prob>F=0.000); and Reichsmark bloc: $F(2,17356)=107.71$ (Prob>F=0.000).
54. P-value=0.000.
55. P-value=0.343.
56. P-value=0.000.
57. P-value=0.000 for both estimates.
58. P-value=0.000 for both estimates. To ensure that these results are not due to the abnormally low levels of trade during the Great Depression, we reanalyzed the data using only 1928 trade as the reference level. The results are robust, with these exceptions: the coefficient on alliances becomes positive and statistically significant for the pre-1928 period (p-value=0.048); its treatment effect is insignificant (p-value=0.960).

Table 3.3. Effects of GATT membership on industrial-country trade

GATT founding members	–6%
Privileged group	94%*
Commonwealth bloc	51%*
Sterling bloc	–34%*
Reichsmark bloc	72%*
Gold bloc	17%*
Exchange-control bloc	–0.01%*

Notes: *significant at 1 percent.

the sterling, Commonwealth, and Reichsmark blocs (2003, 11). The pattern differs, however, in other cases: the trade of gold and exchange-control bloc members was indistinguishable from that of other countries until they actually became bloc members, after which it increased significantly.[59]

Conclusion

Recent empirical studies of the postwar trade regime disagree about its effects, a disagreement that primarily reflects differences in how its members are defined. Studies that code only states that formally acceded to the regime as members show that the GATT/WTO did not have any significant impact on their trade. Studies that use a broader definition conclude that the postwar regime did indeed exert a significant impact on their trade.

In this chapter we have examined the effects of the GATT from the perspective of the rules that governed negotiations under its auspices. Thus, we focused on the small set of countries that the principal supplier rule benefited. Using both interwar and postwar data and defining members broadly, our results show that the distribution of the benefits of GATT membership was severely skewed: the postwar regime privileged trade expansion among members of a very small set of states. We also show that the GATT regime replaced the interwar system de jure but not de facto, as several interwar blocs continued to influence trade patterns after 1945.

Our findings on the effects of the GATT raise questions about the utility of international institutions. The trade regime has been perhaps the paradigmatic example of a welfare-enhancing international institution, even though conventional wisdom has long held that its principal beneficiaries

59. The Ritschl and Wolf results are sensitive to model specification. When they control for trade diversion, they find that trade within the Commonwealth bloc, for example, increases significantly after its formation (2003, 24). Eichengreen and Irwin find that the formation of the Commonwealth and Reichsmark blocs exerted a positive and significant effect on the trade of its members, while the formation of the currency blocs did not (1995, 15).

were the industrial countries. We show that its benefits were even more narrowly concentrated and that the regime coexisted with the system it was intended to supplant. Thus, our analysis suggests that what fueled the postwar regime was an effort to enhance the welfare of the major trading nations, rather than an attempt to resolve market-failure problems. As a result, the GATT can be understood primarily as an exercise in great power diplomacy, which determined the course of global trade governance and produced lasting distributive consequences for the global trading system.

4

A Matter of Timing

WTO Accession and International Trade

The World Trade Organization (WTO) was established in 1995, following the Uruguay Round of negotiations under the General Agreement on Tariffs and Trade (GATT). As the "first construct in a new post–Cold War architecture of international cooperation" (Ostry 1997, 238), the WTO's "clear" legal status and mandate was regarded as "the crossing of an important threshold in international trade relations" (Gallagher 2005, 2). The WTO renewed and incorporated the GATT of 1994 but is in itself a new legal entity. Unlike the GATT, which was "provisional," the WTO is a formal intergovernmental agreement with the status of an international treaty. The WTO formalized a great many of the subjects covered in the GATT in separate agreements and thus vastly expanded the scope of the institutional arrangements governing trade among its members. These agreements, moreover, were linked in a "single undertaking," requiring members to accept the full set of agreements concluded in the Uruguay Round.

The focus of this chapter is on the effects of WTO membership on new entrants to the regime, that is, those countries that acceded to the WTO following its establishment in 1995. The analysis compares the impact of WTO membership on these countries' trade relations with other WTO members, both old and new. In doing so, this chapter engages the broader debate on the success of the GATT/WTO in expanding trade among its members. In asking whether membership indeed comes with the benefits of a boost in trade with other institutional participants, this chapter focuses specifically on the impact of the WTO, the GATT's successor regime. Though the

GATT remains an integral part of the WTO, the WTO as a whole is vastly different from its predecessor, in terms of its legal status, its scope of institutional jurisdiction, and the rules it embodies for global trade governance.

The analysis in this chapter on the trade-creating effects of the WTO is motivated by the vast change in the nature of the accession process for new entrants, given the influx of transition economies into the global trade regime after the end of the Cold War and a qualitative shift in ideas about what may best promote trade liberalization. Thus the terms of accession that have attended new applicants to the regime reflect the substantially broader scope of the WTO's mandate, in particular the requirements for fulfilling obligations of the "new" issue areas that also became formalized in the WTO's various agreements. Existing GATT members acceded to the successor regime with a commitment to the "single undertaking" that obligated member states to all WTO agreements. However, the accession of existing GATT members to the WTO was more or less automatic, while new applicants acceding after the formal establishment of the WTO were subject to a substantially more stringent accession process that necessitated change in trade-related domestic regulations. The terms of accession for new members indicate more broadly a qualitative shift in the nature of global trade governance, from governance of "barriers at the border" to "behind-the-border regulations" necessitated by the host of new issues now under the WTO mandate. At the same time, accession cases under the WTO reflect a qualitative shift in views about how trade liberalization may best be achieved, with greater attention now directed to the importance of domestic regulatory changes as a force for trade liberalization and expansion. Thus this chapter advances the argument that *how* states become members of this institution may well influence how they fared in their trade relations, and the analysis evaluates the impact on trade of these new accession cases.

The analysis evaluates this argument using quantitative methods, differentiating WTO members by the timing of their accessions and assessing their impact on trade. It distinguishes among three kinds of WTO members: (1) "standing members," who became members of the GATT before the start of the Uruguay Round, the last round of trade negotiations under the old regime, and "succeeded" to the WTO in 1995, the first year of the WTO; (2) the "early adopters," who became GATT members during the Uruguay Round and gained membership in the first year of the WTO; and (3) the "later entrants," who acceded in 1996 or later via the lengthy, complex, and stringent formal accession process that has become the norm for entry into the WTO. The empirical analysis evaluates how each group's trade has fared under the regime, both with members of the same group as well as with other groups. The analysis also concentrates on the extent of trade creation, or the degree to which trade expanded after states entered the regime. The results of the analysis show that membership in the WTO has had divergent effects on international trade, expanding trade for later members but having weak or even negative effects on trade between industrialized and developing countries. These divergent effects are the economic consequences of the politically charged process of accession to the regime.

The following section discusses the evolution of the accession process in the trade regime, moving from terms of entry that emphasized the reduction of "barriers at the border" under the GATT to "behind-the-border regulations" after the establishment of the WTO. A case study of China's accession process into the WTO demonstrates how these changes translated into practice for one of the WTO's most important new entrants. The subsequent quantitative analysis section assesses the effect of WTO membership on all its new entrants since the establishment of the regime.

The Changing Terms of Membership:
From the GATT to the WTO

Accession rules under the WTO reflect a fundamental shift in the broad principles governing trade and promoting trade expansion. As the WTO's predecessor, the GATT promoted trade expansion through the reduction of trade barriers—known as "barriers at the border" in the form of tariffs and quantitative restrictions. Under the WTO, however, the emphasis has shifted to "behind-the-border regulations" (Barton, Goldstein, Josling, and Steinberg 2006, 125–152) and overall trade liberalization in accession applicants. The shift is in part a consequence of a transformation that began in the early 1990s after the debt crisis of the 1980s and the changing role of the International Monetary Fund, as well as another important systemic change—the fall of the Berlin Wall and the subsequent end to the Cold War (Ostry 2002). These events ushered in a new economic policy paradigm emphasizing deregulation, privatization, and liberalization, otherwise known as the Washington Consensus, as essential for promoting and sustaining economic growth. This emergent economic policy paradigm, in turn, influenced the course of the Uruguay Round and resulted in a transformation of the multilateral trading system and global trade governance. Attending the creation of the WTO was a qualitative shift in emphasis from reduction of tariffs and quantitative restrictions to liberalization of the trade-related institutional infrastructure of national economies, namely domestic regulatory and legal systems.

Removing barriers to trade and factor flows between countries came to be regarded as a function of laws, regulations, and administrative capacity. Economic regulatory reform became the centerpiece of the "new" issues that dominated the Uruguay Round.[1] In services, for example, the General Agreement on Trade in Services (GATS) reflected a move away from "*negative* regulation"—what governments must *not* do to impede trade, to "*positive* regulation"—what governments *must* do to promote trade and factor flows (Ostry 2002, 11). This emphasis on positive regulation was evident in the intellectual property rights regime, which included not only standards for domestic laws but also enforcement mechanisms to ensure the exercise of property rights.[2] The shift away from border barriers to behind-the-border regulations now entailed transformations in the institutional infrastructure of developing countries in particular, reaching far into the domestic realm to include governance mechanisms, administrative and regulatory systems, and legal systems.

This was consistent with the expanded scope of the WTO and the "single undertaking" to which countries committed themselves upon gaining membership. Accession negotiations under the WTO have thus reflected the vastly broader scope of the trade regime, encompassing not only border measures but also a great many domestic policy issues. These include export subsidies for industrial and agricultural goods as well as intellectual property rights and expansion of the jurisdictional scope of the regime to areas previously excluded or neglected, such as agriculture, services, textiles, and clothing. At the same time, the accession process has also been significantly affected by the particular countries that comprise the group of new applicants. These include a significant number of transition, or former centrally planned economies, including China, Russia and other

1. The Tokyo Round negotiations did involve domestic regulations in the area of subsidies and antidumping measures, resulting in the *Understanding Regarding Notification, Consultation, Dispute Settlement and Surveillance,* designed to promote transparency and increase legalization. However, the Uruguay Round greatly expanded positive regulation in both substantive and procedural law, owing to the inclusion of "new" issues such as intellectual property rights (Ostry 2002, 18). The Trade-Related Intellectual Property Rights (TRIPs) Agreement, for example, requires the publication of laws, regulation, administrative services, and enforcement procedures.

2. Developing countries argued during the Uruguay Round, however, that such commitments were likely to affect their domestic political and economic systems significantly. The codification of international standards on intellectual property rights, for example, would require domestic legislation to be brought in line with WTO commitments, which some considered an "attack" on the economic base of many developing countries (Wilkinson 2006, 91). The agreement on trade-related investment measures (TRIMS), for another, was perceived to be an instrument for promoting large-scale investment liberalization and extensive regulation by the WTO (Sauvé 2000, 85).

former Soviet republics, the Baltic countries, and Cambodia, Vietnam, and Laos. As the WTO, like the GATT before it, was designed to regulate trade among market economies, accession of these transition economies has lent greater complexity to the negotiations (Michalopoulos 1998; Langhammer and Lücke 1999). Moreover, it has been argued that WTO applicants have increasingly become subject to accession requirements that call for liberalization measures that surpass those of incumbent members (Broude 1998).

Accession under the GATT

In the earliest days of global trade governance under the GATT, the twenty-three original members, or Contracting Parties, examined the terms of accession at the Annecy Round in 1949, immediately after the first Geneva Round. Indeed, one of the main objectives of the meeting was to examine more closely the terms of accession for new members. The Annecy Round established *The Annecy Protocol of Terms of Accession to the General Agreement on Tariffs and Trade*. Its provisions concerned the accession of the first ten new countries to the GATT, which acceded under Article XXXIII,[3] and specified that accession would take place when (1) two-thirds of the existing members have signed the accession protocol for a particular applicant country; and (2) the acceding country puts into effect the tariff schedules negotiated as part of the accession process.[4] The State Department's analysis of the accession protocol emphasized the importance of reducing trade barriers to achieve trade expansion on a nondiscriminatory basis, an important economic foreign policy goal of the United States at this time (U.S. Department of State 1949, 2, 4).

Accession for prospective members under the GATT took place in relatively short order, as membership was approved chiefly on the basis of tariff schedules. Once negotiations on tariff schedules were complete, they were incorporated into a formal document approving the accession of the particular applicant and submitted for approval to existing members. The Working Party that was designated played a minimal role under the GATT's

---

3. "A government not party to this Agreement, or a government acting on behalf of a separate customs territory possessing full autonomy in the conduct of its external commercial relations and of the other matters provided for in this Agreement, may accede to this Agreement, on its own behalf or on behalf of that territory, on terms to be agreed between such government and contracting parties."

4. The ten countries acceding at this time—Denmark, the Dominican Republic, Finland, Greece, Haiti, Italy, Liberia, Nicaragua, Sweden, and Uruguay, became members under Article XXXIII of the GATT, which provides for accession based on terms agreed upon by the applicant country and the Contracting Parties (U.S. Department of State 1949, 236).

accession procedures, fostering discussion on the particular accession case and providing a forum for raising issues related to the applicant.

Accession under the GATT also extended membership to former colonies under Article XXVI:5(c).[5] This provision granted GATT membership in a way that was somewhat outside the usual accession route. Where colonial powers were willing to sponsor an application by a former colony for membership in the GATT, accession was granted on an automatic basis on the "terms and conditions previously accepted by the metropolitan government on behalf of the territory in question." That is, tariff schedules previously negotiated by the colonizer on behalf of its former colony before the latter's formal membership would continue to apply. Such provisions concerning former colonies reflected the interests of Europe's colonizers vis-à-vis their respective overseas territories.

Accession under Article XXVI:5(c) was thus close to automatic. Former colonies had already been applying GATT provisions in their trade practices on an ad hoc basis, so the costs of de facto membership were low. Through the sponsorship of their former colonizers, many former colonies were granted de facto membership indefinitely.[6] This status was granted on the condition that GATT members would apply its rules and provisions to de facto members on a reciprocal basis. De facto members received, in turn, many of the benefits of the GATT, in spite of fewer obligations and rights than formal members.[7]

During the Uruguay Round, launched in September 1986 at Punta del Este, GATT members and especially the powerful developed countries directed their efforts toward expanding the agenda of trade liberalization. This required increasing the scope of GATT negotiations, and the Uruguay Round covered the widest range of trade issues of any round, resulting in a Final Act that included not only GATT 1994 but also sixty agreements, annexes, decisions, and understandings. Reflecting this new commitment to wide-ranging trade liberalization by GATT members, accession cases came under increasing scrutiny, as increasing importance was attached to international trade regulation in applicant countries.

5. "If any of the customs territories, in respect of which a contracting party has accepted this Agreement, possesses or acquires full autonomy in the conduct of its external commercial relations and of the other matters provided for in this Agreement, such territory shall, upon sponsorship through a declaration by the responsible contracting party establishing the above-mentioned fact, be deemed to be a contracting party." Originally Article XXVI: 4, this provision was amended at the Annecy meeting by the Protocol modifying Part II and Article XXVI of the GATT.

6. De facto status for many countries was retained until the establishment of the WTO, which eliminated this membership provision.

7. For example, while de facto members participated in tariff negotiations and other GATT sessions, they could not vote or have recourse to the GATT's dispute settlement mechanism.

Accession under the WTO

The formal provisions governing accession to the WTO maintain the inclusiveness of its predecessor. The WTO, like the GATT, advocates universal membership, and any state or customs territory that is fully autonomous in the conduct of trade policy may apply to become a member of the WTO. In spite of the inclusiveness of the WTO's membership provisions, in practice the accession process for new entrants is far more stringent and intrusive in terms of the liberalization programs that applicants must adopt. Indeed, the WTO Secretariat's technical note on the accession process indicates that negotiating membership under the regime is "much more complex" than under the GATT and attributes this change to the increased scope and coverage of the WTO Agreement.[8] The process is very different from that under the GATT regime, in which new members simply agreed not to enact new legislation that would be inconsistent with the regime's principles and provisions, thus grandfathering existing trade restrictions (Barton, Goldstein, Josling, and Steinberg 2006).

While GATT applicants largely focused on the negotiation of tariff reductions in their accession process, WTO applicants negotiate not only tariff concessions but also commitments in many different sectors, many of which entail active legislative reform. Indeed, a striking difference of WTO accession cases is the submission of a "legislative action plan" from an applicant country detailing information on legislative changes and new laws and regulations governing trade that are an integral part of the terms of accession (Lanoszka 2001, 583). The wide scope of issues now covered as a result of the Uruguay Round means that accession under the WTO is far more complex, with far-reaching and long-term consequences for the applicant country. The inherent complexity of the accession process under the WTO makes the experience more rigorous and demanding. Applicants are subject to preconditions before membership is formally approved. This "WTO conditionality" requires that members at the time of accession have a national economy that is consistent with WTO rules. Those who have applied for membership but whose policies and regulations are not consistent with WTO rules are required to implement reforms in order to make them so.

The formal provision governing WTO accession is codified in Article XII:[9]

> Any State or separate customs territory possessing full autonomy in the conduct of its external commercial relations and of the other matters provided

---

8. WT/ACC/10/Rev.3, 1, 28 November 2005. See also WT/AC/10/Rev.3, 10, 28 November 2005.

9. Marrakesh Agreement Establishing the World Trade Organization.

for in this Agreement and the Multilateral Trade Agreements may accede to this Agreement, *on terms to be agreed between it and the WTO.* Such accession shall apply to this Agreement and the Multilateral Trade Agreements annexed thereto. (emphasis added)

The provision lacks precision (Abbott, Keohane, Moravcsik, Slaughter, and Snidal 2001). It is vague and general, and it contains no specific accession criteria, with the result that it may be subject to differing interpretations. Such imprecision makes the legal side of the accession process problematic, but it has also made the accession process uneven, with each case differing from the next. Article XII provides leeway for demands on the part of existing members. At the extreme, accession becomes less about WTO consistency than about the interests of the existing members. Applicant countries may well find themselves with little negotiating power and may be pressured simply to accept the terms of accession presented to them.

New accession cases under the WTO involve the establishment of a Working Party consisting of major trading partners that oversees the application process and stipulates the conditions necessary for the applicant to make its policies WTO-consistent.[10] The Working Party begins its deliberations once an applicant submits a Memorandum on the Foreign Trade Regime that details its laws and regulations governing international commerce. It evaluates the memorandum and mediates questions and replies between the acceding government and existing WTO members on the basis of this memorandum. All Working Parties on accession cases include representatives from the United States, the European Union, Japan, Australia, and Switzerland, in order to ensure consistency across cases and to represent the interests of the WTO's major trading states.[11] Other WTO members may participate only in cases of particular interest, namely those that may be most affected by the results of the accession negotiations (Michalopoulos 1998; Langhammer and Lücke 1999, 843).

After the evaluation of the applicant's memorandum and its replies to the questions raised by WTO members, the terms of accession are negotiated through a series of bilateral negotiations between the applicant and

10. Detailed information on the accession process and the accession cases up to Saudi Arabia's accession in 2005 are provided in the *Technical Note on the Accession Process,* WT/ACC/10/Rev.3, 28 November 2005. Available at www.wto.org/english/thewto_e/acc_e/acc_e.htm, accessed 6 August 2008.

11. Available at http://www.wto.org/english/thewto_e/acc_e/cbt_course_e/c4s2p2_e.htm#fnt68, accessed 5 May 2009. According to information on the WTO website, these countries make up over 60 percent of world trade.

its major trading partners. After the negotiations are completed and the Working Party achieves consensus on the final accession package, namely the Report of the Working Party with a draft Decision and Protocol of Accession and its Annexes, it is forwarded to the General Council, which approves and adopts the draft Decision. As was the case under the GATT, an applicant's accession also requires approval by two-thirds of existing members. Thirty days after it accepts the Protocol of Accession, the accession applicant formally becomes a member of the WTO.

The new rules governing WTO accession cases have been subject to extended discussion and controversy in Ministerial Conferences and General Council meetings.[12] The decision to allow applicants, for example, to participate in Working Party meetings as observers has been viewed positively as a way to provide greater transparency in the process. The "legislative action plans" now submitted by accession applicants provide valuable support for ongoing internal economic reforms. At the same time, however, the length of the process has led to some concern that the number of new WTO members would otherwise have been higher, and general agreement exists that though this does not mean the process is not effective, the body should be focused on expediting accession for applicants. More controversial, however, are the market access issues that new applicants must now negotiate with existing members. New WTO members are required to bind policy instruments such as tariffs on merchandise imports, subsidies on agricultural production, and regulations on market access for services to levels agreed upon with current members. However, some acceding countries were subject to more stringent obligations than existing WTO members, making it a kind of "WTO-plus" obligation.[13] In the case of tariffs on industrial goods, existing WTO members have required that acceding countries bind tariffs to no more than about 10 percent (Langhammer and Lücke 1998, 847). Yet one study has shown that the actual rate applied by current WTO members ranges from 13 to 34 percent (Finger, Ingco, and Reincke 1996).

Regarding "WTO-plus" obligations, criticism and controversy have also surrounded the accession of developing countries that request transition periods, invoking "special and differential treatment" under the Enabling Clause, an institutional mechanism adopted in 1979 under the GATT specifically designed to provide greater leeway for developing countries'

---

12. Singapore (December 1996); Geneva (May 1998); Seattle (December 1999); and Doha (2001) with declarations adopted in Singapore, Geneva, and Doha. Discussions at General Council meetings resulted in the adoption in December 2002 of Guidelines for LDC Accessions to facilitate and expedite accessions for least-developed countries.

13. WT/AC/10/Rev.3, 37. Accessed 15 December 2009.

obligations to the regime. Original WTO members, that is, GATT members who became signatories of the WTO Agreement and thus were founding members of the successor regime, were granted transition periods to assist in adjusting to the new obligations. While many original WTO members were automatic beneficiaries of transition periods, such provisions have not been made for accession applicants, and in some cases it was argued that "legitimate claims" for special and differential treatment had not been granted.[14] Those supporting the current and stricter practice on transitions and special and differential treatment, on the other hand, have contended that new entrants are already familiar with the obligations of the WTO Agreement, and therefore any such arrangements for acceding governments should have a clear justification with explicitly defined conditions and timeframes.

Case Study: China's WTO Accession

The case of China's accession to the WTO aptly illustrates the features of the WTO's accession process, in particular the notable changes in the terms of accession for new WTO entrants. In large part, China's accession was "a matter of timing." As Sylvia Ostry notes, "If China had joined the GATT in the 1980s, the negotiations would have centered on traditional trade issues or border barriers.... But the transformation of the system wrought by the Uruguay Round and its after-effects rather dramatically changes the conditions for accession, and also changes the likely impact of Chinese accession on the WTO as well as the impact of the WTO on China" (2002, 9). China was a landmark accession case for the WTO in several respects. As the fourth-largest trading nation in the world at the time of its accession, China drew the attention of the trading world as a rising economic powerhouse from the ranks of the developing world whose accession would make its mark in the evolution of the trade regime.[15] At the same time and equally important, China was an important example of a "nonmarket economy" (NME) and, as was the case for NMEs acceding before it, presented challenges to the WTO system of integrating centrally planned economies on their way to a market-oriented economic system. China was singled out by the United States and its western allies as an exemplar of a transition economy, so its accession application was treated quite differently from that

---

14. Ibid.

15. In 2001, the year of its accession to the WTO, China was the fourth-largest importer and exporter in world merchandise trade, excluding intra-EU trade. From *International Trade Statistics 2002*, Table 1.6, available at www.wto.org/english/res_e/statis_e/its2002_e/section1_e/i06.xls, accessed 12 August 2008.

of Russia in subsequent years, to which the United States resisted granting even observer status during the Uruguay Round (Feng 2006, 140).

China's "long march" to WTO membership spanned almost sixteen years, beginning in July 1986 during the Uruguay Round when it submitted its accession application (Ostry, Alexandroff, and Gomez 2002).[16] It was the longest accession negotiation on record and reportedly the most arduous negotiation in the history of the GATT/WTO system (Gertler 2002, 22). The Working Party for the Accession of China into the WTO concluded its work after eighteen meetings between 1995 and 2001 (Alexandroff and Gomez 2002, 231). It produced a Working Party report of several hundred pages, a significant portion of which was incorporated into China's accession protocol. The Protocol of Accession for China was also the longest on record, comprising some 900 pages and 343 numbered paragraphs, with nine annexes, including China's Goods and Services Schedules (Alexandroff 2002, 211; Alexandroff and Gomez 2002, 231).[17] China's protocol consisted of an unusually lengthy main text of 11 pages on the procedures and technical matters related to China's accession, distinguishing it from other WTO accession cases which included no more than two pages of standardized provisions (Qin 2003, 488). The seventeen sections of the protocol's main text covered not only China's commitments on WTO rules but also a set of special provisions to apply in China's trade relations with other WTO members.

Under the rule of the Kuomintang, China had been a founding member of the GATT, but following the revolution in 1949 and the Kuomintang's retreat to Taiwan, the Chiang Kai-Shek government in 1950 announced its withdrawal from the GATT. Although the Mao Zedong government in Beijing never officially acknowledged this withdrawal from the GATT, in July 1986, nearly forty years later, the People's Republic of China formally notified the GATT of its desire to resume its status as a Contracting Party and to renegotiate the terms of its membership. The Working Party on China's Status was established in March 1987 and had its first meeting in October 1987. The Working Party met on over twenty occasions under the GATT but reached no conclusion on China's terms of accession.

---

16. The shortest accession process under the WTO was for membership of the Kyrgyz Republic, which took two years and ten months overall.

17. In contrast, when Poland became a GATT member in 1967, the Protocol of Accession and the Report of the Working Party together ran only ten pages. Among WTO accessions, Mongolia's (1996) Protocol of Accession and Report of the Working Party, the shortest on record for the WTO period, added up to thirty pages while that of Albania (2000) comprised sixty pages (Lanoszka 2001, 583).

Significant progress on China's accession had been made soon after its application, but the Tiananmen Square incident in 1989 derailed the negotiations for almost two and a half years. There was no activity on the accession front during this time. China participated in the Uruguay Round negotiations, with a view to joining the regime as a founding member of the WTO, though it was unsuccessful in doing so. The GATT Working Party was converted to the WTO Working Party on the Accession of China in December 1995.[18] At the Doha Ministerial in Qatar in November 2001, the same meeting at which the Doha Round was launched, the General Council formally received the Report of the Working Party with a draft Decision and Protocol of Accession. On 11 November 2001, the government of the People's Republic of China notified the WTO that it had accepted and was in compliance with its WTO agreements. Pursuant to WTO rules on accession, thirty days later, on 11 December 2001, the PRC became the WTO's 143rd member.[19]

The main figure in the politics of China's accession was undoubtedly the United States. According to Hui Feng, "Of all the foreign governments that Beijing had to deal with in its WTO agenda, the United States [was] certainly the most important factor in its accession equation." Indeed, the United States was "crucial" to China's successful accession (2006, 139). U.S. support of China's domestic economic reform, the granting of normal trade relations, that is, permanent MFN status for China in 2000, and even pressure from the European Union, Japan, and Canada to conclude negotiations with the United States first and foremost all made China's negotiations with the United States the key factor in its chances for a successful accession application. U.S. support of China's accession was regarded by the latter as a strong indicator of the Western world's acceptance of China into the international community. The United States, for its part, felt it had a strong stake in the continuation of China's domestic economic reforms and sought as well to improve China's record on human rights and arms proliferation. The vote on permanent normal trade relations (PNTR) with China was regarded by David Dreier, chairman of the House Rules Committee, as "the most important vote cast in the 213-year history of the United States of America" (quoted in Feng 2006, 149).[20] Not only did PNTR

18. The Chairman of the Working Party, Ambassador Pierre-Louis Girard of Switzerland, presided over China's accession case for its entire sixteen-year duration.

19. Taiwan became a WTO member a day later, as China-Taipei, thus concluding the politically charged twin accession cases of Taiwan and the PRC.

20. The PNTR bill was approved in the House, as H.R. 4444 (237 to 197) on 24 May 2000, and in the Senate (83 to 15) on 19 September 2000, and it was signed into law by President Clinton on 10 October 2000.

status for China level the ground for its exports to the United States, it also greatly facilitated China's WTO accession.

China's bilateral negotiations with the United States, the most important among the thirty-seven parties with which China had to negotiate, were heavily politicized from the start and influenced by the diplomatic relations between the two countries and their respective domestic politics. The conclusion of the U.S.-China bilateral agreement in November 1999 was preceded in May by the accidental bombing of China's Embassy in Belgrade by NATO forces, which cast a pall over the negotiations. Also significant in U.S. trade politics was its rising trade deficit with China, which had reached $57 billion by 1998, second only to the U.S. trade deficit with Japan (Feng 2006, 142). There was mounting political pressure on Congress and the Clinton administration to debate the economic consequences of China's WTO accession for the United States. The bilateral accord with the United States involved a comprehensive set of issues covering virtually all aspects of the Chinese economy, from trade in goods to services, investment, and intellectual property rights. It entailed sweeping reforms for liberalization of China's market, specifying sector-by-sector liberalization measures and a commitment to subject Chinese firms to increased international competition. The negotiations also reached further into China's domestic institutions in promoting transparency though the installation of legal and administrative policies and institutions to resolve trade disputes. For China, its accession to the WTO was "not only paralleled but also intertwined with" the progress of its domestic economic reform (Feng 2006, 162). WTO membership was an "external anchor" for its domestic reform program, which began in the late 1970s under Deng Xiaoping (Ostry 2002, 19).

The U.S.-China bilateral accord was the keystone in China's WTO accession, as agreements with other WTO members depended on its successful conclusion. Indeed, China's repeated attempts to bypass the United States and divide the Western bloc by concluding agreements with Japan, the European Union, and other negotiating partners before an agreement was reached with the United States were unsuccessful, as these countries refused to conclude any agreement with China until one had been reached with the United States (Crothall 1994). Though the European Union viewed favorably China's ongoing economic reform process and argued for greater flexibility in negotiations, it nevertheless turned away in July 1996 a Chinese delegation led by Long Yongtu, who led China's WTO accession negotiations and approached the EU for a bilateral agreement before concluding one with the United States (Yang in Feng 2006, 151). The United States, the EU, and Japan held confidential talks in 1994 to coordinate their position regarding China's WTO accession when the latter sought to gain membership as a founding member of the WTO (Zarocostas in Liang 2002, 702). The United States Trade Representative continued to coordinate informally after 1997 with Canada, Australia, and the European Union to ensure consistency in their responses to China's WTO accession application (Pearson 2001). The EU concluded its talks with China in May 2000, after the U.S.-China bilateral agreements was reached in November 1999.[21]

In all, China concluded bilateral agreements with thirty-seven WTO members that expressed an interest in market-access negotiations.[22] These bilateral agreements, which included China's consolidated Schedules of Concessions and Commitments to the GATT 1994 as well as its Schedule of Specific Commitments to the General Agreement on Trade in Services (GATS), became China's Goods and Services Schedules and were attached as Annexes to China's Protocol of Accession following review by the Working Party. The commitments resulting from China's bilateral negotiations became part of the terms of its accession to the WTO and were extended to all WTO members on an MFN basis.

The Protocol of Accession for China, which also incorporates a substantial portion of the Working Party Report, contains provisions that reach to the depths of domestic trade legislation and trade practices to bring them into conformity with WTO rules.[23] As has been the standard in the accession cases that came before, the protocol commits China to bringing national measures into conformity with the trade regime's rules. Specifically, China is required to ensure that its trade practices are consistent with WTO rules at the national and subnational levels, such as in the imposition of customs fees and internal taxes (Section 11). The protocol also requires that China bring domestic technical regulations, standards, and conformity assessment procedures in line with the WTO's Technical Barriers to Trade Agreement (Section 13). Furthermore, as a "later entrant" without recourse to developing country exceptions and concessions in the WTO, China received no transition period for eliminating export subsidies and concessions, as provided for developing countries in the Agreement on

21. The U.S.-China bilateral agreement was concluded in November 1999 and signed on 3 March 2000. The E.U.-China bilateral agreement was signed in June 2001.

22. They included: Argentina, Australia, Brazil, Canada, Chile, Columbia, Costa Rica, Cuba, the Czech Republic, Ecuador, the European Union (fifteen members before expansion in 2005), Guatemala, Hungary, Iceland, India, Indonesia, Japan, Korea, the Kyrgyz Republic, Latvia, Malaysia, Mexico, New Zealand, Norway, Pakistan, Peru, the Philippines, Poland, Singapore, the Slovak Republic, Sri Lanka, Switzerland, Thailand, Turkey, the United States, Uruguay, and Venezuela.

23. WT/L/432, 23 November 2001. Available at www.wto.org/english/thewto_e/acc_e/completeacc_e.htm#chn, accessed 21 May 2008.

Subsidies and Countervailing Measures. The protocol specifies the elimination of all export subsidies upon accession and codifies China's agreement not to invoke provisions of the Agreement on Subsidies and Countervailing Measures that grant special treatment for developing countries.

China's commitments extended to domestic laws and regulations concerning trade that reflected the wide scope of the WTO's jurisdiction, including transparency in information provision and publication of domestic legislation; judicial review providing for independent review of trade-related administrative decisions; uniform administration of the WTO Agreements in both the national and subnational governments; and national treatment, that is treatment "no less favorable" than that accorded to domestic economic actors in the areas of goods, services, and intellectual property rights.[24] In the area of foreign investment, China's commitments under the Trade-Related Investment Measures (TRIMs) Agreement was unprecedented in specifying investment liberalization policies, including prohibition of "performance requirements of any kind" and of restricting investment to protect domestic industries (Qin 2003, 503).

Last but not least, the China protocol contained key provisions concerning market economy practices and transition review mechanisms. As did other transition economies or NMEs in the process of moving toward market-oriented economic systems, China also made commitments to economic reform in an effort to integrate its economy into the market-based multilateral trading system. Beyond providing certification of compliance with WTO rules and information on a continuing basis on the status of its privatization program, China also committed to allow market prices to prevail in "*every sector*," though with exceptions (Qin 2003, 505); to eschew government influence in the decisions of state-owned and state-invested enterprises; and to liberalize China's trade regime through legislative reform within three years of accession. Though these obligations are "WTO-plus" in that they go beyond the requirements of the WTO Multilateral Trade Agreements, they are typical of the commitments attending accession of NMEs under the WTO regime (Qin 2003, 505). Though in many respects China's terms of accession were consistent with those of preceding NME cases under the WTO, in the area of transitional review its commitments were the most stringent on record. Going well beyond what is required of other WTO members under the Trade Policy Review Mechanism, China's accession protocol contained special transitional review mechanisms that included provisions for an unprecedented nine reviews of its economy in

---

24. Article III, General Agreement on Tariffs and Trade. See also Trade-Related Investment Measures (TRIMs) Agreement, Article 2.

the first ten years: an annual review for eight years followed by another in the tenth year after its accession.[25]

China's accession thus illustrates some of the major features of accession terms applied to "later entrants," as contrasted with "standing members" and "early adopters." China's entry into the regime entailed commitments that were common to latecomers to the WTO regime and to NME accession cases in terms of their obligations toward domestic legislative and regulatory reforms, "behind-the-border" commitments that went far beyond the "barriers at the border" that marked accession cases under the GATT regime. The next section turns to the consequences of such accessions under the WTO and, using quantitative analysis, evaluates the extent of their success in expanding trade under the WTO regime.

Research Design

The features of the accession process under the WTO, as contrasted with that of the GATT and illustrated above in the case of China's accession, motivate this analysis on the impact of the WTO on international trade. If the changes in the terms of accession under the WTO, now emphasizing reforms in trade-related regulatory mechanisms as well as tariff reductions, have been successful in liberalizing the economies of new members, they would have the effect of expanding the trade of new WTO members, both among the new entrants and between the new entrants and the existing WTO member countries.

Standing Members, Early Adopters, and Later Entrants in the WTO

Given significant differences in accession processes and requirements between the GATT and the WTO, members of the trade regime may be broadly classified into "standing members," "early adopters," and "later entrants," as outlined above. The appendix lists the countries in each group and their accession dates for the GATT and/or the WTO. The "standing members," former members of the GATT, obtained membership before 1986 under the old accession rules and were later invited in the Agreement Establishing the WTO signed in Marrakesh in April 1994 to join the new organization,

---

25. By comparison, under the Trade Policy Review Mechanism, the largest traders—the United States, the EU, Japan, and Canada—are reviewed every two years. The sixteen next largest trading nations are reviewed every four years, and other countries are reviewed every six years, with longer periods allowed for the least-developed economies (Qin 2003, 507).

subject to ratification of the Agreement to which are attached all other agreements, decisions, and understandings. That is, a "standing member" is a GATT Contracting Party that became a founding member of the WTO on 1 January 1995 when it ratified the WTO agreement and the linked agreements in a "single undertaking," and accepted and annexed to the GATT 1994 and the GATS its commitment to concessions on trade in goods and services. These "standing members" comprise the first and largest set of accessions taking place under the WTO.

The second group are the "early adopters." This group consists of those countries that gained membership during the Uruguay Round (1986–1994) and the first year of the WTO (1995), and it is notable in two ways. First, these developing countries, in particular those that became members toward the end of the Uruguay Round, joined with a view to wielding influence over the final set of agreements leading to the establishment of the WTO (Gallagher 2005, 13; Michalopoulos 1999, 117). Participation in the Uruguay Round allowed them a voice, even if not a powerful one, in negotiating for rights and benefits under the new regime. Second, accession to the WTO held definite advantages to being among the "early adopters," especially for those with "least developed country" status. The complex accession process was especially challenging for these applicants, and they were granted leeway in meeting the conditions for accession commensurate with their level of development, financial or trade positions, and administrative and institutional capabilities.[26] Transition periods, for example, were readily granted to those with least-developed country status, allowing greater flexibility in bringing their foreign trade regulations in line with WTO rules.[27]

The third group of WTO members, the "later entrants," was subject to the more complicated and extensive accession process, which entailed negotiating the terms with existing WTO members. Though equal with all other members once membership has been obtained save for any special conditions negotiated during the accession process, "later entrants" were subject to the full acceptance requirement of all WTO agreements and did not automatically qualify for the implementation concessions that developing country members enjoyed at the time of the WTO's establishment in 1995. Nor were the transition arrangements that characterized accession cases during the Uruguay Round readily granted to many WTO applicants.

26. The *Uruguay Round Decision on Measures in Favor of Least-Developed Countries* exempted least-developed countries from commitments and concessions that are "inconsistent with their individual development, financial and trade needs." http://www.wto.org/english/docs_e/legal_e/31-dlldc_e.htm, accessed 15 December 2009 See also WTO document WT/L/508 (20 January 2003), "Guidelines for Accession of Least-Developed Countries."
27. WT/ACC/10/Rev.3, 2 and 15, 28 November 2005.

Few transition arrangements have been granted to WTO applicants, and these have been limited in nature and granted only for specific periods of time. This group of WTO members was subject to terms of accession that were the most complex and far-reaching in terms of domestic regulations on trade.[28]

Analysis: Effects on International Trade

The analysis presented in the following pages provides a comparison of these three groups in terms of the benefits of trade expansion enjoyed under the WTO. In doing so, the analysis builds on a set of controversial findings in the literature that challenge the trade-creating effects of the GATT and the WTO. Among current studies, Rose (2004) found that overall, trade "cannot be dependably linked" to GATT/WTO membership. Upon closer examination, Rose (2004), Gowa and Kim (2005), and Subramanian and Wei (2005) found that when GATT members are divided into industrial and nonindustrial countries, the GATT has had a positive and significant effect only on trade among the former countries. That is, the GATT expanded trade among industrial countries but had little if any impact on trade among nonindustrial countries or between industrial and nonindustrial countries. This is in spite of the "enabling clause," the special and differential treatment accorded to the developing countries within the GATT regime. These findings have been challenged in Tomz, Goldstein, and Rivers (2007) and Goldstein, Rivers, and Tomz (2007), the argument being that the GATT extended rights and obligations to countries who were not formal members of the regime. These studies find that for these members of "institutional standing," the GATT significantly aided trade expansion in the post–World War II period.

The analysis presented here further develops the arguments and findings in the existing literature in two ways. First, it focuses specifically on the impact of the WTO. Given the establishment of a formal organization to govern trade and the greatly expanded scope of issues now covered under the regime, the question arises as to its consequences for trade among its members, both old and new. Second, the analysis is devoted in particular to examining how developing countries have fared under the regime, differentiated by the timing of their membership. The rationale for distinguishing among "standing members," "early adopters," and "later entrants"

---

28. WT/ACC/10/Rev.3, 28 November 2005.

is due to the increasingly complex and, indeed, intrusive dimensions of accession proceedings. Trade negotiation rounds under the previous GATT regime emphasized the reduction of "barriers at the border," as members bargained over tariff rates and quantitative restrictions. Less attention was directed to the compatibility of domestic laws with WTO agreements. The more stringent accession requirements of the WTO, on the other hand, call for the active enactment of legislation that is WTO-consistent, reflecting perhaps the changing view that trade liberalization policies legislated in the domestic political arena must precede any trade-creating benefits conferred by inclusion in the regime. From this perspective, then, the expected trade-creating benefits of the WTO should be greater the later one joins the regime.

Data

The sample analyzed consists of pairs of countries, or dyads, observed annually between the years 1948 to 2004, covering the GATT era and the first ten years of the WTO. Trade is measured by the sum of the exports and imports from country a to country b. As the sample of analysis consists of non-directed dyads, these figures also represent, respectively, imports and exports of country b from country a. The trade data, calculated in constant U.S. dollars (2000), were obtained from IMF's *Direction of Trade Statistics* (DOTS).[29] Countries comprising the dyads include members of the interstate system, as identified by the Correlates of War 2 Project (COW2) and subject to data availability.[30] The sample includes only system members as data on the political variables are available only for these states. The variable of interest, WTO membership, is defined in terms of formal membership where countries have completed the process of accession.

Model Specifications

The dependent variable is the (natural) log of bilateral trade volume: the sum of exports and imports between country i and country j in a given

---

29. Trade values were converted to constant U.S. dollars (2000) using the U.S. GDP (chained) price index, obtained from the GPO, available at www.gpoaccess.gov/usbudget/fy05/sheets/hist10z1.xls, accessed 1 September 2007.

30. The COW2 Project defines a system member as a state that either (1) is a UN member; or (2) has a population of more than five hundred thousand and diplomatic missions from at least two major powers. Correlates of War Project (2005), State System Membership List, v2004.1, available at http://correlatesofwar.org, accessed 1 September 2007.

year t.[31] Explanatory variables on the right-hand side include those of the standard gravity model found in the international trade literature, with recent theoretical formulations advanced in Anderson (1979), Helpman and Krugman (1985), Deardorff (1997), and Anderson and van Wincoop (2003), among others. The model is widely utilized in empirical studies to predict the level of trade between two countries.[32] The basic gravity model variables include the logged products of the two countries' GDP and per capita GDP, both in constant U.S. dollars (2000).[33] As measures of economic size and development, respectively, they are both expected to be positively related to trade flows.[34] The model also includes a set of dummy variables to capture the effect of common membership in institutional arrangements that have been shown in studies to affect trade flows.[35] Indicator variables are set to one if the two countries belong to the same preferential trade agreement or share the same currency in a given year, and zero otherwise.[36] Another dichotomous variable equals one if one country is a beneficiary of trade preferences given by the other under the Generalized System of Preferences, which were special agreements negotiated under the auspices of the United Nations Conference on Trade and Development (UNCTAD) to aid developing countries expand their trade vis-à-vis the developed

31. The Methodological Appendix provides a formal presentation of the baseline model analyzed in this chapter.

32. The origins of the gravity model are variously attributable, with its classic formulation for international trade found in Linnemann (1966), which built on work by Tinbergen (1962). For a discussion of the more recent resurgence of interest in the gravity model and its theoretical advances, see Frankel (1997). The basic form of the gravity model specifies bilateral trade flows to be positively related to the product of the two composite countries' GDPs and negatively related to the distance between them. To these basic variables, subsequent studies, discussed below, have added other variables, such as economic size, geographical proximity, cultural similarity, and common institutional arrangements.

33. Data on GDP and GDP per capita were obtained from the Penn World Tables, version 6.2.

34. On the theoretical importance of the product of the GDPs, a proxy for economic size, for trade flows, see Helpman and Krugman (1985). The effect on trade of GDP per capita captures the level of industrialization or development and concomitantly the level of intra-industry trade, which tends to be higher among industrialized countries. See also Grossman and Helpman (1989, 1991) and River-Batiz and Romer (1991) on contributions from endogenous growth theory.

35. On the effects of preferential and free trade agreements, see Frankel (1997), Bhagwati and Panagariya (1996), and Schott (2004) for a survey of the major issues. In the political science literature, see also Mansfield and Pevehouse (2000) and Kono (2002, 2007). On the effects of currency unions, see, for example, Glick and Rose (2002), Rose and van Wincoop (2001), and Nitsch (2002).

36. Data on PTAs were obtained from Mansfield and Pevehouse (2000) and updated using information from the WTO and Arashiro, Marin, and Chacoff (2005). Data for currency unions were obtained from Rose (2004) and extended using Cohen (2004).

world. GSPs have been used widely as a control variable in models of trade (Rose 2004).[37]

The model also includes a set of political variables that have been associated with higher trade flows, including democracy (Mansfield, Milner, and Rosendorff 2000) and alliances (Mansfield and Bronson 1997; Gowa 1994; Gowa and Mansfield 1993). A dummy variable for democracy equals one if both countries in the dyad score 6 or greater in Polity IV's democracy index; similarly, a dichotomous variable for alliance equals one if both countries are members of the same alliance.[38] The model includes as well a control for whether one member of a dyad was ever a colony of the other. Former colony status is incorporated into an interaction term with another dummy variable that equals one for the WTO years (1995–2004), discussed further below, to account for longstanding relations among former colonies and their metropoles and their effects on trade.

The variables of interest include a dummy variable that equals one for the years since the establishment of the WTO (1995) to 2004 and several interaction variables that combine this variable, denoted *WTO Years*, with the three membership groups. *Standing Members* equals one if both countries in the dyad were GATT members who joined before the start of the Uruguay Round (1986); *Early Adopters* equals one if both countries joined during the Uruguay Round and were members in 1995; and *Later Entrants* equals one if both countries joined the WTO after 1995 and were thus subject to the full-length accession process. Each of these member group variables is combined with *WTO Years* in interaction terms to capture the effect of the WTO on their respective trade.[39] The variables represent each group on its own before and after the WTO was created, thus making the WTO a "treatment" for these groups. In addition, the model specifies effects of the WTO on trade between *Standing Members & Early Adopters, Standing Members & Later Entrants,* and *Early Adopters & Later Entrants* between 1995 and 2004 (*WTO Years*). The model includes as well year fixed effects using dummy variables for each year (except one) in the sample. These account for unmeasured

---

37. For studies on the effects of GSPs, see Özden and Reinhardt (2005) and Herz and Wagner (2006). For a study of the U.S. GSP scheme, see Graham (1978).

38. Formal alliances include mutual defense pacts, nonaggression treaties, and ententes. Data for democracy were obtained from the Polity IV database, available at http://www.cidcm.umd.edu/polity/. Data on alliances were obtained from the COW2 Project, available at http://cow2.la.psu.edu/, version 3.03 (Gibler and Sarkees 2002), accessed 1 September 2007. Alliance data from 2000 were extended to 2004 for this analysis.

39. The model specified dummy variables to capture group effects, rather than simply using individual accession dates, to distinguish between the *Standing Members* and *Early Adopters,* as countries in both groups acceded to the WTO in the same year (1995) but were subject to different accession processes.

factors that are year-specific, such as the oil price shocks of the 1970s and 1980s and the years toward the end of the Cold War (1989–1991), that are expected to affect the trade of all countries.

The hypotheses that are tested in the analyses are focused on the qualitative changes in accession rules under the WTO, namely how the shift in emphasis from reducing tariffs and other "barriers at the border" to regulating "behind-the-border barriers" that require domestic reform for trade liberalization have affected trade among WTO members. The timing of membership that differentiates the three groups captures this shift and is a proxy for the changes in accession requirements, which have increased in their degree of stringency for prospective members under the WTO as they now often require extensive domestic reform as a precondition for membership. In terms of expected effects, if the shift in favor of regulating "behind-the-border barriers" has been more successful in boosting trade for those acquiring WTO membership, it would be the case that countries that accede later to the WTO will benefit the most from membership. Thus if WTO membership is associated positively with trade, then the estimates should be highest for the *Later Entrants,* followed by the *Early Adopters,* and finally the *Standing Members.* Similarly for trade between groups, higher gains in trade would be expected for *Standing Member & Later Entrant* pairs than for *Standing Member & Early Adopter* pairs.

In constructing the membership variables, the analysis uses four different classifications of membership that are found in the literature. There is some controversy over how membership should be defined, namely on the issue of de jure or de facto status in the GATT, which has yielded contradictory findings on the effects of the GATT and the WTO on international trade (Rose 2004, 2007; Tomz, Goldstein, and Rivers 2007). No such disagreement exists, however, on defining membership in the WTO, as it eliminated the option of de facto membership and required countries either to obtain formal membership or to lose their benefits.

The first classification employs the official GATT/WTO date of membership, with twenty-three Contracting Parties, or countries, as the founding members.[40] The second employs Rose's (2004) classification, which includes colonies paired with their colonizers as part of the GATT's founding member group.[41] It differs from the official GATT/WTO classification in that it identifies thirty-two "trading entities" as Contracting Parties to the original GATT of 1947. The additional de facto members were included among the founding members due to their "relationship with a founding

---

40. These membership dates were obtained from the WTO website: www.wto.org.
41. Data were obtained from Rose's website: http://faculty.haas.berkeley.edu/arose/.

member" (Rose 2004, 101). The first two classifications are substantially different from the latter two, which include a far larger set of countries in the *Standing Member* group.

The third classification is that found in Tomz, Goldstein and Rivers (2007) and Goldstein, Rivers, and Tomz (2007), among which the latter study argues that institutions such as the GATT extended rights and obligations broadly to nonmembers, creating "institutional *standing*" for current and former colonies of the Contracting Parties and some countries in the process of accession. Utilizing GATT archival material, they propose an alternative membership scheme that includes de facto members and provisional members in the process of accession. Finally, the classification in Gowa and Kim (2005) uses information from both Rose (2004) and an early working version of Tomz, Goldstein, and Rivers (2007) to construct its set of informal (colonial, de facto, and provisional) and formal members.[42] Gowa and Kim code informal members as GATT members as long as they are system members, that is, as of their year of independence. The roster of informal members identified in Gowa and Kim (2004), therefore, do not exactly replicate those in Tomz, Goldstein, and Rivers (2007) but overlap much more than the first two classifications. The appendix lists the countries according to the four classifications.

The analysis employs fixed effects regression analysis to examine changes in bilateral trade before and after the WTO's establishment. This is appropriate for two reasons. First, it accounts for heterogeneity among the units, thus controlling for unmeasured idiosyncratic features of a country-pair's relations that are not captured by more objective and generalizable factors such as economic size (Green, Kim, and Yoon 2001).[43] Second, the comparisons that the analysis seeks to make are longitudinal rather than cross-sectional. That is, the analysis focuses on the extent to which trade increases, decreases, or remains unaffected when countries enter the WTO era. It is less concerned with whether WTO members trade more with each other than with nonmembers, since by 1995 and certainly with the inclusion of more member countries, the vast majority of countries in the international system had already joined the regime.[44] This makes comparisons

42. The author is grateful to Mike Tomz for kindly providing membership data from Tomz, Goldstein, and Rivers (2007).

43. Other studies such as Anderson and van Wincoop (2003) utilize country (rather than dyad) fixed effects as a "multilateral resistance" term to capture individual country-level resistance factors such as transportation costs.

44. As of the end of 2004, as seen from the roster of accession applicants, nonmembers in the process of accession included thirty-one countries: Afghanistan, Algeria, Andorra, Azerbaijan, Bahamas, Belarus, Bhutan, Bosnia and Herzegovina, Cape Verde, Ethiopia, Iran,

between members and nonmembers less meaningful, so the use of fixed effects analysis is more appropriate to assess the longitudinal impact of WTO membership on trade within each dyad.[45]

Results

Table 4.1 reports the first set of results from analysis. The estimates on the group variables in interaction terms—*Standing Members, Early Adopters,* and *Later Entrants*—show the effect of the WTO on the trade of each group with all other members of the WTO in the remaining two groups.[46] The estimates are effects relative to the base group, that is, country pairs consisting of states that remain outside the WTO system (nonmember dyads) or are paired with WTO members (member and nonmember dyads). The columns represent the four different membership classifications: (1) official GATT/WTO membership; (2) Rose (2004); (3) Tomz, Goldstein, and Rivers (2007); and (4) Gowa and Kim (2005).

F-tests on all four classifications reject the null hypothesis that the estimates for the three groups are equal, indicating that the effects of the WTO on the trade of these groups are statistically distinguishable.[47] Among the three groups, estimates for *Later Entrants* are positive and statistically significant, while those for the other two groups vary according to definitions of membership. While all the effects on trade are positive, estimates for *Standing Members* are significant for the WTO and Rose classifications and *Early Adopters* for the Rose; Tomz, Goldstein, and Rivers; and Gowa and Kim classifications. The size of the group and which countries are included lead to differences in the magnitude of the estimates for *Early Adopters,*

Iraq, Kazakhstan, the Lao People's Democratic Republic, the Lebanese Republic, Libya, Montenegro, the Russian Federation, Samoa, São Tomé and Príncipe, Saudi Arabia, Serbia, Seychelles, Sudan, Tajikistan, Tonga, Ukraine, Uzbekistan, Vanuatu, Vietnam, and Yemen. Of these, Saudi Arabia acceded in 2005; Vietnam and Tonga in 2007; and Cape Verde and Ukraine in 2008. Equatorial Guinea submitted its application for accession in 2007.

45. The use of fixed effects analysis, however, precludes the inclusion of time-invariant variables, such as distance, land area, island status, landlocked status, contiguity, common language, and former colony, which are standard control variables in models of trade. Also excluded from the analysis are the dummy variables for the three member groups' main effects, since these also do not vary over time.

46. As the group dummy variables are time-invariant, the main effects for each of the groups become absorbed into the intercept and hence are not generated separately. Because the variable *WTO Years* does vary across time, turning from 0 to 1 in 1995, the analysis generates estimates for the groups in interaction terms.

47. The null hypothesis that is tested is: *Standing Members = Early Adopters = Later Entrants = 0.* For the classification using official GATT/WTO accession dates, $F(2, 12333) = 7.96$ ($p < 0.001$); using Rose's dates, $F(3, 12333) = 3.17$ ($p < 0.042$); using Tomz, Goldstein, and Rivers dates, $F(3, 12333) = 7.16$ ($p < 0.001$); and using Gowa and Kim dates, $F(2, 12333) = 9.07$ ($p < .000$).

Table 4.1. Effects of the WTO on trade by group

Dependent variable: bilateral trade	(1)	(2)	(3)	(4)
Membership classification:	WTO	Rose	TGR	Gowa and Kim
GDP	0.883**	0.873**	0.857**	0.856**
	(0.049)	(0.049)	(0.049)	(0.049)
GDP per capita	0.260**	0.270**	0.293**	0.295**
	(0.048)	(0.048)	(0.048)	(0.048)
Currency union	0.571**	0.571**	0.577**	0.577**
	(0.118)	(0.117)	(0.116)	(0.116)
PTA	0.197**	0.197**	0.199**	0.199**
	(0.028)	(0.028)	(0.027)	(0.027)
GSP	0.028	0.027	0.026	0.026
	(0.031)	(0.031)	(0.031)	(0.031)
Democracy	0.278**	0.273**	0.265**	0.261**
	(0.023)	(0.023)	(0.023)	(0.023)
Alliance	0.117*	0.116	0.116	0.115
	(0.060)	(0.060)	(0.060)	(0.060)
WTO Years	−1.644**	−1.632**	−1.600**	−1.601**
	(0.133)	(0.133)	(0.133)	(0.133)
Former colony × WTO Years	−0.497**	−0.496**	−0.490**	−0.490**
	(0.074)	(0.073)	(0.071)	(0.071)
Standing member × WTO Years	0.106**	0.097**	0.047	0.046
	(0.035)	(0.034)	(0.035)	(0.035)
Early adopters × WTO Years	0.005	0.082*	0.247**	0.286**
	(0.036)	(0.040)	(0.044)	(0.045)
Later entrants × WTO years	0.220**	0.226**	0.234**	0.235**
	(0.049)	(0.049)	(0.049)	(0.049)
Constant	−44.949**	−44.630**	−44.226**	−44.212**
	(1.723)	(1.724)	(1.721)	(1.719)
Observations	223610	223610	223610	223610
R-squared	0.88	0.88	0.88	0.88

Notes: Robust standard errors in parentheses; * significant at 5 percent; ** significant at 1 percent. Fixed effects regression analysis using *areg* in Stata 9.2. Year effects included but not reported.

with Rose's group, the largest with nineteen countries, having the smallest estimate, and the latter two, with fewer countries included—twelve in the Tomz, Goldstein, and Rivers group and fourteen in the Gowa and Kim group—but having larger estimates.

In terms of substantive effects, table 4.1a shows the percentage changes in trade under the WTO regime for the three groups.[48] Overall, these results support the main hypothesis, that changes in the qualitative dimensions of accession proceedings, which occurred with the advent of the WTO, have

48. Figures were calculated using the formula $\%\Delta y = 100*[exp(\beta\Delta x_i)-1]$ (Wooldridge 2006, 198). They indicate the percentage change in trade as a result of a one-unit change in x, that is, a shift from 0 to 1 in the group dummy variables.

Table 4.1a. Percentage changes in trade by group

Group/membership classification	WTO	Rose	TGR	Gowa and Kim
Standing members	11.18%**	10.19%**	4.81%	4.71%
Early adopters	.51%	8.55%*	28.02%**	33.11%**
Later entrants	24.61%**	25.36%**	26.36%**	26.49%**

Notes: * significant at 5 percent; ** significant at 1 percent.

led to benefits for newcomers to the regime in the form of higher trade. Within each of the four columns of membership classifications, the gains in trade with WTO members for *Later Entrants,* ranging from 24.61 percent to 26.3 percent, is much higher relative to those for *Standing Members,* which range from 4.71 percent to 11.18 percent. Trade between *Early Adopters* and other WTO members varies, chiefly between the WTO and Rose classifications and both the Tomz, Goldstein, and Rivers and Gowa and Kim classifications. What the results do show overall is support for the positive effects of changes in the accession process under the WTO regime. For the *Early Adopters* and the *Later Entrants,* there appears to be a "payoff," an expansion of trade, for those willing to submit their economies to the stringent, complex, and lengthy accession process of WTO membership. It would appear that accession requirements, as they have shifted in favor of reform of "behind-the-border regulations" to make them consistent with WTO principles, have been largely successful in boosting trade for the transition and developing countries joining the regime.

Results for the control variables in table 4.1 are consistent across the four definitions of membership and with findings in current studies. Estimates for *GDP* and *GDP per capita* are positive and statistically significant, demonstrating the importance of the size of the economy on trade flows. Country pairs sharing the same currency increase their trade by about 57 percent, and this result is statistically significant. Common membership in a preferential trade agreement also increases trade between two countries, by almost 20 percent. Country-pairs in which one country enjoys preferential treatment for its goods under the GSP system receive no statistically significant gain in trade. Among the political variables included in this analysis, democracy has a positive effect, increasing trade by 26 to 28 percent when both countries in a dyad are democracies. Common membership in a formal alliance, however, is inconclusive, as the results show a significant and positive effect under only one classification—the formal membership classification of the GATT/WTO.

Table 4.2 reports the regression estimates for the effect of WTO membership on trade within individual groups and between groups. By and large, both trade within and between groups experienced gains in the WTO era, as

Table 4.2. The effect of the WTO on trade within and between groups

Dependent variable: Bilateral trade	(1)	(2)	(3)	(4)
Membership classification:	WTO	Rose	TGR	Gowa and Kim
GDP	0.886**	0.873**	0.857**	0.856**
	(0.049)	(0.049)	(0.049)	(0.049)
GDP per capita	0.256**	0.269**	0.292**	0.294**
	(0.048)	(0.048)	(0.048)	(0.048)
Currency Union	0.571**	0.571**	0.574**	0.575**
	(0.118)	(0.117)	(0.117)	(0.117)
PTA	0.197**	0.196**	0.197**	0.197**
	(0.028)	(0.028)	(0.028)	(0.028)
GSP	0.028	0.027	0.027	0.027
	(0.031)	(0.031)	(0.031)	(0.031)
Democracy	0.277**	0.274**	0.263**	0.258**
	(0.023)	(0.023)	(0.023)	(0.023)
Alliance	0.117*	0.116	0.117	0.116
	(0.060)	(0.060)	(0.060)	(0.060)
WTO Years	−1.659**	−1.634**	−1.617**	−1.619**
	(0.133)	(0.133)	(0.133)	(0.133)
Former colony ×	−0.499**	−0.497**	−0.490**	−0.490**
WTO Years	(0.074)	(0.073)	(0.071)	(0.071)
Standing members ×	0.128**	0.104**	0.077*	0.075*
WTO years	(0.038)	(0.038)	(0.037)	(0.037)
Early adopters ×	−0.010	0.106	0.618**	0.653**
WTO years	(0.130)	(0.168)	(0.127)	(0.140)
Later entrants ×	0.476*	0.478*	0.478*	0.479*
WTO years	(0.242)	(0.242)	(0.242)	(0.242)
Standing members &	0.114*	0.169**	0.281**	0.317**
early adopters × WTO years	(0.046)	(0.050)	(0.054)	(0.055)
Standing members &	0.301**	0.296**	0.280**	0.276**
later entrants × WTO years	(0.059)	(0.059)	(0.058)	(0.058)
Early adopters &	0.357**	0.409**	0.577**	0.658**
later entrants × WTO years	(0.132)	(0.141)	(0.153)	(0.158)
Constant	−45.016**	−44.626**	−44.199**	−44.194**
	(1.722)	(1.724)	(1.720)	(1.718)
Observations	223610	223610	223610	223610
R-squared	0.88	0.88	0.88	0.88

Notes: Robust standard errors in parentheses; * significant at 5 percent; **significant at 1 percent. Fixed effects regression analysis using *areg* in Stata 9.2. Year effects included but not reported.

the estimates are generally positive and statistically significant. There are two exceptions to this pattern: the estimates for *Early Adopters* is negative under the official WTO classification and positive under the Rose classification. However, neither estimate is statistically significant, and under the other two classifications—Tomz, Goldstein, and Rivers and Gowa and Kim—the estimate for *Early Adopters* is actually positive and statistically significant.

Table 4.2a presents the substantive results, again in terms of percentage changes in trade under the WTO regime. Relative to the base group,

Table 4.2a. Percentage changes in trade: Within and between groups

Group/membership classification	WTO	Rose	TGR	Gowa and Kim
Standing members	13.66%**	10.96%**	8.00%*	7.79%*
Early adopters	–1.00%	11.18%	85.52%**	92.13%**
Later entrants	60.96%*	61.28%*	61.28%*	61.45%*
Standing members & early adopters	12.08%*	16.07%**	32.45%**	37.30%**
Standing members & later entrants	35.12%**	34.45%**	32.31%**	31.78%**
Early adopters & later entrants	42.90%**	50.53%**	78.07%**	93.09%**

Notes: * significant at 5 percent; ** significant at 1 percent.

it is the latecomers to the regime that have experienced the largest gains in trade. Across all four classifications but with the two exceptions noted above, *Early Adopters* and *Later Entrants* experience higher levels of trade among members of the same group, as compared with *Standing Members.* Trade between countries that are *Early Adopters* increased by over 85 percent under the Tomz, Goldstein, and Rivers classification, and over 90 percent under the Gowa and Kim classification. Trade between *Later Entrants* increased by over 60 percent in all four classifications. In terms of trade between groups as well, the largest increases in trade are again seen for the latecomers, or pairs consisting of *Early Adopters* and *Later Entrants:* their trade increases by anywhere from 42.90 percent under the WTO classification to 93.09 percent under the Gowa and Kim classification. These increases in trade are substantially higher than for the trade between *Standing Members* and each of the other latecomer groups. Trade amongst *Standing Member & Early Adopter* pairs range from 12.08 percent to 37.30 percent, and between *Standing Member & Later Entrant* pairs from 31.78 percent to 35.12 percent. These figures are statistically significant and show that membership in the WTO has had a varied but positive impact on trade creation. This is especially the case for newcomers to the regime.

Persistence of a Distributive Divide

Table 4.3 presents the results of extending the analysis, in keeping with the arguments and findings presented in the previous chapter on the effects of the GATT, to examine the effects of the WTO regime on trade between industrialized and nonindustrialized countries.[49] The purpose of this

49. The list of industrial countries remains the same as in chapter 3 and includes the following twenty-one countries: Australia, Austria, Canada, Denmark, Finland, France, Germany, Greece, Iceland, Ireland, Italy, Japan, Netherlands, New Zealand, Norway, Portugal, Spain,

analysis is to examine closely the effect of the WTO on the trade between industrial countries, all of them *Standing Members,* and the latecomers to the regime. The estimates in table 4.3 show the effect of the WTO regime on the three groups but also where they are further disaggregated according to their level of development. The estimates show the effect of the WTO regime on (1) trade in industrial-country dyads among the *Standing Members;* (2) trade between industrial-country *Standing Members* and each of the latecomer groups, that is, industrial country *Standing Members* paired with *Early Adopters* and *Later Entrants;* and (3) trade in the remaining groups consisting largely of nonindustrial-country dyads.[50]

The estimates for industrial-country standing members are positive and statistically significant across all four membership classifications and show that trade in this subgroup of *Standing Members* has increased since the establishment of the WTO. The estimates for the mixed dyads consisting of industrial and nonindustrial countries are negative and statistically significant, in particular for *Standing Member & Early Adopter* pairs, indicating that their trade has actually decreased under the regime. Finally, the estimates for nonindustrial-country pairs are positive and statistically significant for *Early Adopters* and *Later Entrants* across all four membership classifications and positive and statistically significant for *Standing Members* under the WTO and Rose classifications.

The array of results suggests a varied and interesting set of effects for the WTO regime on trade between the industrialized countries of the North and the nonindustrialized, developing countries of the South. Table 4.3a presents the percentage changes in trade. The industrial countries have generally fared well under the WTO regime, as their trade has increased by at least 12.75 percent under the WTO classification to over 19 percent under the Gowa and Kim classification. In contrast, trade between the developed and developing worlds, represented by the effects for industrialized and nonindustrialized country pairs, has decreased substantially since 1995, by 37.37 percent under the WTO classification to over 46 percent under the Gowa and Kim classification for dyads consisting of industrial country *Standing Members* and nonindustrial country *Early Adopters.* Trade between industrial country *Standing Members* and nonindustrial country *Later Entrants* has also decreased, though the results are not statistically significant across

---

Sweden, Switzerland, the United Kingdom, and the United States. The analysis in this chapter also includes in this group Belgium and Luxembourg, which the IMF categorizes separately beginning in 1997.

50. Those among the *Standing Members* include both mixed pairs of industrial and nonindustrial countries as well as nonindustrial country pairs.

Table 4.3. Effects of the WTO on trade: Industrial and nonindustrial country pairs

Dependent variable: Bilateral trade	(1)	(2)	(3)	(4)
Membership classification	WTO	Rose	TGR	Gowa and Kim
GDP	0.864**	0.866**	0.861**	0.861**
	(0.051)	(0.051)	(0.051)	(0.051)
GDP per capita	0.274**	0.274**	0.287**	0.288**
	(0.049)	(0.050)	(0.050)	(0.049)
Currency union	0.530**	0.529**	0.535**	0.535**
	(0.121)	(0.121)	(0.119)	(0.119)
PTA	0.193**	0.188**	0.192**	0.189**
	(0.027)	(0.028)	(0.027)	(0.027)
GSP	0.042	0.046	0.049	0.049
	(0.031)	(0.031)	(0.031)	(0.031)
Democracy	0.277**	0.276**	0.272**	0.267**
	(0.023)	(0.023)	(0.023)	(0.023)
Alliance	0.120*	0.121*	0.125*	0.125*
	(0.059)	(0.059)	(0.059)	(0.059)
WTO years	−1.629**	−1.636**	−1.624**	−1.624**
	(0.136)	(0.136)	(0.136)	(0.136)
	−0.438**	−0.447**	−0.453**	−0.454**
Former colony × WTO years	(0.078)	(0.078)	(0.076)	(0.076)
Industrial countries:				
Standing members × WTO years	0.120**	0.138**	0.173**	0.174**
	(0.044)	(0.043)	(0.043)	(0.043)
Industrial and nonindustrial countries:				
Standing members & early adopters × WTO years	−0.468**	−0.541**	−0.554**	−0.617**
	(0.060)	(0.068)	(0.075)	(0.078)
Standing members & later entrants × WTO years	−0.225**	−0.197*	−0.164	−0.160
	(0.086)	(0.087)	(0.086)	(0.086)
Nonindustrial countries:				
Standing members × WTO years	0.132**	0.116**	0.053	0.052
	(0.036)	(0.035)	(0.035)	(0.035)
Early adopters × WTO years	0.172**	0.266**	0.418**	0.483**
	(0.046)	(0.050)	(0.054)	(0.055)
Later entrants × WTO years	0.267**	0.256**	0.261**	0.260**
	(0.063)	(0.065)	(0.065)	(0.065)
Constant	−44.277**	−44.352**	−44.335**	−44.335**
	(1.779)	(1.781)	(1.778)	(1.775)
Observations	223610	223610	223610	223610
R-squared	0.88	0.88	0.88	0.88

Notes: Robust standard errors in parentheses; * significant at 5 percent; ** significant at 1 percent. Fixed effects regression analysis using *areg* in Stata 9.2. Year effects included but not reported.

Table 4.3a. Percentage changes in trade: Industrial and nonindustrial countries

Group/membership classification	WTO	Rose	TGR	Gowa and Kim
Industrial countries:				
Standing members	12.75%**	14.80%**	18.89%**	19.01%**
Industrial and nonindustrial countries:				
Standing members & early adopters	−37.37%**	−41.78%**	−42.54%**	−46.04%**
Standing members & later entrants	−20.15%**	−17.88%*	−15.13%	−14.79%
Nonindustrial countries:				
Standing members	14.11%**	12.30%**	5.44%	5.34%
Early adopters	18.77%**	30.47%**	51.89%**	62.09%**
Later entrants	30.60%**	29.18%**	29.82%**	29.69%**

Notes: * significant at 5 percent; ** significant at 1 percent.

all membership classifications, and the magnitude of the effects is more moderate in comparison. Trade for these pairs, among the statistically significant results, decreased by 17.88 percent under the Rose classification to 20.15 percent under the WTO classification.

Finally, for the nonindustrialized countries of the developing world, the effect of the WTO regime has generally been a positive one for the latecomers, as they have experienced substantial increases in trade. For the *Early Adopters,* their trade with other nonindustrialized countries in the other member groups increased by at least 18.77 percent to a high of over 62 percent. *Later Entrants* saw more moderate but still significant increases, as their trade with other nonindustrial countries increased by 29 to 30 percent. The results for the *Standing Members* is less dramatic and less conclusive as well, as under the Tomz, Goldstein, and Rivers and the Gowa and Kim classification this group's trade has been largely unaffected by the WTO regime. Where the results are statistically significant, *Standing Members* have been the least affected of the three groups, registering gains of 14.11 percent to 12.30 percent for the WTO and Rose classifications, respectively.

The results overall speak to the persistence of a distributive divide in terms of the gains in trade achieved through membership in the WTO, one that markedly divides the industrialized countries of the North from the developing countries in the South. In terms of the patterns of trade produced under the regime, trade among industrialized countries has increased under the regime, as has trade among nonindustrialized countries. However, this is greatly offset by the substantial depression in trade between industrialized and nonindustrialized countries. These findings strongly suggest that while the WTO regime has been successful in boosting trade within the developed North and the developing South, it has been largely unsuccessful in promoting trade between the two groups, which is the stated objective of the Doha Development Round, the currently stalled trade negotiations under the WTO. While the success or failure of the Doha Round remains to be seen, as it is still in process, the results of this analysis at the very least show strong support for the need for trade negotiations explicitly designed to redress imbalances in global trade, in particular to address the decreasing trade between industrial and nonindustrial countries.

Conclusion

The analysis in this chapter examined the effects of the World Trade Organization (WTO) on trade among its members in its first decade of existence, in the 1995–2004 period. The analysis focuses on a key variable: the terms of accession. The chapter examines how trade among WTO members was affected by the regime's accession rules and the timing of members' entry into the WTO. The theoretical framework distinguishes between "standing members," or those who were members of the GATT as well as the WTO, the "early adopters," those who entered the regime during the Uruguay Round or in the first year of the WTO's creation, and the "later entrants" who gained membership via the lengthy and complex accession process after 1995. The empirical analysis evaluates how WTO member trade has fared under the regime, both among members of the same group and between members of different groups. The analysis assesses the effect of the WTO on trade creation, or the degree to which trade expanded after states entered into the regime. The results of the analysis show positive but divergent effects among the groups, suggesting that old and new members of the WTO have benefited in different ways from participation in the regime. They also indicate that there may be strong distributive consequences of membership in the WTO, as the effect on trade varies between mixed pairs of industrialized and nonindustrialized countries. Most important, the WTO has been largely unsuccessful in boosting trade between industrial and nonindustrial countries, suggesting the importance of the Doha Round as a way to redress this imbalance.

Conclusion

"Globalization has reached a turning point. The future is a contested terrain
of very public choices that will shape the world economy of the 21st century."
Mazur (2000)

As of this writing, we remain in the era of the "Doha Deadlock," with the
fate of the Doha Round of trade negotiations under the WTO uncertain, if
not dire. In July 2008, trade talks collapsed once again at the end of an in-
tense nine-day meeting of the 153-member global trade governance body.
The latest breakdown in the Doha Round negotiations follows a similar
breakdown in talks two years earlier, in July 2006, when another "time out"
was called, this time by Pascal Lamy, director-general of the WTO. In the
July 2008 talks, aside from the usual tussle over tariff rates and market access for sensitive sectors, the failure of the talks resulted directly from the
disagreement of the United States and two emerging economies—China
and India.

The major issue of contention among the three countries, and ultimately
the one issue of disagreement that led to the collapse of the talks, was that
of "special safeguard mechanisms," what Director-General Lamy referred
to as item 18 of the twenty-item "to-do" list for the meeting's participants.[1]
Specifically, these safeguards would provide an insurance policy of sorts for

---

1. David Loyn. Trade Talks' Failure Ends Doha Dreams. BBC News. Available at http://
news.bbc.co.uk/2/hi/business/7532168.stm, accessed 12 December 2008. Though the issue
of special safeguard mechanisms led directly to the breakdown of the talks, they also produced no agreement on reducing the European Union's tariffs on banana exports from Latin
American countries, which are currently charged import duties, while those from the ACP
(African, Caribbean and Pacific) countries enter the EU market duty free. Nor did the talks
even address the concerns of African countries regarding U.S. subsidies for cotton. Indeed,

difficult economic times, especially for developing countries. These safeguards would include import rules that would allow developing countries to protect their agricultural markets by imposing tariffs on certain goods in the event of a drop in prices or a surge in imports. The disagreement was over the threshold for such a contingency, with the United States arguing that the "safeguard clause" for protecting developing countries' agricultural imports set an excessively low threshold for imposing tariffs.

This collapse of the Doha Round trade talks was lamented as a "collective failure" and "heartbreaking" by the EU Trade Commissioner Peter Mandelsohn.[2] China, one of the two key opponents of the United States during the talk, noted that the breakdown of negotiations was a "serious setback" for the world economy, but it blamed the "selfish and shortsighted behavior" of the world's wealthy nations and cited the unwillingness of the United States and Europe to remove their agricultural subsidies as the real reason for the failure of the talks.[3] Acrimonious exchanges took place among the three major actors in the negotiations—the United States, India, and China—with the U.S. Trade Representative Susan Schwab accusing the others of "blatant protectionism" that provided excessive protection for farmers and failed to open markets.[4] In spite of the efforts of Director-General Pascal Lamy to forge a consensus among the major economies to restart the talks, as recently as December 2008, the WTO announced that following intensive and extensive consultations with the United States, the EU, India, China, and Brazil, no consensus emerged to call for new ministerial talks under the Doha Round banner.[5]

The July 2008 meeting of member countries was the latest installment in the negotiations under the banner of the Doha Round. Following its launch in Doha, Qatar, in 2001, ministerial-level meetings were held in Cancún (2003), Geneva (2004), Hong Kong (2005), and again in Geneva (2006). The Cancún talks collapsed in four days as delegates failed to reach agreement on agricultural subsidies and market access. A general agreement among key economies—the United States, the EU, Japan, and Brazil—to

---

this report notes that by the end of the nine-day meeting, the African countries were not even represented in the core negotiating group.

2. BBC News. World Trade Talks End in Collapse.
Available at http://news.bbc.co.uk/2/hi/business/7531099.stm, accessed 12 December 2008.

3. BBC News. Dismay at Collapse of Trade Talks. Available at http://news.bbc.co.uk/2/hi/business/7532302.stm, accessed 12 December 2008.

4. BBC News. World Trade Talks End in Collapse. Op. cit.

5. BBC News. WTO Abandons Plans for Trade Talks. Available at http://news.bbc.co.uk/2/hi/business/7779748.stm, accessed 17 October 2009.

reduce export subsidies, even if no specific agreement was concluded, was the major achievement in Geneva in 2004. The Hong Kong Ministerial Conference produced an agreement to end agricultural subsidies by 2013 and gave rise to renewed efforts to conclude the Doha Round by its four-year deadline, set for December 2006, six months before the U.S. president's trade-promotion authority was set to expire. Even with an extension of this deadline, the Doha Round talks collapsed once again in Geneva in July 2006, when member countries once more failed to come to agreement on agricultural subsidies, leading to the suspension of the negotiations.

Hopes did rise at the Davos meeting of the World Economic Forum in Switzerland in January 2007. At this gathering of the world's top business leaders, political figures, intellectuals, and journalists, which provided another forum for leading figures to come together, Lamy declared that the key economies were ready to resume the Doha Round negotiations. At the end of June 2007, leaders of four key member countries—the United States, the EU, India, and Brazil—met in Potsdam to reopen talks among themselves in the hopes of reaching an agreement. They had hoped to revive the Doha Round negotiations and, more important, to reach an agreement that would signal progress for the trade talks, just before the U.S. president's trade-promotion authority was set to expire. Also known as fast-track trade negotiating authority, trade-promotion authority expedites the approval process of trade agreements negotiated by the president. It allows U.S. presidents to negotiate trade agreements that can be submitted to Congress for approval, without being subject to amendments or filibuster and within a mandatory deadline. However, once again these leading economies were unable to resolve their longstanding differences over agriculture and farming subsidies. The meeting ended without success, and the U.S. president's trade-promotion authority subsequently expired, on 30 June 2007. Any WTO agreement that could be produced from this Doha Round, however unlikely, now faces greater hurdles as it is now subject to greater legislative oversight in its leading economy—the United States.

Protests against the WTO have become a familiar sight at these meetings as well, and opponents of the trade regime continue unabated in their criticisms, invariably greeting the collapse of the talks with cheers and claiming another victory for the developing world. The Cancún meeting in 2003, in particular, was marred by a suicide on its very first day. Just outside the building where the talks were being held, a 56-year-old rice farmer and former president of the Korean Advance Farmers Federation, wearing a sign emblazoned with the statement "The WTO kills farmers," stabbed himself in the chest and later died in the hospital. In a handout he left behind, he protested the subsidies on agricultural goods from the United States and the EU and described his efforts to organize opposition to economic forces that had become "waves that destroyed our lovely rural communities" (Isaak 2005, 184). The Ministerial Meeting in Hong Kong was marked also by large protests, though on a smaller scale than those seen in Seattle some years before.

The focus of this book has been on the effect of the global trade regime—the GATT and the WTO—on international trade. In this book, it is the critics who have taken center stage, as the analysis offers an assessment of the institutional and empirical bases of their claims against the regime. It takes on the major criticism that is at the heart of the "anti-globalization" movement, namely whether the global trading system is geared toward the rich and powerful to the detriment of the rest of the global economy and especially the developing world. It does so with an investigation into the origins, the evolution, and the consequences of the regime, privileging the explanatory role and theoretical importance of two key variables: power and time. These variables provide important insights into why global trade governance looks the way it does, how the rules of trade embodied in the regime have remained so resilient over the years, and what the impact of these rules on the evolution of the global trading system has been. In doing so, this book's broader theoretical focus is on the distributive consequences of institutional formation, that is, how the construction of global governance mechanisms, in spite of resolving collective action problems among actors, leads to inequalities in the benefits they confer among a regime's participants. The arguments developed in this book thus provide important linkages between the criticisms that have found such favor among opponents of the global trade regime and the distributional issues of institutional design, institutional evolution, and institutional effects.

In contributing to the existing scholarship on the GATT, and on power and institutions more broadly, this book has employed a combination of analytical tools to bridge, and perhaps to synthesize, realist and neoliberal perspectives on the role of international institutions. This is particularly demonstrated in the emphasis on the combination of power and identity that informs the analysis of the GATT's creation under U.S. leadership. It may arguably be labeled as analytical eclecticism; nevertheless, the exercise suggests just how the advances in scholarship can provide the conceptual and analytical tools to consider the questions of power and governance of the international economy in this post–Cold War globalization era.

The findings of this book offer two main responses to the critics of the regime who have provided the "inspiration" for this project. First, the results of the analyses corroborate one of the core findings of this book, that the trade-creating benefits of the GATT and the WTO have indeed been skewed disproportionately in favor of major powers and industrialized countries. Those in the "anti-globalization" camp, synonymous in this case with the opponents of GATT and the WTO, are correct to a certain extent insofar as this institution to promote liberal trade was and remains the main negotiating forum of rich countries, who also happen to be the principal suppliers that form the key negotiating parties of the GATT and the WTO. However, this is less a product of collusion and conspiracy than the outcome of great power politics and the domestic constraints borne by the dominant actor, the United States. The dynamics of great power politics and the particular imprint of U.S. leadership, shaping the initial "rules of the game" in GATT, became over the years embedded and also reinforced in this institution for the governance of the global trading order. Once these factors are taken into account, it is not surprising to find that the distribution of GATT benefits in terms of increased market access has been uneven at best. Indeed, the original institutional design was purposeful and, in significant ways, successful.

Second, as a consequence of the first, there is little question as to the existence of a distributive divide that has resulted from the global trade regime. One may speak of a developmental divide, but this book emphasizes as well the existence, and persistence, of a distributive divide that is a direct product of the design and evolution of the global trade regime. This distributive divide highlights the inequalities in the benefits of trade expansion received from membership in the trade regime. The GATT in particular, due to the power relations that determined its institutional arrangements, led to a distributive divide in which much of the benefits of the trade regime—trade expansion—went to the major powers and leading economies, thus largely leaving out the rest of the participants. In terms of its actual impact on global trade, the WTO as well has been less than successful in promoting trade between the industrialized countries of the North and the developing countries of the South. Indeed, the analysis finds that trade between these two "worlds" has decreased in the WTO era. As the leading economies continue to jostle over agricultural subsidies and market access for industrial goods, the findings of this book further emphasize the importance of the Doha Round in acknowledging the need for trade negotiations explicitly designed to promote trade between the industrial and nonindustrial countries.

Rules and Consequences: Summary of Findings

The arguments and analyses in this book have been developed broadly under the themes of "Rules" and "Consequences," and this section provides a summary of the main findings. Each of the two main parts of this book has focused on a distinct aspect of the story about the GATT and WTO, emphasizing, respectively, the origins and evolution of the GATT/WTO and their impact on international commerce. The first part of the book provided a qualitative analysis of the formation and evolution of the GATT. It advanced arguments on power, especially in the forms of U.S. leadership and great power politics, and how it influenced the construction of the rules of the GATT and contributed to their persistence over time. In chapter 1, the theoretical framework explicitly problematized power as an explanatory factor in institutional design outcomes. It argued that *who designs* is a key issue in institutional design. In the GATT, the institutional preferences of the principal architect, the United States, and how these preferences produced cooperation problems with other leading actors, determined the regime's institutional arrangements. Negotiations at the formation of the GATT produced the power-based bargaining protocol that is the hallmark of trade negotiations under the GATT and as well the WTO, namely bilateral negotiations on a product-by-product basis among principal suppliers.

Chapter 2, continuing the analysis of the "Rules," devoted its attention to the second key variable in this book, that is, on the role of time. In addressing the question of why the GATT changed so little over time, in spite of the large influx of new members from the developing world and the repeated calls for reform, the analysis brought greater attention to the way the institutional arrangements put in place by the powerful nations became entrenched and resistant to change. The chapter identified the major sources of institutional resilience in the global trade regime across the rounds of multilateral trade negotiations, ending with the Uruguay Round and the formation of the World Trade Organization (WTO). The analysis traced the resilience of two power-related institutional features: centralization, in particular the concentration of bargaining power brought about by the principal supplier rule; and flexibility, namely the set of exceptions for agriculture and for free trade areas and customs unions installed at the insistence of the United States.

Part 2, on "Consequences," examined the impact of the rules of trade, namely how trade among countries was affected by membership in the regime. The central findings of the analyses from these chapters are that the major powers and the leading economies were the ones to experience the greatest gains in trade, and even with the advent of the WTO, there has been little change in the distributive divide, and trade between industrial and developing countries continues to remain an important problem to be addressed in the current Doha Round. Chapter 3, coauthored with Joanne Gowa, engages the emerging body of literature on the "benefits of membership" in the global trade regime. It argues that U.S. strategy in the GATT negotiations, influenced by a combination of Cold War imperatives and domestic constraints, led to a highly skewed distribution of benefits from the regime. Quantitative analyses using bilateral data show that the GATT had a strong and significant positive impact on the trade of only a small set of states, namely Canada, France, Germany, the United Kingdom, and the United States. At the same time, it left the discriminatory trade blocs of the interwar era, which the United States had hoped to dismantle, largely intact.

Chapter 4 extended the analysis to examine the effects of the WTO on trade between 1994 and 2004. The central argument of the chapter is that the conditions of membership, coinciding with the timing of membership, matters in the WTO's trade-creation effects. The new conditions of membership characterizing the WTO's accession process reflects the qualitative changes in accession rules that now emphasize reform in "behind-the-border" regulations for prospective members, making it a key variable to explain the effects on trade. Based on the timing of membership, the analytical framework distinguishes between "standing members," those who became WTO members automatically as GATT members; the "early adopters," who joined the GATT during the Uruguay Round and subsequently became WTO members; and the "later entrants" who gained WTO membership after 1995 through a significantly more lengthy and complex process. The results of the quantitative analysis show that these three groups have benefited to varying degrees under the WTO and, perhaps more important, that the regime has been largely ineffective in boosting trade between industrial countries and the developing world. In this connection, the Doha Round becomes all the more important as an effort to redress this imbalance in global trade.

Power, Institutions, and International Trade in the Twenty-First Century

The findings of this book on the effects of the GATT/WTO system on international trade have important implications for broader issues of governance in the globalization era. The current era of the "Doha Deadlock" may well be regarded as a "crisis" of sorts (Wilkinson 2006) for the global trading system, yet it may represent as well a fork in the road as to the direction of global trade governance in the twenty-first century. It is a direction that will be greatly determined by how the world's trading nations, and especially the leading actors among them, will deal with the institutional and great power legacies that have accompanied us into this new century. This post–Cold War era has been one marked by the tragedy of the terrorist attacks of 11 September 2001, and the emerging threat of global pandemics and climate change, and yet the existing network of institutions for global governance is largely the product of a vastly different era. This raises questions as to the viability of these institutions, embedded and entrenched as they are in the Cold War politics that first produced them, and whether these "old" power relations have given way to new ones that call, accordingly, for reform of the institutional landscape. As one of the earliest post–Cold War institutions to promote cooperation among countries in the conduct of trade, the WTO's success—or its failure in promoting liberal trade and expanding commercial ties among countries—carries important implications, highlighting in particular the tensions that exist between economic efficiency and economic justice (Kapstein 2006).

Retreat or Reform?

The existing scholarship in international relations suggests two main directions for the future of global trade governance. One is to retreat from the multilateral trading system as we know it, and instead supplant it with a complex network of bilateral and regional trading arrangements. As much as the WTO represented one of the "clearest" examples of institutional binding on the part of the leading economy—the United States (Ikenberry 2001), the latest suspension of talks and the expiration of the U.S. executive's trade-promotion authority have been attended by a long-term "proliferation" of preferential trade agreements in the post–Cold War era (Mansfield 1998). Many have suggested that the collapse of the Doha Round talks may well signal the end of the multilateral trading system and that global trade governance may devolve into bilateral and other forms of limited trade agreements in which countries focus on individual trade concerns at the expense of a liberal trading system. The repeated failure of the talks and the lack of progress since 2001 over key issues such as farm subsidies and the liberalization of trade in services, especially in banking and telecommunications, have undermined the credibility of the multilateral trade governance body and have led to more movement toward bilateral and regional trade agreements.

The failure of talks under the Doha Round banner has led member countries to declare variously their intention to pursue bilateral agreements, such as the statement from Indian Trade Minister Kamal Nath in July 2006, when the "time out" was called, on his country's intention to pursue separate agreements with the EU and Japan.[6] Indeed, scholars such as Mansfield

---

6. BBC News. In Quotes: The Doha Deadlock. Available at http://news.bbc.co.uk/2/hi/business/5216080.stm, accessed 16 September 2007.

and Milner (1999) have pointed out that an important factor that explains why countries form preferential trade agreements (PTAs) is the lack of success in the multilateral forum of trade negotiations.

Regional and bilateral trading arrangements in the form of PTAs may well signal retreat from the multilateral trading system under the GATT and the WTO. The world now is also increasingly marked by trading blocs, raising concerns that trade is no longer multilaterally oriented but rather regionally or even bilaterally oriented. Arguments for their proposed benefits, whether in security dividends (Mansfield and Pevehouse 2000) or reductions in trade volatility (Mansfield and Reinhardt 2008), have relied almost exclusively on trade-creation effects. However, PTAs may well produce trade-diversion effects (Viner 1950), in which the political and economic benefits of participation in a PTA are offset by the costs of diversion, or reduction, of trade with nonmembers. To the extent that PTAs have strong trade-diversion effects and states are increasingly turning toward such arrangements, the aggregate effect on the global trading system may well be less liberalization in trade, more volatility, and more protectionism (Foroutan 1998). Moreover, the move by the United States in recent years toward preferential trading agreements such as the controversial Central American Free Trade Agreement (CAFTA), has led to warnings that the global trading system may indeed be headed (back) toward discriminatory trading arrangements—and that the U.S. strategic position is likely to be significantly weakened by such a trend (Gordon 2003). As noted earlier, some 380 regional trading agreements (RTAs) have been notified to the WTO as of July 2007, of which 205 are currently in force.[7] The changing landscape of trading arrangements raises important questions as to the extent to which governance of international trade is likely to devolve to these bilateral and regional institutional mechanisms and what impact they will have on the ability of the WTO to continue to govern trade.

The second option is one of reform, but one that entails a radical overhaul of the normative foundations of global governance and calls for a different fundamental bargain among the world's economies. Though this is the prime arena of contestation in which the "antiglobalization" movement and the opponents of the WTO stake their claims and calls for change, the issue of reform of the global trade regime reflects the emergence of important questions regarding power and institutional design in the twenty-first century. One of these is whether the great power politics that drove the GATT's original bargain still holds sway; another is the extent to which the imprint of U.S. leadership in the GATT and later the WTO still carries

---

7. Available at www.wto.org/english/tratop_e/region_e/region_e.htm, accessed 18 October 2007.

weight in this era of globalization. Such questions become all the more pressing given emerging claims of a "tectonic shift" in power relations from figures such as James Wolfensohn, former president of the World Bank.[8] Wolfensohn stated that "economic power is moving eastward" and away from the leading economies, the United States and Europe, and that there is greater need to acknowledge the role of countries such as China and to address social problems in these countries, where high growth has occurred at the expense of poor labor conditions. Indeed, at its extreme, the opponents of the WTO are demanding a fundamental reassessment of the capitalist underpinnings of the current liberal order, a position that has been extensively criticized as "misapprehensions" of the antiglobalization camp (Bhagwati 2002). Nevertheless, those who argue for reform of the global trading system have injected into the debate calls for equity and social justice (Stiglitz and Charlton 2005) and economic justice extending the domestic social compact to the international society (Kapstein 2006).

Leadership in the Twenty-First Century

Whether the Doha Round proceeds to a successful conclusion, and whether the choice is retreat from the multilateralism of the GATT/WTO and the global trading system as we know it or the reorganization of global trade governance under fundamentally different normative foundations that combine the market with some form of distributive justice, the question of leadership, that is, who leads and how that leadership is to be exercised, may well be one of the most pressing questions of our time. While the realist perspective instructs us on the importance of the distribution of power and the neoliberal institutional perspective on how institutions produce cooperation among those that would otherwise not participate, greater attention to the identity and attributes of the powerful actors in the current global arena, as argued in this book, shed light on *how* governance of the global economy, including the successful conclusion of the Doha Round, will likely evolve under their leadership and whether the path will be marked by cooperation or conflict between them.

In this connection, the breakdown of the Doha Round talks in July 2008 strongly reflect an emerging new architecture of power politics in the international economy, in which, at least in the context of the WTO, emergent powers Brazil, India, and China were pitted against the United States. Moreover, while the "go-it-alone" power of the United States dominated the construction of the GATT and other post–World War II institutions, in this

---

8. BBC News. Rich Nations 'Ignore' Power Shift. Available at http://news.bbc.co.uk/2/hi/business/7006172.stm, accessed 26 September 2007.

era of the "Doha Deadlock" many countries, noting the inequalities that the current regime has produced, have begun to advance the position that "no deal is better than a bad deal."[9] Indeed, the breakdown of the latest talks and the dim prospects of concluding the Doha Round are due in great part to this emerging position of the developing countries, now with a stronger voice thanks to rising powers such as Brazil, India, and China and their ability to influence the outcome of multilateral trade negotiations. While scholars continue to debate the status of the United States as an "empire" and examine the features of its hegemony (Lake 2008), others have noted the passing of the unipolar moment of the post–Cold War era, as the formerly undisputed leadership of the United States has given way to the realities of the U.S. financial crisis and perhaps the emergence of the G-20 as the new "enacting coalition" (Gruber 2000) of the twenty-first century.[10]

The membership of the G-20 includes Argentina, Australia, Brazil, Canada, China, France, Germany, India, Indonesia, Italy, Japan, Mexico, Russia, Saudi Arabia, South Africa, South Korea, Turkey, the United Kingdom, the United States, and the European Union. They comprise the world's most powerful countries and representing 85 percent of the global economy, are very much indicative of which countries hold sway in the current international political arena. As the leaders of these economies gathered in Washington, D.C., in November 2008 to deliberate on the reform of international financial institutions such as the International Monetary Fund, the question of "who designs?" is ever more pressing, as we consider the participation of the newly powerful BRIC countries—Brazil, Russia, India, and China—who will likely have a hand in the reform or construction of governance mechanisms in the international financial system. Though the summit produced no substantive plans for restructuring the international financial system, the meeting was notable for "who was there" and the symbolism afforded by the participation of newly powerful developing countries such as the BRIC group as well as Saudi Arabia.[11] Thus, in the governance of the international economy, we may well observe the first of the institutional initiatives in the financial sector, as a result of resolving cooperation problems among this disparate set of leading actors, with significant implications for how these leading actors will now shape the evolution of the WTO and global trade governance more broadly.

9. David Loyn. Op. cit.

10. On the "American Empire," see 2008 forum in International Studies Perspectives 9, no. 3.

11. Andrew Walker. Summit Shows Times Have Changed. BBC News. Available at http://news.bbc.co.uk/2/hi/business/7731889.stm, accessed 17 October 2009.

This book, on "Power and the Governance of Global Trade," has focused on the impact of the GATT and WTO regime, the premier governance mechanism for international trade, on the formation and evolution of the global trading system. It has assessed the institutional and empirical bases of criticisms against it, directing its analyses to the rules of the institution and its consequences for international commerce. The findings indicate the persistence of a distributive divide for the regime's participants, leading to a highly skewed distribution of benefits and a lack of success in promoting trade between industrial and developing countries. The arguments and analyses advanced in this book highlight the role of power and institutions in international trade and, more broadly, in the progress of economic globalization.

Methodological Appendix

This methodological appendix presents information from the quantitative analyses in chapters 3 and 4. For chapter 3, the baseline model, a description of the variables, and the countries included in the analysis are reported. The baseline model and a description of the variables are also reported for chapter 4, as well as the countries defined as *Standing Members, Early Adopters,* and *Later Entrants* according to the four classifications of WTO membership.

Chapter 3

Baseline Model:

$$Log(IMP_{ijt}) = \alpha + \beta_1 \ Log(GDP_i{}^* \ GDP_j)_t + \beta_2 \ Log(GDPPC_i{}^* \ GDPPC_j)_t + \beta_3 \ Log(Distance)_{ijt} + \beta_4 \ Log(Area_i{}^*Area_j)_t + \beta_5 \ (Land \ Contiguity)_{ijt} + \beta_6 \ (Landlocked)_{ijt} + \beta_7 \ (Island)_{ijt} + \beta_8 \ (Common \ Language)_{ijt} + \beta_9 \ (Common \ Colonizer)_{ijt} + \beta_{10} \ (Colony)_{ijt} + \beta_{11} \ (Currency \ Union)_{ijt} + \beta_{12} \ (RTA)_{ijt} + \beta_{13} \ (GSP)_{ijt} + \beta_{14} \ (Both\_GATT)_{ijt} + \beta_{15} \ (One\_GATT)_{ijt} + \Sigma_t \delta_t Year_t + \varepsilon_{ijt}$$

Dependent Variable

- *Log(IMP$_{ijt}$):* natural log of the dollar amount (U.S.) of each country's imports from the other in a given year. There are two observations per country pair in a given year: country a's imports from country b

and, conversely, country b's imports from country a. Data were obtained from the *Direction of Trade Statistics* (DOTS) of the International Monetary Fund. We use the U.S. consumer price index (CPI) to deflate these and convert them to constant dollars (CPI for Urban Consumers, all items; 1982–1984 = 100, from www.economy.com/freelunch).

Independent Variables

- *Log(GDP$_i$* * *GDP$_j$)$_t$*: natural log of the product of the two countries' *GDP* in year t in constant (1984) U.S. dollars.
- *Log(GDPPC$_i$* * *GDPPC$_j$)$_t$*: natural log of the product of the two countries' per capita GDP *(GDPPC)* in year t in constant (1984) U.S. dollars.
- *Log(Distance)$_{ij}$*: natural log of the great-circle distance between countries i and j.
- *Log(Area$_i$*Area$_j$)$_t$*: natural log of the product of the land areas (in square kilometers) of the two countries.
- *Land Contiguity$_{ijt}$*: dummy variable that equals one if the two countries share a land border and zero otherwise.
- *Landlocked$_{ijt}$*: number of landlocked countries within the dyad: 0, 1, or 2.
- *Island$_{ijt}$*: number of island countries within the dyad: 0, 1, or 2.
- *Common Language$_{ijt}$*: dummy variable that equals one if the two countries share a common language and zero otherwise.
- *Common Colonizer$_{ijt}$*: dummy variable that equals one if countries i and j are former colonies of the same country and zero otherwise.
- *Colony$_{ijt}$*: dummy variable that equals one if either country was ever a colony of the other and zero otherwise.
- *Currency Union$_{ijt}$*: dummy variable that equals one if the two countries in the dyad share the same currency in year t.
- *RTA$_{ijt}$*: dummy variable that equals one if the two countries in the dyad belong to the same regional trade agreement (RTA) in year t.
- *GSP$_{ijt}$*: dummy variable that equals one if one country grants preferences to the other, in year t, under the Generalized System of Preferences, agreements negotiated under the auspices of the United Nations Conference on Trade and Development (UNCTAD).
- *Both_GATT$_{ijt}$*: dummy variable that equals one if both countries in the dyad are GATT members in year t.
- *One_GATT$_{ijt}$*: dummy variable that equals one if one country in the dyad is a GATT member in year t.
- $\sum_t \delta_t Year_t$: year fixed effects, or dummy variables for t-1 years.

Countries Included in Table 3.1 Analysis

Algeria	Ecuador	Latvia	Senegal
Angola	Egypt	Lesotho	Seychelles
Antigua &	El Salvador	Liberia	Sierra Leone
Barbuda	Equatorial Guinea	Libya	Singapore
Argentina	Ethiopia	Lithuania	Solomon
Australia	Fiji	Madagascar	Islands
Austria	Finland	Malawi	Somalia
Bahamas	France	Malaysia	South Africa
Bahrain	Gabon	Maldives	Spain
Bangladesh	Gambia	Mali	Sri Lanka
Barbados	Georgia	Malta	St. Kitts & Nevis
Belize	Germany	Mauritania	St. Lucia
Benin	Ghana	Mauritius	Sudan
Bolivia	Greece	Mexico	Suriname
Botswana	Grenada	Mongolia	Swaziland
Brazil	Guatemala	Morocco	Sweden
Bulgaria	Guinea	Mozambique	Switzerland
Burkina Faso	Guinea-Bissau	Myanmar	Syria
Burundi	Guyana	Namibia	Tanzania
Cameroon	Haiti	Nepal	Thailand
Canada	Honduras	Netherlands	Trinidad &
Cape Verde	Hungary	New Zealand	Tobago
Central African	Iceland	Nicaragua	Tunisia
Republic	India	Niger	Turkey
Chad	Indonesia	Nigeria	Uganda
Chile	Iran	Norway	United Arab
China	Iraq	Oman	Emirates
Colombia	Ireland	Pakistan	United
Comoros	Israel	Panama	Kingdom
Congo,	Italy	Papua New	United States
Democratic	Jamaica	Guinea	Uruguay
Republic of	Japan	Paraguay	Vanuatu
Costa Rica	Jordan	Peru	Venezuela
Côte d'Ivoire	Kenya	Philippines	Yemen,
Cyprus	Korea,	Poland	Republic Of
Denmark	Republic of	Portugal	Yugoslavia,
Djibouti	Kuwait	Romania	Socialist Federal
Dominica	Lao People's	Rwanda	Republic of
Dominican	Democratic	Samoa	Zambia
Republic	Republic	Saudi Arabia	Zimbabwe

Chapter 4

Baseline Model:

$$Log(Trade_{ijt}) = \alpha + \beta_1 \, Log(GDP_i * GDP_j)_t + \beta_2 \, Log(GDPPC_i * GDPPC_j)_t + \beta_3$$
$$(Currency \, Union)_{ijt} + \beta_4 (PTA)_{ijt} + \beta_5 (GSP)_{ijt} + \beta_6 (Democracy)_{ijt} + \beta_7 (Alliance)_{ijt} +$$
$$\beta_8 \, (WTO \, Years)_{ijt} + \beta_9 \, (Fomer \, Colony)_{ijt} + \beta_{10} \, (Former \, Colony * WTO \, Years)_{ijt} +$$
$$\beta_{11}(Standing \, Members)_{ijt} + \beta_{12}(Early \, Adopters)_{ijt} + \beta_{13}(Later \, Entrants)_{ijt} +$$
$$\beta_{14}(Standing \, Members * WTO \, Years)_{ijt} + \beta_{15}(Early \, Adopters * WTO \, Years)_{ijt} +$$
$$\beta_{16}(Later \, Entrants * WTO \, Years)_{ijt} + \Sigma_t \delta_t Year_t + \varepsilon_{ijt}$$

Dependent Variable:

- $Log(Trade_{ijt})$: natural log of the dollar amount (U.S.) of bilateral trade between country i and country j in a given year t. Data were obtained from the *Direction of Trade Statistics* (DOTS) of the International Monetary Fund. Trade values were converted to constant U.S. dollars (2000) using the U.S. GDP (chained) price index, obtained from the Government Printing Office (GPO): www.gpoaccess.gov/usbudget/fy05/sheets/hist10z1.xls.

Independent Variables

- $Log(GDP_i * GDP_j)_t$: natural log of the product of the two countries' *GDP* in year t in constant (2000) U.S. dollars. Data obtained from the Penn World Tables, 6.2.
- $Log(GDPPC_i * GDPPC_j)_t$: natural log of the product of the two countries' per capita GDP (*GDPPC*) in year t in constant (2000) U.S. dollars. Data obtained from the Penn World Tables, 6.2.
- *Currency Union$_{ijt}$*: dummy variable that equals one if the two countries in the dyad share the same currency in year t. Data obtained from Rose (2004) and extended using Cohen (2004).
- *PTA$_{ijt}$*: dummy variable that equals one if the two countries in the dyad belong to the same regional trade agreement (RTA) in year t. Data obtained from Mansfield and Pevehouse (2000) and updated using information from the WTO and Arashiro (2005).
- *GSP$_{ijt}$*: dummy variable that equals one if one country grants preferences to the other in year t under the Generalized System of Preferences, agreements that were negotiated under the auspices of the United Nations Conference on Trade and Development (UNCTAD). Data compiled from the *Generalized System of Preferences List of Beneficiaries* from the United Nations Conference on Trade and Development (UNCTAD), various years.
- *Democracy$_{ijt}$*: dummy variable that equals one if both countries in the dyad have a score of 6 or higher in Polity IV's democracy index.

www.cidcm.umd.edu/polity/, accessed December 2006. Available as of November 2009 at www.systemicpeace.org/polity/polity4.htm.

- *Alliance$_{ijt}$:* dummy variable that equals one if both countries in the dyad are members of the same alliance. Formal alliances include mutual defense pacts, nonaggression treaties, and ententes. Data obtained from the COW2 Project, www.correlatesofwar.org/, version 3.03 (Gibler and Sarkees), accessed December 2006. Values for 2000, the last year for which data are available, were extended to 2004 for the analysis.
- *WTO Years$_{ijt}$:* dummy variable that equals one for the years 1995 to 2004, from the first year of the WTO to the most current year included in the analysis.
- *Former Colony$_{ijt}$:* dummy variable that equals one if either country was ever a colony of the other and zero otherwise.
- *Former Colony*WTO Years$_{ijt}$:* interaction term to capture the effect of the *WTO Years* on *Former Colony* trade.
- *Standing Members$_{ijt}$:* dummy variable that equals one if both countries acceded to the GATT but before 1986, the beginning of the Uruguay Round, and zero otherwise.
- *Early Adopters$_{ijt}$:* dummy variable that equals one if both countries joined the GATT during the Uruguay Round (1986–1994) or in the first year of the WTO (1995), and zero otherwise
- *Later Entrants$_{ijt}$:* dummy variable that equals one if both countries acceded to the WTO in 1996 or after, and zero otherwise.
- *Standing Members*WTO Years$_{ijt}$:* interaction term to capture the effect of the *WTO Years* on *Standing Members*
- *Early Adopters*WTO Years$_{ijt}$:* interaction term to capture the effect of the *WTO Years* on *Early Adopters*
- *Later Entrants*WTO Years$_{ijt}$:* interaction term to capture the effect of the *WTO Years* on *Later Entrants*
- $\sum_t \delta_t Year_t$: year fixed effects, or dummy variables for *t-1* years.

Note on Baseline Model Specifications

As fixed effects analysis is employed to estimate the models in chapter 4, the baseline model does not include time-invariant variables such as distance, land area, contiguity, landlocked status, island status, common language, and whether two countries had a common colonizer. *Former Colony* status and the three group variables—*Standing Members, Early Adopters,* and *Later Entrants*—are also time—invariant. However, their interaction terms are not, as the variable *WTO Years* shifts from zero to one beginning in 1995. The main effects of these four variables are thus included in the baseline model specifications but no estimates are generated as they drop out of the analysis.

Classification of *Standing Members, Early Adopters and Later Entrants*

A. Classification Using Official GATT/WTO Accession Dates

Standing Members (80)

Argentina	Dominican	Kuwait	Senegal
Australia	Republic	Luxembourg	Sierra Leone
Austria	Egypt	Madagascar	Singapore
Bangladesh	Finland	Malawi	South Africa
Barbados	France	Malaysia	Spain
Belgium	Gabon	Maldives	Sri Lanka
Belize	Germany	Malta	Suriname
Brazil	Ghana	Mauritania	Sweden
Burkina Faso	Greece	Mauritius	Switzerland
Burundi	Guyana	Myanmar	Tanzania
Cameroon	Hungary	Netherlands	Thailand
Canada	Iceland	New Zealand	Togo
Central African	India	Nicaragua	Trinidad &
Republic	Indonesia	Nigeria	Tobago
Chile	Ireland	Norway	Turkey
Colombia	Israel	Pakistan	Uganda
Côte d'Ivoire	Italy	Peru	United Kingdom
Cuba	Jamaica	Philippines	United States
Cyprus	Japan	Poland	Uruguay
Denmark	Kenya	Portugal	Zambia
	Korea, Republic of	Romania	Zimbabwe

Early Adopters (31)

Antigua & Barbuda	Dominica	Liechtenstein	Slovak Republic
Bahrain	El Salvador	Macao	Slovenia
Bolivia	Guatemala	Mali	St. Lucia
Botswana	Guinea	Mexico	St. Vincent & the
Brunei	Guinea-Bissau	Morocco	Grenadines
Costa Rica	Honduras	Mozambique	Swaziland
Czech Republic	Hong Kong	Namibia	Tunisia
Djibouti	Lesotho	Paraguay	Venezuela

B. Classification Using Rose (2004)

Standing Members (88)

Antigua & Barbuda	Barbados	Burundi	Chile
Argentina	Belgium	Cameroon	Colombia
Australia	Belize	Canada	Côte d'Ivoire
Austria	Brazil	Central African	Cyprus
Bangladesh	Burkina Faso	Republic	Denmark

Djibouti	Ireland	Myanmar	St. Lucia
Dominica	Israel	Netherlands	St. Vincent & the
Dominican	Italy	New Zealand	Grenadines
Republic	Jamaica	Nicaragua	Suriname
Egypt	Japan	Nigeria	Sweden
Finland	Kenya	Norway	Switzerland
France	Korea, Republic of	Pakistan	Tanzania
Gabon	Kuwait	Peru	Thailand
Germany	Luxembourg	Philippines	Togo
Ghana	Madagascar	Poland	Trinidad &
Greece	Malawi	Portugal	Tobago
Guinea-Bissau	Malaysia	Romania	Turkey
Guyana	Maldives	Senegal	Uganda
Hong Kong	Malta	Sierra Leone	United Kingdom
Hungary	Mauritania	Singapore	United States
Iceland	Mauritius	South Africa	Uruguay
India	Morocco	Spain	Zambia
Indonesia	Mozambique	Sri Lanka	Zimbabwe

Early Adopters (19)

Bahrain	El Salvador	Mali	Slovenia
Bolivia	Guatemala	Mexico	Swaziland
Botswana	Guinea	Namibia	Tunisia
Costa Rica	Honduras	Paraguay	Venezuela
Czech Republic	Lesotho	Slovak Republic	

C. Classification Using Tomz, Goldstein, and Rivers (2007)

Standing Members (99)

Antigua & Barbuda	Chile	Guinea-Bissau	Macao
Argentina	Colombia	Guyana	Madagascar
Australia	Côte d'Ivoire	Hong Kong	Malawi
Austria	Cuba	Hungary	Malaysia
Bahrain	Cyprus	Iceland	Maldives
Bangladesh	Denmark	India	Mali
Barbados	Djibouti	Indonesia	Malta
Belgium	Dominica	Ireland	Mauritania
Belize	Dominican	Israel	Mauritius
Botswana	Republic	Italy	Mozambique
Brazil	Egypt	Jamaica	Myanmar
Brunei	Finland	Japan	Namibia
Burkina Faso	France	Kenya	Netherlands
Burundi	Gabon	Korea, Republic of	New Zealand
Cameroon	Germany	Kuwait	Nicaragua
Canada	Ghana	Lesotho	Nigeria
Central African	Greece	Liechtenstein	Norway
Republic	Guinea	Luxembourg	Pakistan

Peru	South Africa	Sweden	Turkey
Philippines	Spain	Switzerland	Uganda
Poland	Sri Lanka	Tanzania	United
Portugal	St. Lucia	Thailand	Kingdom
Romania	St. Vincent & the	Togo	United States
Senegal	Grenadines	Trinidad &	Uruguay
Sierra Leone	Suriname	Tobago	Zambia
Singapore	Swaziland	Tunisia	Zimbabwe

Early Adopters (12)

Bolivia	El Salvador	Mexico	Slovak Republic
Costa Rica	Guatemala	Morocco	Slovenia
Czech Republic	Honduras	Paraguay	Venezuela

D. Classification Using Gowa and Kim (2005)

Standing Members (94)

Antigua &	Dominican	Luxembourg	Singapore
Barbuda	Republic	Madagascar	South Africa
Argentina	Egypt	Malawi	Spain
Australia	Finland	Malaysia	Sri Lanka
Austria	France	Maldives	St. Lucia
Bahrain	Gabon .	Mali	St. Vincent & the
Bangladesh	Germany	Malta	Grenadines
Barbados	Ghana	Mauritania	Suriname
Belize	Greece	Mauritius	Swaziland
Belgium	Guinea	Morocco	Sweden
Botswana	Guinea-Bissau	Mozambique	Switzerland
Brazil	Guyana	Myanmar	Tanzania
Burkina Faso	Hungary	Netherlands	Thailand
Burundi	Iceland	New Zealand	Togo -
Cameroon	India	Nicaragua	Trinidad &
Canada	Indonesia	Nigeria	Tobago
Central African	Ireland	Norway	Tunisia
Republic	Israel	Pakistan	Turkey
Chile	Italy	Peru	Uganda
Colombia	Jamaica	Philippines	United
Côte d'Ivoire	Japan	Poland	Kingdom
Cyprus	Kenya	Portugal	United States
Denmark	Korea, Republic of	Romania	Uruguay
Djibouti	Kuwait	Senegal	Zambia
Dominica	Lesotho	Sierra Leone	Zimbabwe

Early Adopters (12)

Bolivia	El Salvador	Mexico	Slovak Republic
Costa Rica	Guatemala	Namibia	Slovenia
Czech Republic	Honduras	Paraguay	Venezuela

E. Later Entrants (21, Common to All Classifications)

Albania	Ecuador	Lithuania	Panama
Armenia	Estonia	Macedonia	Saudi Arabia
Bulgaria	Georgia	Moldova	Taiwan
Cambodia	Jordan	Mongolia	
China	Kyrgyzstan	Nepal	
Croatia	Latvia	Oman	

References

Abbott, Andrew. 1997. Of Time and Space. *Social Forces* 75, no. 4: 1149–1182.

Abbott, Kenneth W., Robert O. Keohane, Andrew Moravcsik, Anne-Marie Slaughter, and Duncan Snidal. 2001. The Concept of Legalization. In *Legalization and World Politics*, ed. Judith L. Goldstein, Miles Kahler, Robert O. Keohane, and Anne-Marie Slaughter. Cambridge, MA: MIT Press.

Aldcroft, Derek H. 1981. *From Versailles to Wall Street, 1919–1929.* Berkeley: University of California Press.

Alexandroff, Alan S. 2002. A Transitional Review Mechanism: Has an Effective Multilateral Mechanism Been Created? In *China and the Long March to Global Trade: The Accession of China to the World Trade Organization,* ed. Sylvia Ostry, Alan S. Alexandroff, and Rafael Gomez. London: Routledge.

Alexandroff, Alan S., and Rafael Gomez. 2002. Conclusion: Where Do We Go From Here? In *China and the Long March to Global Trade: The Accession of China to the World Trade Organization,* ed. Sylvia Ostry, Alan S. Alexandroff, and Rafael Gomez. London: Routledge.

Alt, James E., Jeffry Frieden, Michael J. Gilligan, Dani Rodrik, and Ronald Rogowski. 1996. The Political Economy of International Trade: Enduring Puzzles and an Agenda for Inquiry. *Comparative Political Studies* 29, no. 6: 689–717.

Anderson, James. 1979. A Theoretical Foundation for the Gravity Equation. *American Economic Review* 69, no. 1: 106–116.

Anderson, James E., and Eric van Wincoop. 2003. Gravity with Gravitas: A Solution to the Border Puzzle. *American Economic Review* 93, no. 1: 170–192.

——. 2004. Trade Costs. *Journal of Economic Literature* 42, no. 3: 691–751.

Arashiro, Z., C. Marin, and A. Chacoff. 2005. *Challenges to Multilateralism: The Explosion of PTA's.* Sao Paulo: Institute for International Trade Negotiations.

Arthur, Brian. 1994. *Increasing Returns and Path Dependence in the Economy.* Ann Arbor: University of Michigan Press.

Bachrach, P., and M. S. Baratz. 1962. Two Faces of Power. *American Political Science Review* 56, no. 4: 947–952.

Bagwell, Kyle, and Robert W. Staiger. 1999. An Economic Theory of the General Agreement. *American Economic Review* 89, no. 1: 215–248.

———. 2002. *The Economics of the World Trading System.* Cambridge, MA: MIT Press.

Baier, Scott L., and Jeffrey H. Bergstrand. 2007. Do Free Trade Agreements Actually Increase Members' International Trade? *Journal of International Economics* 71, no. 1: 72–95.

Baldwin, David A. 1971. Money and Power. *Journal of Politics* 33, no. 3: 578–614.

———. 1979. Power Analysis and World-Politics: New Trends Versus Old Tendencies. *World Politics* 31, no. 2: 161–194.

Barbieri, Katherine, Omar Keshk, and Brian Pollins. 2008. Correlates of War Project Trade Data Set Codebook, Version 2.01. Online: http://correlatesofwar.org.

Barbieri, Katherine, and Jack S. Levy. 1999. Sleeping with the Enemy: The Impact of War on Trade. *Journal of Peace Research* 36, no. 4: 463–479.

Barnett, Michael, and Raymond Duvall. 2005a. Power in Global Governance. In *Power in Global Governance,* ed. Michael Barnett and Raymond Duvall. Cambridge, UK: Cambridge University Press.

———. 2005b. Power in International Politics. *International Organization* 59, no. 1: 39–75.

Barton, John H., Judith L. Goldstein, Timothy E. Josling, and Richard H. Steinberg. 2006. *The Evolution of the Trade Regime: Politics, Law, and Economics of the GATT and the WTO.* Princeton: Princeton University Press.

Baumgartner, Frank R., and Bryan D. Jones. 1993. *Agendas and Instability in American Politics.* Chicago: University of Chicago Press.

Bhagwati, Jagdish. 1990. Multilateralism at Risk: The GATT is Dead, Long Live GATT. *The World Economy* 13, no. 2: 149–169.

———. 2002. Coping With Antiglobalization: A Trilogy of Discontents. *Foreign Affairs* January/February. http://fullaccess.foreignaffairs.org/20020101facomment6552/jagdish-n-bhagwati/coping-with-antiglobalization-a-trilogy-of-discontents.html.

Bhagwati, J. N., and D. A. Irwin. 1987. The Return of the Reciprocitarians: United States Trade Policy Today. *World Economy* 10, no. 2: 109–130.

Bhagwati, Jagdish, and Arvind Panagariya. 1996. Preferential Trading Areas and Multilateralism: Strangers, Friends, or Foes. In *The Economics of Preferential Trade Agreements,* ed. Jagdish Bhagwati and Arvind Panagariya. Washington, DC: EAI Press.

Bidwell, Percy. 1956. *What the Tariff Means to American Industries.* New York: Harper and Brothers.

Black, J. 1959. Argument for Tariffs. *Oxford Economic Papers,* New Series, Volume 11, No. 2: 191–208.

Blundell, Richard, and Monica Costa Dias. 2000. Evaluation Methods for Non-Experimental Data. *Fiscal Studies* 21, No. 4: 427–468.

Boin, Arjen. 2008. Mapping Trends in the Study of Political Institutions. *International Studies Review* 10, no. 1: 87–92.

Broude, T. 1998. Accession to the WTO—Current Issues in the Arab World. *Journal of World Trade* 32, no. 6: 147–166.

Bulmer, Simon, and Martin Burch. 1998. Organizing for Europe: Whitehall, the British State, and European Union. *Public Administration* 76, no. 4: 601–628.

Burley, Anne-Marie. 1993. Regulating the World: Multilateralism, International Law, and the Projection of the New Deal Regulatory State. In *Multilateralism Matters: The*

Theory and Praxis of an Institutional Form, ed. John Gerard Ruggie. New York: Columbia University Press.

Büthe, Tim. 2002. Taking Temporality Seriously: Modeling History and the Use of Narratives as Evidence. *American Political Science Review* 96, no. 3: 481–493.

Butler, Michael A. 1998. *Cautious Visionary: Cordell Hull and Trade Reform, 1933–1937.* Kent, Ohio: Kent State University Press.

Calvert, Randall L. 1995. Rational Actors, Equilibrium, and Social Institutions. In *Explaining Social Institutions,* ed. Jack Knight and Itai Sened. Ann Arbor: University of Michigan Press.

Camps, M. 1964. *Britain and the European Community, 1955–1963.* Princeton: Princeton University Press.

Caporaso, James A. 1992. International Relations Theory and Multilateralism: the Search for Foundations. *International Organization* 46, no. 3: 599–632.

Carey, John M. 2000. Parchment, Equilibria, and Institutions. *Comparative Political Studies* 33, nos. 6–7: 735–761.

Chase, Kerry. 2006. Multilateralism Compromised: The Mysterious Origins of General Agreement Article XXIV. *World Trade Review* 5, no. 1: 1–30.

Cheng, I-Hui, and Howard J. Wall. 2004. Controlling for Heterogeneity in Gravity Models of Trade and Integration. Federal Reserve Bank of St. Louis Working Paper 1999–010E.

Cohen, Benjamin J. 2004. *The Future of Money.* Princeton: Princeton University Press.

Coleman, William D. 1998. From Protected Development to Market Liberalism: Paradigm Change in Agriculture. *Journal of European Public Policy* 5, no. 4: 632–651.

Correlates of War 2 Project. 2003. State System Membership List, v2002.1. Online: http://cow2.la.psu.edu.

Cowhey, Peter F. 1993. Elect Locally—Order Globally: Domestic Politics and Multilateral Cooperation. In *Multilateralism Matters: The Theory and Praxis of an Institutional Form,* ed. John Gerard Ruggie. New York: Columbia University Press.

Cox, Gary. 1997. *Making Votes Count: Strategic Coordination the World's Electoral Systems.* Cambridge, UK: Cambridge University Press.

Crick, W. F. 1951. International Financial Relations: Some Concealed Problems. *International Affairs* 27, no. 3: 297–305.

Crothall, Geoffrey. 1994. China Hints at Bypassing U.S. in GATT Talks. *South China Morning Post (3 March),* 1.

Culbertson, William Smith. 1937. *Reciprocity: A National Policy for Foreign Trade.* New York: McGraw-Hill.

Curzon, Gerard. 1965. *Multilateral Commercial Diplomacy: The General Agreement on Tariffs and Trade and Its Impact on National Commercial Policies and Techniques.* New York: Frederick A. Praeger.

Curzon, Gerard, and V. Curzon. 1976. The Management of Trade Relations in the General Agreement. In *International Economic Relations of the Western World 1959–1971: Volume 1, Politics and Trade,* ed. Andrew Shonfield. London: Oxford University Press.

Dahl, Robert Alan. 1957. The Concept of Power. *Behavioral Science* 2: 201–215.

———. 1991. *Modern Political Analysis.* Englewood Cliffs, NJ: Prentice Hall.

Dam, Kenneth W. 1970. *The General Agreement: Law and International Economic Organization.* Chicago: University of Chicago.

David, Paul. 1985. Clio and the Economics of QWERTY. *American Economic Review* 75, no. 3: 332–337.

——. 1994. Why Are Institutions "Carriers of History"? Path Dependence and the Evolution of Conventions, Organizations, and Institutions. *Structural Change and Economic Dynamics* 5, no. 2: 205–220.

——. 2000. Path Dependence, Its Critics, and the Quest for "Historical Economics." In *Evolution and Path Dependence in Economic Ideas: Past and Present,* ed. P. Garrouste and S. Ioannides. Cheltenham: Edward Elgar.

Deardorff, Alan. 1997. Determinants of Bilateral Trade: Does Gravity Work in a Classical World? In *The Regionalization of the World Economy,* ed. Jeffrey Frankel. Chicago: University of Chicago Press.

Destler, I. M. 2005. *American Trade Politics.* 4th ed. Washington, DC: Institute for International Economics.

Deudney, Daniel H. 2007. *Bounding Power: Republican Security Theory from the Polis to the Global Village.* Princeton: Princeton University Press.

Diebold, Jr., William. 1952. *The End of the ITO.* Princeton: International Finance Section, Department of Economics and Social Institutions, Princeton University.

——. 1988. The History and the Issues. In *Bilateralism, Multilateralism, and Canada in U.S. Trade Policy,* ed. William Diebold Jr. Washington, DC: Council on Foreign Relations.

Eckes, Alfred E., Jr., and Thomas W. Zeiler. 2003. *Globalization and the American Century.* Cambridge, UK: Cambridge University Press.

Eichengreen, Barry, and Douglas A. Irwin. 1995. Trade Blocs, Currency Blocs, and the Reorientation of World Trade in the 1930s. *Journal of International Economics* 38, nos. 1–2: 1–24.

——. 1998. The Role of History in Bilateral Trade Flows. In *The Regionalization of the World Economy,* ed. Jeffrey Frankel. Chicago: University of Chicago Press.

Eichengreen, Barry, and Jeffrey Sachs. 1985. Exchange-Rates and Economic-Recovery in the 1930s. *Journal of Economic History* 45, no. 4: 925–946.

Fearon, James D. 1998. Bargaining, Enforcement, and International Cooperation. *International Organization* 52, no. 2: 269–305.

Feinstein, Charles H., Peter Temin, and Gianni Toniolo. 1997. *The European Economy between the Wars.* Oxford: Oxford University Press.

Feis, Herbert. 1948. The Geneva Proposals for an International Trade Charter. *International Organization* 2, no. 1: 39–52.

Feng, Hui. 2006. *The Politics of China's Accession to the World Trade Organization: The Dragon Goes Global.* London: Routledge.

Finger, J. M. 1979. Trade Liberalization: A Public Choice Perspective. In *Challenges To a Liberal International Economic Order,* ed. Ryan C. Amacher, Gottfried Haberler, and Thomas D. Willett. Washington, DC: American Enterprise Institute.

Finger, J. M., Merlinda D. Ingco, and Ulrich Reincke. 1996. *The Uruguay Round: Statistics on Tariff Concessions Given and Received.* Washington, DC: World Bank.

Finlayson, Jock A., and Mark W. Zacher. 1983. The General Agreement and the Regulation of Trade Barriers: Regime Dynamics and Functions. In *International Regimes,* ed. Stephen D. Krasner. Ithaca: Cornell University Press.

Fiorentino, Roberto V., Luis Verdeja, and Christelle Toqueboeuf. 2007. The Changing Landscape of Regional Trade Agreements: 2006 Update. Discussion Paper No. 12. Geneva: World Trade Organization Secretariat.

Foroutan, Faezeh. 1998. Does Membership in a Regional Preferential Trade Arrangement Make a Country More or Less Protectionist? World Bank Policy Research Working Paper No. 1898.

Frankel, Jeffrey A. (with Ernesto Stein and Shang-Jin Wei). 1997. *Regional Trading Blocs in the World Economic System.* Washington, DC: Institute for International Economics.

Frieden, Jeffry A. 1999. Actors and Preferences in International Relations. In *Strategic Choice and International Relations,* ed. David A. Lake and Robert Powell. Princeton: Princeton University Press.

Gallagher, Peter. 2005. *The First Ten Years of the WTO: 1995–2005.* Cambridge, UK: Cambridge University Press.

Gardner, Richard N. 1956[1980]. *Sterling-Dollar Diplomacy in Current Perspective: The Origins and the Prospects of Our International Economic Order. With Revised Introduction.* New York: Columbia University Press.

Garrett, Geoffrey, and Barry R. Weingast. 1993. Ideas, Interests, and Institutions: Constructing the EC's Internal Market. In *Ideas and Foreign Policy: Beliefs, Institutions, and Political Change,* ed. Judith Goldstein and Robert O. Keohane. Ithaca: Cornell University Press.

Gavin, Francis J. 2004. *Gold, Dollars, and Power: The Politics of International Monetary Relations, 1958–1971.* Chapel Hill: University of North Carolina Press.

General Agreement on Tariffs and Trade. 1947. United Nations Treaty Series Volume 55, Registration number 814 (Registered *ex officio* on 30 May 1950).

General Agreement on Tariffs and Trade. 1969[86]. *Basic Instruments and Selected Documents, Volume IV.* Geneva: GATT. Available at http://www.wto.org/english/docs_e/legal_e/gatt47_e.pdf.

Gertler, Jeffrey L. 2002. Negotiating China's Protocol of Accession. In *China and the Long March to Global Trade: The Accession of China to the World Trade Organization,* ed. Sylvia Ostry, Alan S. Alexandroff, and Rafael Gomez. London: Routledge.

Gibler, Douglas M., and Meredith Sarkees. 2002. Coding Manual for v3.0 of the Correlates of War Formal Interstate Alliance Data set, 1816–2000. Version 3.03 Typescript.

Gilligan, Michael J. 1997. *Empowering Exporters: Reciprocity Delegation and Collective Action in American Trade Policy.* Ann Arbor: University of Michigan.

Glick, Reuven, and Andrew K. Rose. 2002. Does a Currency Union Affect Trade? The Time-Series Evidence. *European Economic Review* 46, no. 6: 1125–1151.

Glickman, David L. 1947. The British Imperial Preference System. *Quarterly Journal of Economics* 61, no. 3: 439–470.

Goldstein, Judith. 1988. Ideas, Institutions, and American Trade Policy. *International Organization* 42, no. 1: 179–217.

———. 1993. Creating the General Agreement Rules: Politics, Institutions, and American Policy. In *Multilateralism Matters: The Theory and Praxis of an Institutional Form,* ed. John Gerard Ruggie. New York: Columbia University Press.

Goldstein, Judith L., Douglas Rivers, and Michael Tomz. 2007. Institutions in International Relations: Understanding the Effects of the GATT and the WTO on World Trade. *International Organization* 61, no. 1: 37–67.

Gordon, Bernard K. 2003. A High-Risk Trade Policy. *Foreign Affairs* 82, no. 4: 105–118.

Gourevitch, Peter Alexis. 1999. The Governance Problem in International Relations. In *Strategic Choice and International Relations,* ed. David Lake and Robert Powell. Princeton: Princeton University Press.

Gowa, Joanne. 1994. *Allies, Adversaries, and International Trade.* Princeton, NJ: Princeton University Press.

Gowa, Joanne, and Soo Yeon Kim. 2005. An Exclusive Country Club: The Effects of the GATT on Trade, 1950–94. *World Politics* 57, no. 4: 453–478.

Gowa, Joanne, and Edward D. Mansfield. 1993. Power Politics and International Trade. *American Political Science Review* 87, no. 2: 408–420.

Graham, Thomas R. 1978. The U.S. Generalized System of Preferences for Developing Countries: International Innovation and the Art of the Feasible. *American Journal of International Law* 72, no. 3: 513–541.

Green, Donald P., Soo Yeon Kim, and David H. Yoon. 2001. Dirty Pool. *International Organization* 55, no. 2: 441–468.

Greif, Avner. 2006. *Institutions and the Path to the Modern Economy: Lessons from Medieval Trade, Political Economy of Institutions and Decisions.* Cambridge, UK: Cambridge University Press.

Grieco, Joseph M. 1993. Understanding the Problem of International Cooperation: The Limits of Neoliberal Institutionalism, and the Future of Realist Theory. In *Neorealism and Neoliberalism: The Contemporary Debate*, ed. David A. Baldwin. New York: Columbia University Press.

Grossman, Gene, and Elhanan Helpman. 1989. Product Development and International Trade. *Journal of Political Economy* 97: 1261–1283.

———. 1991. *Innovation and Growth in the Global Economy.* Cambridge, MA: MIT Press.

Gruber, Lloyd. 2000. *Ruling The World: Power Politics and The Rise Of Supranational Institutions.* Princeton: Princeton University Press.

———. 2005. Power Politics and the Institutionalization of International Relations. In *Power in Global Governance*, ed. Michael Barnett and Raymond Duvall. Cambridge, UK: Cambridge University Press.

Haggard, Stephan. 1988. The Institutional Foundations of Hegemony: Explaining the Reciprocal Trade Agreements Act of 1934. *International Organization* 42, no. 1: 91–119.

Hardin, Russell. 1989. Why a Constitution? In *The Federalist Papers and the New Institutionalism*, ed. Bernard Grofman and Donald Wittman. New York: Agathon.

Hart, Michael. 1998. *Fifty Years of Canadian Tradecraft: Canada at the GATT 1947–1997.* Ottawa: Centre for Trade Policy and Law.

Hathaway, Dale. 1997. *Agriculture and the GATT: Rewriting the Rules.* Washington, DC: Institute for International Economics.

Hausman, Jerry A., and William E. Taylor. 1981. Panel Data and Unobservable Effects. *Econometrica* 49, no. 6: 1377–1398.

Hawkins, Harry C. 1951. *Commercial Treaties and Agreement: Principles and Practice.* New York: Rinehart and Co.

Helpman, Elhanan, and Paul Krugman. 1985. *Market Structure and Foreign Trade.* Cambridge, MA: MIT Press.

Herz, Bernhard, and Marco Wagner. 2006. Do the World Trade Organization and the Generalized System of Preferences Foster Bilateral Trade? Unpublished manuscript.

Hill, Bernard. 1984. *Common Agricultural Policy: Past, Present, and Future.* London: Routledge.

Hirschman, Albert O. 1945[1980]. *National Power and the Structure of Foreign Trade.* Berkeley: University of California Press.

———. 1970. *Exit, Voice, and Loyalty; Responses to Decline in Firms, Organizations, and States.* Cambridge, MA: Harvard University Press.

Hiscox, Michael J. 1999. The Magic Bullet? The RTAA, Institutional Reform, and Trade Liberalization. *International Organization* 53, no. 4: 669–698.

Hoda, Anwarul. 2001. *Tariff Negotiations and Renegotiations under the GATT and the WTO: Procedures and Practices.* Cambridge, MA: Cambridge University Press.

Hoekman, Bernard M., and Michel M. Kostecki. 2001. *The Political Economy of the World Trading System: The WTO and Beyond.* 2nd edition. Oxford: Oxford University Press.

——. 1995. *The Political Economy of the World Trading System: from GATT to WTO.* Oxford: Oxford University Press.

Horn, Henrik, Giovanni Maggi, and Robert Staiger. 2006. Trade Agreements as Endogenously Incomplete Contracts. National Bureau of Economic Research Working Paper No. 12745.

Hudec, Robert E. 1975. *The General Agreement Legal System and World Trade Diplomacy.* New York: Praeger.

Ikenberry, John G. 1992. A World Economy Restored: Expert Consensus and the Anglo-American Postwar Settlement. *International Organization* 46, no. 1: 289–321.

——. 2001. *After Victory: Institutions, Strategic Restraint, and the Rebuilding of Order after Major Wars.* Princeton: Princeton University Press.

ITO (International Trade Organization). 1948. *International Organization* 2, no. 1: 133–136.

Irwin, Douglas. 1995. The GATT in Historical Perspective. *AEA Papers and Proceedings* 85, no. 2: 323–328.

——. 1993. Multilateral and Bilateral Trade Policies in the World Trading System: An Historical Perspective. In *New Dimensions in Regional Integration,* ed. Jaime De Melo and Arvind Panagariya. Cambridge: Centre for Economic Policy Research.

Irwin, Douglas A., and Randall S. Kroszner. 1999. Interests, Institutions, and Ideology in Securing Policy Change: The Republican Conversion to Trade Liberalization after Smoot-Hawley. *Journal of Law and Economics* 42, no. 3: 643–673.

Irwin, Douglas A., Petros C. Mavroidis, and Alan O. Sykes. 2008. *The Genesis of the GATT (The American Law Institute Reporters Studies on WTO Law).* Cambridge, UK: Cambridge University Press.

Isaak, Robert A. 2005. *The Globalization Gap: How the Rich Get Richer and the Poor Get Left Further Behind.* New York: Prentice Hall.

Johnson, D. G. 1973. *World Agriculture in Disarray.* London: Fontana/Collins.

Josling, Timothy E., Stefan Tangerman, and T. K. Warley. 1996. *Agriculture in the GATT.* London: Macmillan.

Kaiser, David E. 1980. *Economic Diplomacy and the Origins of the Second World War: Germany, Britain, France and Eastern Europe, 1930–1939.* Princeton: Princeton University Press.

Kapstein, Ethan B. 2006. *Economic Justice in an Unfair World: Toward a Level Playing Field.* Princeton: Princeton University Press.

Keohane, Robert O. 1984. *After Hegemony: Cooperation and Discord in the World Political Economy.* Princeton: Princeton University Press.

Knight, Jack. 1992. *Institutions and Social Conflict: Political Economy of Institutions and Decisions.* Cambridge: Cambridge University Press.

Knorr, Klaus. 1948. The Bretton Woods Institutions in Transition. *International Organization* 2, no. 1: 19–38.

Kock, Karin. 1969. *International Trade Policy and the GATT, 1947–1967.* Stockholm: Almqvist and Wiksell.

Kono, Daniel Y. 2002. Are Free Trade Areas Good for Multilateralism? Evidence from the European Free Trade Association. *International Studies Quarterly* 46, no. 4: 507–527.

——. 2007. When Do Trade Blocs Block Trade? *International Studies Quarterly* 51, no. 1: 165–181.

Koremenos, Barbara, Charles Lipson, and Duncan Snidal. 2001a. Rational Design: Looking Back to Move Forward. *International Organization* 55, no. 4: 1051–1082.

————. 2001b. The Rational Design of International Institutions. *International Organization* 55, no. 4: 761–799.

Krasner, Stephen D. 1991. Global Communications and National Power: Life on the Pareto Frontier. *World Politics* 43, no. 3: 336–366.

Lake, David A. 1999. *Entangling Relations: American Foreign Policy in Its Century.* Princeton: Princeton University Press.

————. 2008. The New American Empire? *International Studies Perspectives* 9, no. 3: 281–289.

Langhammer, R. J., and M. Lücke. 1999. WTO Accession Issues. *World Economy* 22, no. 6: 837–873.

Lanoszka, Anna. 2001. The World Trade Organization Accession Process: Negotiating Participation in a Globalizing Economy. *Journal of World Trade* 35, no. 4: 575–602.

Lasswell, Harold D. 1936. *Politics: Who Gets What, When, How?* New York: P. Smith.

Lasswell, Harold D., and Abraham Kaplan. 1950. *Power and Society: A Framework for Political Inquiry.* New Haven: Yale University Press.

Li, Quan, and David Sacko. 2002. The (Ir)Relevance of Militarized Interstate Disputes for International Trade. *International Studies Quarterly* 46, no. 1: 11–43.

Liang, Wei. 2002. China's WTO Negotiation Process and its Implications. *Journal of Contemporary China* 11, no. 33: 683–719.

Linneman, Hans. 1966. *An Econometric Study of International Trade Flows.* Amsterdam: North-Holland.

Lipson, Charles. 1983. The Transformation of Trade: the Sources and Effects of Regime Change. In *International Regimes,* ed. Stephen D. Krasner. Ithaca: Cornell University Press.

Lohmann, Susanne, and Sharyn O'Halloran. 1994. Divided Government and U.S. Trade Policy: Theory and Evidence. *International Organization* 48, no. 4: 595–632.

Ludema, Rodney D., and Anna Maria Mayda. 2005. Do Countries Free Ride on MFN? Center for Economic Policy Research (CEPR) Discussion Papers, No. 5160.

Lukes, Steven. 1974. *Power: A Radical View.* New York: Macmillan.

Mahoney, James. 2000. Path Dependence in Historical Sociology. *Theory and Society* 29, no. 4: 507–548.

Mansfield, Edward D. 1998. The Proliferation of Preferential Trading Arrangements. *Journal of Conflict Resolution* 42, no. 5: 523–543.

Mansfield, Edward D., and Rachel Bronson. 1997. Alliances, Preferential Trading Arrangements, and International Trade. *American Political Science Review* 91, no. 1: 94–107.

Mansfield, Edward D., and Helen V. Milner. 1999. The New Wave of Regionalism. *International Organization* 53, no. 3: 589–627.

Mansfield, Edward D., Helen V. Milner, and Peter Rosendorff. 2000. Free to Trade: Democracies, Autocracies, and International Trade. *American Political Science Review* 94, no. 2: 305–321.

Mansfield, Edward D., and Jon C. Pevehouse. 2000. Trade Blocs, Trade Flows, and International Conflict. *International Organization* 54, no. 4: 775–808.

Mansfield, Edward D., and Eric Reinhardt. 2008. International Institutions and the Volatility of International Trade. *International Organization* 62, no. 4: 621–652.

March, James G., and Johan P. Olsen. 1989. *Rediscovering Institutions: The Organizational Basis of Politics.* New York: Free Press.

————. 1998. The Institutional Dynamics of International Political Orders. *International Organization* 52, no. 4: 943–969.

Martin, Lisa L. 1992a. *Coercive Cooperation: Explaining Multilateral Economic Sanctions.* Princeton: Princeton University Press.

Mathis, James H. 2002. *Regional Trade Agreements in the GATT-WTO: Article XXIV and the Internal Trade Requirement.* Norwell, MA: Kluwer Law International.

Mátyás, Lázló. 1997. Proper Econometric Specification of the Gravity Model. *The World Economy* 20, no. 3: 363–368.

Mazur, Jay. 2000. Labor's New Internationalism. *Foreign Affairs* 79, no. 1 (January/February).

McFarland, Andrew S. 1969. *Power and Leadership in Pluralist Systems.* Stanford: Stanford University Press.

Michalopoulos, Constantine. 1999. The Integration of Transition Economies into the World Trading System. Manuscript. Washington, DC: World Bank.

———. 1999. The Developing Countries in the WTO. *The World Economy* 22, no. 1: 117–143.

Mikesell, Raymond Frech. 1994. *The Bretton Woods Debates: A Memoir.* Princeton, N.J.: International Finance Section, Dept. of Economics, Princeton University.

Miller, Gary. 2000. Rational Choice and Dysfunctional Institutions. *Governance* 13, no. 4: 535–547.

Milward, Alan S. 2000. *The Reconstruction of Western Europe, 1945–51,* 2d. ed. Berkeley: University of California.

Moe, Terry M. 1984. The New Economics of Organization. *American Journal of Political Science* 28, no. 4: 739–777.

———. 2005. Power and Political Institutions. *Perspectives on Politics* 3, no. 2: 215–233.

Moravcsik, Andrew. 1997. Taking Preferences Seriously: A Liberal Theory of International Politics. *International Organization* 51, no. 4: 513–553.

———. 1998. *The Choice for Europe: Social Purpose and State Power from Messina to Maastricht.* Ithaca: Cornell University Press.

Morrow, James D. 1994. Modeling the Forms of International Cooperation: Distribution versus Information. *International Organization* 48, no. 3: 387–423.

Nagel, Jack H. 1975. *The Descriptive Analysis of Power.* New Haven: Yale University Press.

Nau, Henry R. 2002. *At Home Abroad: Identity and Power in American Foreign Policy.* Ithaca: Cornell University Press.

———. 2003. Identity and the Balance of Power in Asia. In *International Relations Theory and the Asia-Pacific,* ed. G. John Ikenberry and Michael Mastanduno. New York: Columbia University Press.

Neal, L. 1979. Economics and Finance of Bilateral Clearing Agreements—Germany, 1934–8. *Economic History Review* 32, no. 3: 391–404.

Newey, W., and K. West. 1987. A Simple Positive Semi-Definite, Hetersoscedasticity and Autocorrelation Consistent Covariance Matrix. *Econometrica* 55, no. 3: 703–708.

Nitsch, Volker. 2002. Honey, I Shrunk the Currency Union Effect on Trade. *The World Economy* 215, no. 4: 457–474.

North, Douglass C. 1990. *Institutions, Institutional Change, and Economic Performance.* Cambridge, UK: Cambridge University Press.

Notter, Harley. 1949. *Postwar Foreign Policy Preparation 1939–1945.* Publication 3580. Washington, DC: U.S. Department of State.

Oatley, Thomas H. 2001. Multilateralizing Trade and Payments in Postwar Europe. *International Organization* 55, no. 4: 949–969.

Oatley, Thomas H., and Robert Nabors. 1998. Redistributive Cooperation: Market Failure, Wealth Transfers, and the Basle Accord. *International Organization* 52, no. 1: 35–54.

O'Rourke, Kevin H., and Jeffrey G. Williamson. 1999. *Globalization and History: Evolution of a Nineteenth-Century Atlantic Economy.* Cambridge: The MIT Press.

Ostry, Sylvia. 1997. *The Post–Cold War Trading System: Who's on First?* Chicago: University of Chicago Press.

———. 2002. The WTO: Post Seattle and Chinese Accession. In *China and the Long March to Global Trade: The Accession of China to the World Trade Organization,* ed. Sylvia Ostry, Alan S. Alexandroff, and Rafael Gomez. London: Routledge.

Ostry, Sylvia, Alan S. Alexandroff, and Rafael Gomez, eds. 2002. *China and the Long March to Global Trade: The Accession of China to the World Trade Organization.* London: Routledge.

Oye, Kenneth A. 1992. *Economic Discrimination and Political Exchange: World Political Economy in the 1930s and 1980s.* Princeton: Princeton University.

Özden, Çaglar, and Eric Reinhardt. 2005. The Perversity of Preferences: GSP and Developing Country Trade Policies, 1976–2000. *Journal of Development Economics* 78, no. 1: 1–21.

Pahre, Robert. 2001. Most-Favored-Nation Clauses and Clustered Negotiations. *International Organization* 55, no. 4: 859–890.

Patterson, Gardner. 1966. *Discrimination in International Trade, The Policy Issues: 1945–1965.* Princeton: Princeton University Press.

Pearson, Margaret M. 2001. The Case of China's Accession to GATT/WTO. In *The Making of Chinese Foreign and Security Policy in the Era of Reform, 1978–2000.* Ed. D. M. Lampton. Stanford: Stanford University Press.

Persson, Torsten. 2001. Currency Unions and Trade: How Large Is the Treatment Effect? *Economic Policy* 16, no: 33: 435–448.

Pierson, Paul. 2004. *Politics in Time: History, Institutions, and Social Analysis.* Princeton: Princeton University Press.

Polacheck, Solomon William. 1978. Dyadic Disputes: An Economic Perspective. *Papers, Peace Science Society (International)* 28: 67–80.

Pollard, Robert A. 1985. *Economic Security and the Origins of the Cold War, 1945–1950.* New York: Columbia University Press.

Pollins, Brian M. 1989. Does Trade Still Follow the Flag? *American Political Science Review* 83, no. 2: 465–480.

Pomfret, Richard. 1988. *Unequal Trade: The Economics of Discriminatory International Trade Policies.* Oxford: Basil Blackwell.

Putnam, R. D. 1988. Diplomacy and Domestic Politics: The Logic of Two-Level Games. *International Organization* 42, no. 3: 427–460.

Qin, Julia Ya. 2003. "WTO-Plus" Obligations and Their Implications for the World Trade Organization Legal System: An Appraisal of the China Accession Protocol. *Journal of World Trade* 37, no. 3: 483–522

Ritschl, Albrecht, and Nikolaus Wolf. 2003. Endogeneity of Currency Areas and Trade Blocs: Evidence from the Inter-War Period. Discussion Paper Series, No. 4112. London: Centre for Economic Policy Research.

River-Batiz, Luis A., and Paul Romer. 1991. International Trade and Endogenous Growth. *Quarterly Journal of Economics* 106, no. 2: 531–555.

Rose, Andrew K. 2004. Do We Really Know that the WTO Increases Trade? *American Economic Review* 94, no. 1: 98–114.

———. 2007. Do We Really Know that the WTO Increases Trade? Reply. *American Economic Review* 97, no. 5: 2019–2025.

Rose, Andrew K., and Eric van Wincoop. 2001. National Money as a Barrier to International Trade: The Real Case for Currency Union. *American Economic Review* 91, no. 2: 386–390.

Rosendorff, B. Peter, and Helen V. Milner. 2001. The Optimal Design of International Trade Institutions: Uncertainty and Escape. *International Organization* 55, no. 4: 829–857.

Ruggie, John Gerard. 1982. International Regimes, Transactions, and Change: Embedded Liberalism in the Postwar Economic Order. *International Organization* 36, no. 2: 379–415.

——. 1992. Multilateralism: The Anatomy of an Institution. *International Organization* 46, no. 3: 561–598.

Sachs, Jeffrey D. and Andrew Warner. 1995. Economic Reform and the Process of Global Integration. In *Brookings Papers on Economic Activity*, eds. William C. Brainard and George L. Perry. Washington: Brookings Institution.

Sauvé, Pierre. 2000. Developing Countries and the GATS 2000 Round. *Journal of World Trade* 34, no. 2: 85–92.

Schnietz, Karen E. 2000. The Institutional Foundation of U.S. Trade Policy: Revisiting Explanations for the 1934 Reciprocal Trade Agreements Act. *Journal of Policy History* 12, no. 4: 417–444.

Schott, Jeffrey J. 2004. *Free Trade Agreements: U.S. Strategies and Priorities*. Washington, DC: Institute for International Economics.

Sebenius, James K. 1991. Designing Negotiations toward a New Regime: The Case of Global Warming. *International Security* 15, no. 4: 110–148.

Snyder, Richard C. 1940. Commercial Policy as Reflected in Treaties from 1931 to 1939. *American Economic Review* 30, no. 4: 787–802.

Sprout, Harold Hance, and Margaret Tuttle Sprout. 1956. *Man-Milieu Relationship Hypotheses in the Context of International Politics*. Princeton: Center of International Studies, Princeton University.

Srinivasan, T. N. 1998. *Developing Countries and the Multilateral Trading System: From the GATT to the Uruguay Round and the Future*. Boulder, CO: Westview.

Steinberg, Richard H. 2002. In the Shadow of Law or Power? Consensus-Based Bargaining and Outcomes in the GATT/WTO. *International Organization* 56, no. 2: 339–374.

Stiglitz, Joseph E., and Andrew Charlton. 2005. *Fair Trade for All: How Trade Can Promote Development*. New York: Oxford University Press.

Stinchcombe, Arthur. 1968. *Constructing Social Theories*. New York: Harcourt.

Subramanian, Arvind, and Shang-Jin Wei. 2003. The WTO Promotes Trade, Strongly But Unevenly. NBER Working Paper 10024.

——. 2007. The WTO Promotes Trade, Strongly But Unevenly. *Journal of International Economics* 72, no. 1: 151–175.

Taussig, F. W. 1892. Reciprocity. *Quarterly Journal of Economics* 7, no. 1: 26–39.

Tinbergen, Jan. 1962. An Analysis of World Trade Flows. In *Shaping the World Economy*, ed. Jan Tinbergen. New York: Twentieth Century Fund.

Tomz, Michael, Judith L. Goldstein, and Douglas Rivers. 2007. Do We Really Know That the WTO Increases Trade? Comment. *American Economic Review* 97, no. 5: 2005–2018.

Tussie, Diane. 1987. *The Less Developed Countries and the World Trading System: A Challenge to the GATT*. London: Frances Pinter.

Tyers, R., and K. Anderson. 1992. *Disarray in World Food Markets: A Quantitative Assessment*. Cambridge: Cambridge University Press.

U.S. Department of State. 1947. *Analysis of the General Agreement on Tariffs and Trade.* Washington, DC: United States Government Printing Office.

———. 1948. *Havana Charter for an International Trade Organization.* Publication 3206. Washington, DC: U.S. Department of State.

———. 1949. *Analysis of Protocol of Accession and Schedules to the General Agreement on Tariffs and Trade Negotiated at Annecy, France, April–August 1949.* Washington, DC: Government Printing Office.

United States Tariff Commission. 1948. *Operation of the Trade Agreements Program, 1934–1948, Parts I–III.* Washington, DC: United State Government Printing Office.

———. 1957. *Operation of the Trade Agreements Program, 9th Report, July 1955–June 1956.* Washington, DC: Government Printing Office.

———. 1958. *Operation of the Trade Agreements Program, 10th Report, June 1956–June 1957.* Washington, DC: Government Printing Office.

Verdier, Daniel. 1994. *Democracy and International Trade: Britain, France, and the United States, 1860–1990.* Princeton: Princeton University.

Viner, Jacob. 1950. *The Customs Union Issue.* New York: Carnegie Endowment for International Peace.

Weingast, Barry R., Judith Goldstein, and Michael A. Bailey. 1997. The Institutional Roots of American Trade Policy: Politics, Coalitions, and International Trade. *World Politics* 49, no. 3: 309–338.

Wendt, Alexander. 2001. Driving with the Rearview Mirror: On the Rational Science of Institutional Design. *International Organization* 55, no. 4: 1019–1049.

Wilcox, Clair. 1949. *A Charter for World Trade.* New York: Macmillan.

Wilkinson, Rorden. 2006. *The WTO: Crisis and the Governance of Global Trade.* London: Routledge.

Winters, L. A. 1989. Patterns of World Trade in Manufactures: Does Trade Policy Matter? In *Causes of Changes in the Structure of International Trade, 1960–85,* ed. J. Black and A. Macbean. London: Macmillan.

Wooldridge, Jeffrey M. 2006. *Introductory Econometrics: A Modern Approach, 3rd Edition.* Cincinnati: South-Western.

Zamagni, Vera. 1993. *The Economic History of Italy 1860–1990: Recovery after Decline.* Oxford: Oxford University Press.

Zeiler, Thomas W. 1999. *Free Trade, Free World: The Advent of General Agreement.* Chapel Hill: University of North Carolina Press.

Index